THE AMNESIA GIRL!

GERRI R GRAY

Also by Gerri R Gray

Gray Skies of Dismal Dreams (HellBound Books, 2018)

Contributor to:

Beautiful Tragedies (HellBound Books, 2017)
Demons, Devils & Denizens of Hell 2 (HellBound Books, 2017)

THE AMNESIA GIRL!

GERRI R GRAY

A HellBound Books Publishing LLC Book
Houston TX

A HellBound Books LLC Publication

Copyright © 2017 by HellBound Books Publishing LLC
All Rights Reserved

Cover and art design by HellBound Books Publishing LLC

No part of this book may be reproduced, stored in a retrieval system, or transmitted by any means, electronic, mechanical, photocopying, recording or otherwise without written permission from the author This book is a work of fiction. Names, characters, places and incidents are entirely fictitious or are used fictitiously and any resemblance to actual persons, living or dead, events or locales is purely coincidental.

www.hellboundbookspublishing.com

Printed in the United States of America

Acknowledgements

Many thanks to Brandy Yassa for her excellent editing work, and to my publisher, James H Longmore, for making this book a reality!

Cover and art design by
HellBound Books Publishing LLC

Edited by Brandy Yassa

The Amnesia Girl!

Dedication

To Birtie, for royal blue laughter and the magic of Wilva.
And also to my Honey Bear, for encouraging me all the way.

The Amnesia Girl!

THE AMNESIA GIRL!

The Amnesia Girl!

Contents

A Rude Awakening
Lunatics Need Not Explain
Group Therapy
The Fall of Freud
Friends in Low Places
An Emotional Wreck
An Unbalanced Diet
Spaced Out
Warped Minds
Tales From the Fuhrerbunker
WARP Versus FRUMP
Molotov Cocktails and Pink Champagne
The Leopard's Lair
Simply Smashing
Bringing Down the House

The Amnesia Girl!

Chapter One

A Rude Awakening

"Farika. What a beautiful name. I've never known anyone named Farika before. Do you believe in déjà vu?" asked a voice, which had the odd distinction of sounding familiar, while at the same time unrecognizable. It paused for a brief moment, and then continued to ramble. "I read somewhere that our names define who we are, so I guess that makes you unusual. But unusual in a good way, I'm sure. If you read my psychiatric assessments and psychometric evaluations, you'll find that I'm defined as a borderline personality disorder coupled with foreign accent syndrome, which is somewhat uncommon; but psychobabble is nothing but porn for shrinks. I consider myself to be pretty normal, in an insane kind of way, but then, don't all mental patients? My name is Mara Marhoe. Remember me? I'm your roomie."

The Amnesia Girl!

Farika slowly opened her eyes and an unfamiliar world began to seep into her senses until a flood of disorientation permeated the totality of her brain. Gripped by grogginess, she could make out the blurry outline of a heavyset woman sitting at the foot of her bed. Gradually the haziness cleared, like fog burning away, and she sat up and looked around at her bleak and unfamiliar surroundings. It appeared to be a hospital room containing two matching beds, two matching nightstands, and two matching chairs. On the wall next to her bed was a window that was covered by vertical metal bars that had long ago been painted white but were now discolored and paint-peeling. Cracks in several of the window's twelve small panes distorted the rays of hazy morning sunlight that beamed in.

She could see that the woman sitting on her bed was in her early twenties, short, and extremely plump. Her reddish-colored hair was cut in a short pixie style and she wore a pair of plastic-framed glasses that were held together at the front with what appeared to be a thin strip of white masking tape. She smiled at Farika and lit up a cigarette.

"Did you know," said Mara Marhoe, "that the name Farika means a 'tranquil leader?' You look pretty tranquil to me. Maybe it's just the tranquilizers they give you here, who knows? Anyway, I looked you up in this big black book full of names and that's how I know. Hey, speaking of books, have you ever read one called *The Bell Jar*? A woman who put her head in a gas oven wrote it. Have you ever put your head in a gas oven?"

Farika's racing heart began to thump violently within her chest like a fist pounding frantically against the inside of a coffin lid after a premature burial. A cold sweat dampened her forehead. A wave of panic shot through her body like a shockwave until a fiery ball of terror exploded like a bomb inside her mind, puncturing her thoughts with its jagged pieces of shrapnel. "Where am I?" Farika cried out, as her eyes widened fearfully and then darted around the room as if searching for a clue. "How did I get here? Is this some kind of hospital? Oh my God, who am I? Why can't I remember anything?"

Mara Marhoe took a deep drag on her cigarette and then slowly let out the smoke. "This whole place is like a goddamn bell jar," she declared, oddly detached. "Once it comes down over your head, you can't get out. You're trapped like a rat. Your air gets all used up, you can't breathe, and, finally, you drop dead. But they aren't going to make me stick my head in some frigging oven. No way! I'll get those bastards first, all of them, and then broil *their* heads in the oven, with a shiny red apple in their grinning mouths; a *poisoned* apple, of course." She cracked an impish grin, took another drag on her cigarette, and then quivered like a humongous Jell-o mold as a fit of maniacal laughter rocketed from her mouth along with a chaotic puff of smoke.

"Oh my God, you're out of your mind!" Farika screamed as she threw back the covers and scrambled out of bed. "Stay away from me! You're sick in the head! Don't come near me!" The uncarpeted floor felt like a smooth sheet of ice against the bottom of Farika's bare feet as she sprinted towards the door. "Help!" she cried out. "Somebody help me! This woman's insane!"

Mara Marhoe took another drag on her cigarette and sat with her eyes glued to the terrified girl; her laughter intensified until it was dripping deviously.

Farika flung the door open and found herself in a long corridor of muted green and gray, where drugged patients stumbled about in a strange zombie-like fashion; some mumbling to themselves, and some staring off into space as if in a trance. She quickly made her way down the hallway, hoping to find a passageway leading to freedom. However, to her dismay, all she found was one locked door after another.

She spied an elderly gray-haired man sitting by himself, humming, in a wheelchair that was parked alongside a wall, upon which hung an odd finger-painting of smiling two-headed children dancing around a tree that bore a human face with a fanged mouth. As he hummed a tune that Farika did not recognize, he stared down at the floor, smiling.

"Help me, please," Farika begged him. Her voice reverberated with desperation. "Tell me how I can get out of here. I don't belong in this place. There's been a mistake."

The old man's humming immediately ceased and he slowly raised his head to make eye contact with Farika. Without warning, he jumped out of the wheelchair, his hands seized Farika's breasts, and he yelled out madly in an Irish brogue: "Tits are the Devil's doorknockers!"

Farika let out a loud scream. She quickly managed to free her bosoms from the old man's discourteous grasp and then took off running. Within a matter of moments, a team of mental health technicians, clad in sterile white uniforms apprehended her, pumped her full of sedatives, and returned her to her room, where she found Mara Marhoe sitting in the same location as before, smoking what was left of her cigarette.

"Welcome home, Farika," she said, before inserting her butt into an empty 'un-cola' can of shimmering green and lighting up a fresh cigarette.

"How did you know my name?" asked Farika, her speech sounding slightly slurred as the full effects of the sedatives that had been forced into her began to take hold. She eyed Mara Marhoe with suspicion.

Mara Marhoe blew a smoke-ring and then stabbed it with her middle finger. Her bloated belly gave off a loud rumbling sound, followed by a curious high-pitched squeal that sounded neither human nor animal. "You have to watch what you say in your sleep around here," she whispered almost inaudibly. "The walls have ears… literally. And in case you haven't already figured it out for yourself, the TVs here have eyes. Not everyone can see them, of course, but I can. They watch our every move."

Farika climbed out of bed and attempted to stand on her feet. Her legs felt as weak as her mind felt confused, and her body felt as though it was floating an inch or two above the floor. She slowly made her way across the room, nearly losing her balance at one point, while Mara Marhoe continued to sit on the bed and watch her every move like a gigantic, smoke-blowing hawk. At the other side of the room, near the door leading to the hallway, she found a small lavatory consisting of just a toilet and a wall-mounted sink, surmounted by an old chrome faucet with white porcelain handles.

Attached to the wall above the sink was a mirror that showed an unfamiliar reflection - a young woman whose ivory facial features were framed by long tresses of raven-black hair. A pair of strange, dark-green eyes stared back at her from the glass, as though wondering who she was. Her pale lips parted as if to speak, but no sound emerged.

In her head, she could hear a man's voice. It was singing:

> *Farika, child with an angel's face,*
> *Farika, lost in time and in space,*
> *Farika, my Farika...*

And then everything faded to black.

* *

The Amnesia Girl!

"A question that sometimes drives me hazy: Am I, or are the others, crazy?" asked a cheerful male voice. "That's my favorite quote by Albert Einstein. Did you know that he married his cousin and that one of their sons was committed to a mental institution?"

Farika opened her eyes. Standing next to her bed was a young mustachioed doctor in a white lab coat. She thought to herself how handsome he looked and, for a fleeting moment, fantasized that he was a knight in shining armor come to whisk her away to some romantic realm of happily-ever-after. Around his neck was a stethoscope and clutched in his hand was a clipboard.

Farika glanced around the room in search of her rambling roommate but there was no sign of her. She gently rubbed her sleepy eyes and wondered if Mara Marhoe had simply been a figment of her imagination.

"Good morning, Farika. I'm Doctor Scholl. And how are we feeling this morning?" the doctor asked.

Farika sat up. "Where am I? What happened? Please tell me!"

The doctor dragged a chair over to Farika's bedside and sat down. "There's no need to panic, young lady. You're in Midtown Psychiatric Hospital."

"Psychiatric hospital?"

Doctor Scholl nodded his head and offered an empathetic smile. "You appear to be suffering from retrograde amnesia. Let me explain to you what that is. The main feature of this disorder is the impaired ability to recall past events and previously familiar information."

"Amnesia? I don't understand. How could something like that have happened to me?" asked Farika. "Was I hurt in a car accident or something?"

"Amnesia can result from any number of things that damage the areas of the brain vital for memory processing," explained the doctor. "When you were first brought in, we ran tests to determine if you might have suffered a stroke or a heart attack, as both of those can deprive the brain of an adequate supply of oxygen, resulting in memory loss. Happens all the time. We also checked for possible brain tumors and even carbon monoxide poisoning. The results all came back negative."

Tears began to well up in Farika's eyes. "I feel like I'm trapped in a nightmare that I can't wake up from. Doctor, I'm so scared!"

"Calm yourself," the doctor urged. "Everything is all right. I just need to ask you a few questions. Do you know what year this is?"

"1974," replied Farika. "I think."

"Yes, very good," commended the doctor. "And who is the President of the United States?"

"Richard Milhous Nixon."

The doctor smiled. "Yes. You're doing very well." He then began firing off a round of important questions that left Farika feeling shaken and disconcerted. "Now, what is your last name? Where and when were you born? What is the name of the street you live on? Have you ever had mayonnaise and Kaopectate smeared all over the bottoms of your feet and licked off by a grown man dressed up as a baby?"

Farika thought long and hard, but her mind was blank. "I don't know. I don't know. I can't remember!"

"Have you used drugs of any kind – prescription or recreational?"

"I can't remember," replied Farika. A look of panic suddenly swept across her face. "Oh, my God! Could I be experiencing some kind of nightmarish drug trip? Maybe somebody slipped me some bad LSD! Maybe this place and all the weird people in it are simply one big, freaky hallucination!"

Doctor Scholl cracked a slight smile as if amused by

Farika's theory. "I can assure you that everything you perceive to be unreal is, in fact, quite real. And vice versa. Now, tell me, have you been experiencing any severe headaches or strange urges to trample a man while wearing red thigh-high boots with six-inch stiletto heels?"

"No, I don't think so," replied Farika after pondering the question for about ten seconds. "But I have been experiencing these strange dream-like visions. They're sort of like dreams, only they happen when I'm awake."

"Go on," prompted the doctor, as he jotted something down on his clipboard.

"Well, in these dreams, or whatever they are, I feel like I'm being pursued by someone or something and my life is in great danger. And then I hear a man's voice off in the distance somewhere and he's singing my name over and over. I don't know who this man is, but his voice is sweet and melodic and very comforting. He keeps singing and his voice grows louder and louder until my head starts to buzz and feel like it's about to explode. Then the dream ends. I don't know what any of it means."

Farika listened to the scribbling sound of the doctor's pencil and thought to herself how odd her words just sounded. She was sure if she had heard the same words uttered from someone else's lips she would have thought them mad as a hatter. She was suddenly overcome by a wave of anxiety and secretly feared that the doctor would think she was completely insane and commit her to some dungeon-like, padded room in the bowels of the psychiatric hospital for the rest of her life.

"Very interesting," the doctor remarked as he finished writing. He raised up the bottom half of the top sheet of paper attached to his clipboard and read something that was written on the sheet underneath it. He removed his eyeglasses and looked into Farika's eyes.

"According to your chart, you were physically examined by three of our resident doctors – Doctor Flushing, Doctor Farfle, and Doctor Fertuitus – and, according to their reports, you don't appear to have suffered any head injuries. So, it's quite possible that your amnesia is what we call dissociative, or psychogenic. It's quite rare and typically stems from a great emotional shock or trauma. However, in most cases, the loss of personal memories and autobiographical information lasts only for a short period of time."

"I see," Farika responded, feeling somewhat relieved. "So, tell me, doctor, how long will my amnesia last? When can I expect to get my memory back?"

"It's impossible to say. Amnesia can be short term, or it can be permanent." Doctor Scholl put his glasses back on and his gaze shifted down to Farika's feet. "You have very provocative feet. What size shoe do you wear?" he asked.

"I honestly can't remember," Farika answered, puzzled by the doctor's question. "I'm guessing a seven or an eight, but I'd have to take off one of my shoes and look inside to find the actual size."

Doctor Scholl promptly instructed Farika to remove both of her shoes so he could inspect her feet. He then inquired if she was familiar with reflexology, and she shook her head to indicate that she wasn't. "Reflexology is an ancient Oriental technique that utilizes pressure-point massage on the feet to promote healing in other parts of the body," he explained, as he began rubbing and pressing deeply on the sole of one of Farika's bare feet with the tips of his thumbs and fingers.

"Will this foot massage help me to regain my memory?" Farika asked.

"We must explore all avenues of therapy," the doctor

wheezed as his finger movements grew more vigorous and the lenses of his glasses began to steam up. His breathing soon grew heavy and a small trickle of drool escaped from the corner of his mouth. His tongue darted across his lips in a lizard-like fashion.

The reflexology treatment felt quite interesting to Farika and was beginning to relieve some of her pent-up stress. She closed her eyes and allowed the back of her head to sink into the marshmallow-softness of her pillow. All of a sudden, she felt the weird sensation of something warm and wet and her eyelids flew open, providing her with the startling sight of the doctor suckling the big toe of her left foot. Farika let out a shriek and instinctively pulled her foot away from Doctor Scholl's mouth; however, the demented doctor grabbed hold of it and continued to slurp, all the while moaning deliriously, in spite of the amnesiac's protests. After coming up for air, he cried out: "You have the hallux of a goddess!"

Just when Farika had convinced herself that her reflexology session couldn't get any stranger, the door to her room flew open and a snaggletoothed Japanese man with a *chonmage* haircut like a samurai, dashed in on all fours, barking wildly, like an excited dog. Farika let out a gasp as he made a frenzied beeline to Doctor Scholl's leg and proceeded to hump it in a furious manner.

Looking rather annoyed, the doctor withdrew his mouth from Farika's big toe and snapped, "Please control yourself, Mister Hiroshima! Can't you see that I'm in the middle of a therapy session with a patient? How can I hope to plant her tender young feet firmly on the road to recovery with you interrupting us like this?"

Doctor Scholl's words were to no avail; the crazed patient merely barked in defiance and continued to hump his leg. Disgusted, the doctor shook his leg violently in a fruitless attempt to free it from the clutches of its sexually-aroused assailant, as he shouted out for a nurse to come at once, adding, with a tone of urgency, "Mister Hiroshima is in heat again!"

Within a matter of moments, a vinegar-faced nurse rushed into the room with her right hand firmly wrapped around the handle of an electric cattle prod. Her very presence seemed to strike fear in the heart of the mad humper, and he immediately released his grip on the doctor's leg, cowered next to Farika's bed, and let out a series of whimpers. The nurse quickly proceeded to place a leather dog collar with an attached leash around his neck and then led him, on all fours, out of the room. Before disappearing from view, she zapped his buttocks with the prod, which caused him to yelp out in pain, and then, with an evil grin on her face, she remarked, "If you insist on behaving like a dog, then you'll be treated like a dog. Now heel, Mister Hiroshima!"

Doctor Scholl looked down at his wristwatch. "I'm afraid that concludes our session for today, Farika. I hope I didn't get off on the wrong foot with you. I will see you again the day after tomorrow. In the meantime, I will arrange for a strong sedative."

"Thank you," said Farika. "But I really don't think I need a sedative."

"It's not for *you*," replied the doctor as he exited the room.

Chapter Two

Lunatics Need Not Explain

"You can't trust them," Mara Marhoe warned in a whispering voice as her eyeballs scanned the dining room.

Farika looked up from her dismal tuna fish sandwich and gazed around the room, wondering whom Mara Marhoe was referring to.

Despite its bright yellow walls, the room possessed a dark and depressing atmosphere. About two-dozen patients belonging to various ages, genders and races, sat at old metal tables that had been arranged into four long rows. Some consumed their meals in silence while some chatted with others, discussing all matters of things, ranging from the latest psychotropic drugs to Julie Nixon Eisenhower's ovarian cyst. At one table, a smiling woman sat rocking an invisible baby, while at another, a man was busy having a conversation with his plastic pepper shaker. Farika could overhear him telling it the directions to the Statue of Liberty. Every now and then his voice was drowned out by the sound of an elderly lady with no teeth, who was mumbling something to herself, and the intermittent bursts of wild laughter from a lazy-eyed, crotch-rubbing man who sat alone at a table, the next row over.

Farika looked across the table at Mara Marhoe. "Whom, exactly, are you talking about?" she asked curiously.

"Shhh! They'll hear you," Mara Marhoe snapped. She took another look around the dining room to make sure nobody was listening. When she felt it was safe to answer, she replied, "Doctor I and that creepy Nurse Mars bitch, that's who. He's the head perv in this can of mixed nuts and she's his devoted concubine. Whatever you do, Farika, take care not to get on her bad side. She's bad news!"

"Bad news?" asked Farika. "What do you mean?"

"What I mean is, she likes to inflict pain on her victims. It gets her off, big time. There's a rumor going around that she has a torture chamber downstairs in the basement, where she carries out all kinds of sadistic acts and psychotronic mind control experiments, like the Nazis did back in the 1940s. And while psycho Mars is busy getting her kicks, Doctor I observes all the lurid action and jots down notes in that little blue book that he always carries around with him."

Farika secretly hoped that Mara Marhoe was either pulling her leg or spouting delusions. The possibility that her roommate's story carried with it any grains of truth was a frightening thought that caused goose bumps to spring up on her arms. She was about to ask her friend about the doctor's little blue book, when a grinning, straggly-haired woman with frighteningly dark circles underneath her eyes, and a food tray in her bony hands, approached the table and asked Farika if she could sit down next to her.

An expression of rage instantaneously erupted on Mara Marhoe's face. "Shove off, bitch!" she growled, with a mouth full of food. "The lady and I are in the middle of a private conversation. Go sit your moldy old ass down somewhere else."

"Screw you, potbellied pig!" hissed the straggly-haired woman in a scratchy-sounding voice. "Who lit the string on *your* tampon?" She reluctantly took a chair at a nearby table, where she sat with her eyes firmly affixed upon Farika. She then gave her a wink and proceeded to tongue her tuna fish sandwich in a rather lewd manner.

"Who *is* that strange woman?" Farika asked Mara Marhoe in a hushed voice.

"She's no one you want to be hanging around with. Trust me," replied Mara Marhoe. "She used to be a well-known beautician. Her mind snapped after some creep raped her and then she went on a psychotic murder rampage at a beauty parlor, stabbing everyone to death with a rat-tail comb. It was a real bloodbath! And then they sent her here."

Gazing at the obscenely gesturing woman from out of the corner of her eye, Farika gasped, "Oh, how horrible!" With a disgusted sigh, she put down her sandwich, which tasted less appealing with each and every nibble that she forced herself to take.

The man conversing with his plastic pepper shaker suddenly grabbed hold of it and began dashing it angrily against the top of his table, while shouting at it, "You bastard! I've already explained to you three fucking times which subway train you take to get to the South Ferry Station! Don't ask me to explain it to you again!"

The dining room went silent for a few seconds, and then, from the table next to the one that Farika and Mara Marhoe were sitting at, a Puerto Rican woman with glazed eyes and a pink, quilted housecoat blurted out,

"It's such a joy to be insane; lunatics need not explain!" She repeated the rhyme again and again, and then, one by one, the other patients in the dining room began chanting it along with her and banging their metal trays against their metal tables in rhythm to it.

> *"It's such a joy to be insane; lunatics need not explain!*
> *It's such a joy to be insane; lunatics need not explain!*
> *It's such a joy to be insane; lunatics need not explain!"*

Using his chair as a step stool, the man with the plastic pepper shaker climbed up onto the top of his table and began disrobing, tossing his clothes into the air with wild abandon. Within a matter of seconds, he was completely naked. He then latched onto his long, drooping penis with his hand and waved it wildly in Farika's direction while maniacally screaming out Abraham Lincoln's 'Gettysburg Address' at the top of his lungs. His face then took on a strange, reddish tint, which rapidly advanced into an intense shade of crimson. His eyes bugged. Veins in his neck and forehead bulged and pulsated. His body vibrated violently, as if he were in the throes of a seizure of some sort, and from his flesh emanated a pungent odor similar to singed hair. He generated a peculiar crackling noise, and then his body, which was now a dark, crimson color from head to toe, burst into a bright, and sizzling, ball of fire.

Farika's eyes widened in horror and she frantically leapt from her seat, accidentally knocking her chair to the floor. "Holy crap!" she shrieked, while pointing her index finger at the human fireball. "That man over there just burst into flames! Somebody do something!"

Unfazed by the quivering heap of flaming flesh that was filling the dining room with foul-smelling billows of greasy, black smoke, Mara Marhoe stared down at her paper plate while stuffing the last bits of her sandwich into her mouth. "Calm your areolas, Amnesia Girl," she demanded, while continuing to masticate her food. "It's just a simple case of spontaneous human combustion. Don't you ever read the *National Enquirer*, or are you some kind of illiterate?"

Farika picked up her chair and sat back down. "Just a simple case of spontaneous human combustion?" she echoed, as though in disbelief of her own two ears. "How is that physically possible? And how can you just sit there and be so apathetic about it? People just don't go around bursting into flames every day for no apparent reason. It's not a normal thing! It defies logic!" She wasn't sure if Mara Marhoe had tuned her out or was unable to hear her over the lunatic chant, which, by now, had reached a fevered pitch.

Half a minute passed and then, with her voice devoid of even the slightest trace of emotion, Mara Marhoe nonchalantly stated, "That's the second one at Midtown within the past six months."

A fire alarm suddenly sounded throughout the building and a robust and dark-skinned nurse, accompanied by an even more robust and dark-skinned orderly, burst through the double-swinging doors of the smoke-filled dining room.

"Smoking is not permitted in the dining room!" the nurse shouted, but her voice could barely be heard over the loud, riotous chanting and tray banging. She clapped her hands together and shouted louder, "Stop this noise at once or you'll all be put into straightjackets and sedated! Don't screw with me!"

One of the patients, a hippie girl with long, braided hair and wire-rimmed glasses, made a sudden lunge at the nurse, screaming out a plethora of obscenities -- some quite colorful -- and attempted to strike her in the head with her metal food tray. She was immediately subdued by the orderly, and then, within a matter of moments, sedated by the nurse and removed from the dining room by a team of mental health technicians who arrived with a padded, stainless steel gurney equipped with a multitude of leather restraints that would have delighted the most hardcore aficionado of bondage and discipline. By now the chanting and banging had stopped.

Unable to finish the rest of her meal and feeling increasingly queasy, Farika pushed herself away from the table. The metal legs of her hard plastic chair produced an odd screeching noise, not unlike a cry for help, as they slid across the green- and gray-checkered linoleum floor. At that same moment, somewhere in the mist-enshrouded expanse of Farika's mind, the identical noise sounded.

She returned, alone, to her dismal room and gazed out of the dismal, barred window that was almost entirely obscured by a thick layer of dirt that had, over the years, collected on the opposite side of the panes. She could make out the shapes of great, grimy smokestacks atop sinister-looking factory buildings that had been erected during the Industrial Revolution and from which arose billowing grayish-white, steamy clouds like smoke signals of distress. Surrounding them were weathered, brick high-rises that stood like silent sentries guarding their well-kept secrets behind tattered window shades and curtains. *The view of the outside is almost as dismal as the view of the inside*, she thought to herself.

As the minutes stretched into what seemed like hours, Farika pondered the mystery of herself, hoping to find even the smallest fragment of a clue. But whatever memories her brain might have retained of her now-forgotten past were as grayish-white and opaque as the smokestack clouds that rose high into the air with the promise of forming into something substantial, only to dissipate into nothingness.

Mara Marhoe's words began to slowly seep into Farika's head and she thought how at one time she probably would have found the far-fetched rambling of an abnormal mind to be darkly humorous. How she knew that, she wasn't sure. She just seemed to know it with a good amount of certainty. However, all the things Mara Marhoe had told her about strange, psychotronic experiments and mind control did not leave her with even the slightest urge to laugh. Instead, they filled her with a sense of dread.

The sound of white, rubber-soled shoes echoed in the seemingly endless hall outside of Farika's room and grew louder with each step until they reached her door and then took on the solid form of a raven-haired, middle-aged woman who possessed pale skin and cadaverous eyes. She was dressed all in white with a black, metal name tag that was pinned to her clinical-looking uniform just above her left breast. It identified her as Nurse Mars. Farika instantly recognized her as the nurse who had zapped Mister Hiroshima with the cattle prod earlier in the day.

"And how are we feeling today?" came a voice from between the nurse's dark red lips.

"I want to go home," Farika whimpered in a frightened, almost childlike, little voice.

"And where is home?" asked Nurse Mars.

"I don't know," Farika replied, her voice with filled despair. "I don't know." The sound of her own words unleashed an uncontrollable trickle of tears from her eyes, and she wept in front of the white uniform with the black name tag.

Nurse Mars produced a hypodermic syringe and a small glass bottle that held a clear liquid, and as she proceeded to prepare for the giving of an injection, she grimly stated, "Well, until you are once again in full possession of your memory, I'm afraid this mental health facility will have to be your home. But don't despair. It's the finest one in all of New York City and you'll get plenty of tender loving care here." Her lips then formed into a chilling grin and she held up the filled syringe. Her thumb was positioned on its plunger. "This will help you sleep," she said. "The doctor ordered it especially for you. And maybe, just maybe, when you wake up you'll find that your amnesia has resolved itself."

With a quick sting, she injected the mysterious substance that the doctor had ordered into Farika's arm, reminded her that she had a group therapy session in the morning, and then, with her mission accomplished, she departed the room, turning once again into nothing but the sound of white, rubber-soled shoes that echoed down the endless hall until they faded into the distant, distorted jumble of voices, moaning, ringing bells, and shutting doors.

Farika stared up at the dingy ceiling and her eyes focused on a long, crooked crack that ran through the plaster. As she grew drowsy, she wondered how many other patients before her had stared up at that same crack, perhaps wondering the same thing. *Where were all of those people now and what had become of them? Were some of them cured? Had some died? Were they still patients, perhaps confined to some padded room in the asylum, where the doctors lock away the incurable, so they needn't be reminded of their failures as healers? Or maybe, just maybe, they had vanished in the middle of the night?*

As a tear welled up in Farika's left eye, the crack on the ceiling appeared to quiver for a moment and then stopped. Farika stared up at it, greatly curious. She felt puzzled, but was quite sure that she had observed it move, albeit ever so slightly. And then, to her astonishment, it began to move once again – only this time it was wriggling in a constant serpentine fashion. Its strange, snakelike movements soon took on the appearance of a sidewinder, and Farika rubbed her eyes in disbelief. *This can't be possible*, she thought. *Am I having a dream?* The crack then widened in one spot and from it, emerged a buzzing, black housefly, which flew down and landed on the wall in front of Farika. It proceeded to rapidly increase in size until it was as large as a vulture. Farika was mesmerized by this peculiar, winged creature and was unable to take her eyes from it. It then began to speak as a human being does, but in an uncanny, buzzing voice, and it said, "Hello, Farika."

"Who are you?" Farika asked the enormous fly, her voice growing weak and raspy as the mysterious injection slowly propelled her mind into a spaced-out stupor. "*What* are you?"

"They call me the Superfly, baby."

"Are you real?"

"I'm as real as you are," replied the fly. "But reality doesn't impress me one bit, baby, so don't go getting yourself all hung up on it. It's merely a persistent illusion. Just ask Albert Einstein."

"I don't understand," said Farika.

"Of course you don't. Life can only be understood when viewed backwards," the fly philosophized. "In time you will come to learn that understanding what things mean is not nearly as important as understanding what things *don't* mean. Dig what I'm saying? You will also find out for yourself that to understand is to suffer. That's the hardest lesson of them all, but I fear you'll be learning it sooner rather than later."

"You're speaking in riddles," complained Farika,

sounding slightly annoyed. "I'm not sure I can believe anything you tell me."

The buzzing of the fly grew ear-piercingly loud, and it let out a laugh. "You're on the brink of disaster, baby. You can choose to believe in yourself if you're so inclined, or you can choose to believe in nothing. In the end, they both add up to the same thing. My time grows short, as does my patience with you."

"Then buzz off!" retorted Farika as her eyelids grew heavy and her vision started to blur. Suddenly, the intense buzzing from the fly's beating wings ceased and the Superfly mysteriously vanished into the ethers.

Just then, Farika thought she heard Mara Marhoe laughing from somewhere off in the distance. The laughter echoed and had a peculiar distortion about it. After a few moments, which seemed like an eternity, it trailed off and was gone. "It's a joy to be insane," Farika whispered to herself. Then, within her drowsing mind she heard a replay of Nurse Mars' voice reminding her of group therapy in the morning. That voice, too, sounded distorted. However, the prospect that the group therapy session might open a door for her, in more ways than one, soothed her with a momentary glimmer of hope. She closed her eyes and drifted into a dreamless, velvet slumber.

Chapter Three

Group Therapy

The heavy, recessed, paneled door with the chipped glass knob stood silent and ajar, and taped to the center of its middle panel was a sheet of white paper upon which was written in black ink: "Group Therapy. 9:00 am - 10:00 am."

Farika slowly opened the door and peeked inside. She counted six people, men and women, whom she assumed were patients, sitting in a semi-circle on chairs with straight chrome legs and red plastic seats and backs that appeared hard and uncomfortable. Some of them were talking amongst themselves in low, almost whispering, voices, while some tapped their fingers and checked their wristwatches, and others sat catatonically, staring into space. One of the six people, a curly-haired, middle-aged lady wearing cat-eye glasses bejeweled with tiny rhinestones, smiled and motioned with her hand for Farika to come and sit down on the empty chair next to her. She did so, and then two more people filed into the room and took seats.

Anxiety raced through Farika's body and she tried to hide her nervousness from the others in the room. As much as Mara Marhoe sometimes bothered her, she was now wishing that the woman, despite all of her ludicrous ramblings, was sitting there with her to offer her some sort of moral support. There wasn't one familiar face in the entire group and this left Farika feeling insecure and vulnerable.

A lanky, bespectacled man in a white lab coat that matched the color of his receding, wavy hair entered the room and took a seat in a chair that faced the semi-circle of people. An opening in his neatly trimmed beard revealed his pinkish lips, which were wrapped tightly around a dark brown, wooden pipe. In one of his hands was a black notebook with a gold pen attached to it. He crossed his legs and removed the pipe from his mouth, placing it in a clear glass ashtray on a small table next to him. Farika studied his face and guessed his age to be somewhere between fifty and sixty years old.

He cleared his throat and once he was confident that he had everyone's undivided attention, he began to speak in an almost melodic, foreign-sounding accent, complete with a rolling R. "Good morning, everybody," he began, "and welcome to group therapy. For those of you who do not know who I am, allow me to introduce myself. My name is Doctor Ivan Iotaplutoniumenzymaticastrophe. But it may be much easier for some of you to address me simply as Doctor I."

The group emitted a collective sigh of relief.

Doctor I continued, "I am the head psychiatrist of this mental health facility and, as some of you may already know, I am also the author of *The Joy of Insanity* - a soon-to-be-published treatise on the benefits of mental illness and the therapeutic application of insanity as an art form."

Farika was startled to hear the sound of someone clapping his or her hands, and looked over to where the sound was coming from. She saw Nurse Mars standing inside the room near the door, and she was giving the doctor a standing ovation. Farika thought it odd that she hadn't seen the nurse enter the group therapy room.

With a smile that seemed to be bursting with great pride, Nurse Mars looked at the group and chirped, "You should all consider yourselves extremely lucky to be under the care of a brilliant psychiatrist like Doctor I. The man is an undisputed genius!"

Doctor I thanked her without turning to look at her and then continued to speak to the group. "Now, with that said, let me move on to say that group therapy can be a rewarding experience for many patients, and numerous therapeutic benefits can be reaped from it. But first you must free yourself from all inhibitions and allow yourself to share your deepest, darkest thoughts and feelings with the group." His eyes met with Farika's and he held his gaze upon her and said, with a slight smile, "This includes your wet dreams and your sexual fantasies. The filthier and more perverted they are, the better. Don't leave out any details." He stroked his beard.

At that moment Farika experienced a wave of uneasiness that came over her, washing away any tiny particles of hope that she had brought with her to the session. She felt like she was sitting before the group, exposed in all her nakedness, and, in an odd way, almost violated by the white-haired man's words. It didn't help that Nurse Mars was glaring at her with a look that could have killed. Farika could sense invisible daggers with poisoned tips thrusting into her and ripping her open. Nurse Mars turned and left the room. But the daggers remained.

"There is no need to be shy or embarrassed," the doctor continued. He then took his eyes off of Farika and said to the group in general, "Openly discussing these issues helps to put your problems into perspective, and you may find that it can also aid you in strengthening your relationship skills, reduce any feelings of isolation you may be experiencing, and help you to find your voice. Remember, we are all here to act as a support network and provide a sounding board during the course of the next hour. Now, starting with the gentleman to my left and working clockwise, will you please introduce yourself to the rest of the group and describe yourself in one or two sentences."

"My name is Mister Feldman, Elliott Feldman," said the man at the left end of the semi-circle. "And since the age of eight I've been plagued by horrible recurring nightmares involving a large homosexual squid that possesses a huge phallus at the end of each tentacle. And they're not even circumcised! It's just horrible."

"I've had that same dream too," blurted out a man from the other side of the semi-circle. "It's pretty common."

The lady with the cat-eye glasses leaned over towards Farika and whispered in her ear, "I'll bet anything he has an overbearing mother. There's always an overbearing mother behind neuroses like that."

The black woman sitting to the right of Elliott Feldman rolled her eyes in annoyance before speaking. "My name is LaTaurus Jackson," she said, staring straight ahead to avoid eye contact with anyone. "I've been diagnosed with psychophobia, kleptomania, anorexia, pyromania, and Tourette syndrome, just to name a few."

Sitting to her right was a woman with drab clothes and wild eyes. "My name is Zora Zenith and right now, at this very moment, my head is swimming with homicidal thoughts."

The man to her right was well-groomed, and wore a snooty look on his face. "Butch Picasso," he said, slicking down his hair. "I shouldn't even be here. I'm an extremely important person and this is all just a big waste of my valuable time."

The lady with the cat-eye glasses leaned over towards Farika and whispered into her ear, "Narcissistic personality disorder with fragile self-esteem issues and delusions of grandeur. He probably grew up thinking vaginas had teeth."

The woman sitting to the right of Butch Picasso licked her lips and said, with a heavy Spanish accent, "*Hola*, I'm Sybil Santana and I have abnormal sexual impulses. I feel compelled to tell the group that I have an uncontrollable urge at this moment to insert a coffee pot plug into my *panocha*!"

"Cockmunching cuntsicle!" LaTaurus screamed out, as her head ticced to the left.

"That's very impressive, Miss Santana," Doctor I complimented. "It pleases me very much to see you making such wonderful progress in overcoming your avoidant personality disorder!"

The mousy, withdrawn-looking woman sitting next to Sybil spoke next. "My name is Bianca Tortellini and I'm a housewife from Massapequa. I suffer from haphephobia, which is the fear of being touched... and I can also move objects with my mind."

Next in line to introduce himself to the group was a distinguished-looking gentleman with a pencil-thin mustache and wavy hair. "Howdy, folks," he said with a sparkling smile. "I'm Hugh Hayward. I've had electroconvulsive therapy nine times for my obsessive–compulsive personality disorder, and I'm an all-around nice guy."

"Fart hole maggot!" LaTaurus screamed out, as her

head ticced to the right.

The butterflies in Farika's stomach were multiplying at great speed as her turn to introduce herself to the group drew closer. She found herself starting to feel nauseous and fantasized about jumping out of her seat and running out the heavy, recessed, paneled door with the chipped glass knob to some safe, dark spot where she could curl herself up into a fetal position and hide.

"Hello, everybody," said the lady with the cat-eye glasses. "My name is Sylvia Sylvers. I'm a self-loathing, unpublished poetess with suicidal tendencies." She then cracked a smile and announced proudly, "I've tried to kill myself three times in the past week!"

"I must applaud you, Mrs. Sylvers," said Doctor I, clapping his hands. "Since you've been attending group therapy, you have reduced your suicide attempts by over fifty percent!"

The moment of truth had finally arrived, and all eyes were upon Farika. She nervously cleared her throat. "My name is Farika. I can't tell you my last name because I can't remember what it is. You see, I'm an amnesiac. And other than that, I'm not really sure how to describe myself to all of you, because I haven't yet discovered who I am, or should I say was."

"I really must protest!" complained Butch Picasso. "Those were more than one or two sentences. I counted. Who do you think you are, someone special like me?"

Farika began to laugh, assuming that Butch Picasso was joking. However, she quickly figured out by the perturbed look on his face that he was genuinely agitated. "I'm terribly sorry," she said. "I didn't realize..."

"Now dear, there's no need for you to say you're sorry," said Sylvia in a motherly tone, as she patted Farika's arm. "Don't you pay any attention to that rude man over there. He puts the "ass" in asylum."

"Amnesia!" exclaimed Sybil Santana. "Ooh, how

thrilling! I've always wanted to try that."

"With all due respect," said Farika, "it's not really something that I would call thrilling. It's no picnic not being able to remember your own identity or past. I feel like my whole life has been erased and I'm just an empty canvas. And the possibility that my memory might never return is terrifying."

"Terrifying?" asked Zora Zenith, angrily. "You want to know what terrifying really is? Hearing fifty voices screaming inside your head all at once is terrifying! Seeing rats that really aren't there crawling out of your nipples is terrifying! Waking up day after day and knowing that the only way out of the private hell you're trapped in is to jump out the window is terrifying. You don't know the first thing about feeling terrified, bitch!"

"I'm sorry," said Farika, feeling embarrassed and unnerved. "I didn't mean to upset you."

"Dangling tit nugget!" LaTaurus screamed out.

"Not as sorry as you will be," growled Zora Zenith. "I've been diagnosed with over one hundred different personalities and they're all telling me to kill you."

"Do I detect some feelings of aggression there, Zora?" asked Doctor I.

"Zora isn't here, Doctor I" replied Zora Zenith in a distinctly different voice. "I'm Laura."

"And where is Zora, Laura?" asked the doctor, jotting down notes.

"She's with Nora and Cora. I'm not supposed to tell you this, but they're plotting how they're going to kill the amnesia girl."

"Oh my God!" cried Farika.

"I don't know about anybody else, but I'm feeling one of my panic attacks coming on!" cried Sylvia Sylvers.

"It's all so horrible," moaned Elliott.

"I've never seen so many screwed-up white people in

all my life," LaTaurus stated, shaking her head from side to side.

Sybil Santana chimed in, "I feel compelled to tell the group that amputees make me hot and LaTaurus rhymes with clitoris!"

"Shut the hell up, you taco-bending cockroach!" yelled LaTaurus, jumping up from her seat with both fists clenched and ready for action. "I've had my fill of your goddamn stupidity for one day! I'd love to rip out your eyeballs and shove them right up your asshole!"

Sybil let out a loud scream, buried her face in the palms of her hands and wept.

"Everybody, please control yourselves!" Doctor I yelled. He furiously tapped his gold pen against his notebook until the room returned to silence.

At that moment, a creak sounded and all eyes shifted towards the heavy, recessed paneled door with the chipped glass knob. It slowly opened and then Mister Hiroshima timidly crept into the room without uttering a word.

"Good morning, Mister Hiroshima," exclaimed Doctor I, as he motioned to the newcomer with his hand. "I'm delighted you could join our happy little group this morning. Please have a seat over there with the others."

Mister Hiroshima made his way to the center of the room where the other patients were seated. He bowed as he passed by each one of them and then he suddenly dropped down onto all fours and started crawling around, sniffing each person in a dog-like fashion. When he got to Bianca Tortellini, glistening beads of perspiration suddenly appeared on his pasty forehead, like drops of morning dew clinging to the petals of a lotus flower, and he began to pant furiously. He sprung up from the floor, locking his legs and arms tightly around the housewife's leg, and proceeded to hump away.

Bianca Tortellini's mouth dropped open wide and from it, resounded a blood-curdling scream. "Don't touch me!" she shrieked in absolute terror. "You vile thing! Let go of me! Oh, God! My flesh is burning! Your touch is repulsive! Stop it! Stop it right now! Oh, God! I can't breathe! I swear I'll spew vomit!"

Sybil Santana began to fondle her own breasts as she watched intently. "Ooh, *Madre Maria*, I think I'm going to ovulate!"

LaTaurus' head ticced. "Orifice clit mangler!" she screamed out.

Sylvia Sylvers stretched herself across Hugh Hayward's lap and repeatedly struck Mister Hiroshima on his back with one of her shoes, while Doctor I eagerly jotted down notes in his little blue book. However, her footwear attack only served to step-up the Asian man's excitement and his humping motion switched into overdrive. Bianca Tortellini began to hyperventilate. The horrified housewife's face turned a ghastly shade of white and the pupils of her bugging eyes began to emanate a strange, reddish glow.

A thunderous roaring noise rose up from out of nowhere and permeated the room, causing Farika and several others to cover their ears with their hands. Two of the light bulbs in the overhead light fixture exploded with a loud pop, eliciting a startled gasp from most of the group therapy patients and showering everyone in the room with hundreds of tiny shards of white glass. An unoccupied chair rose up into the air on its own accord, and then flew violently into a wall, knocking a framed picture of poker-playing dogs from its hook. It crashed to the floor and broke into pieces. Books then began to fly from their shelves. They hurled across the room like projectiles, prompting everyone to duck and cover their heads. Some of the women began to scream. Knick-knacks, ashtrays and a desk lamp were next in line to become airborne. Some of the flying objects struck a few of the patients, while others smashed into the walls.

"Clusterfuck spunk-bubble sniffer!" LaTaurus screeched uncontrollably, as her head ticced violently from side to side.

Mister Hiroshima let out a loud howl. His eyes bulged frightfully from their sockets and his body quivered violently as though he were undergoing electrocution. He released his grip on Bianca Tortellini's leg and then collapsed onto the floor in a crumpled heap, unconscious.

All at once, the roaring noise stopped, and the bombardment came to a sudden halt. The strange, reddish glow that had lit up the housewife's eyes quickly faded. Her breathing returned to normal and she sat calmly in her chair, smiling cheerfully as though nothing out of the ordinary had just transpired.

Doctor I peered down at his wristwatch and announced that the hour was up. "Our next group session will be three days from now. Thank you all for coming this morning. I believe we made a good deal of progress today."

Farika rose from her seat and quickly headed for the door. She felt worse now than she did before the session started and was worried about the threats made against her by Zora Zenith and her multiple personalities. But, before she could reach the relative safety of the hallway, Hugh Hayward stepped in front of her and blocked her exit from the group therapy room. He smiled at her bashfully and said, "I hope you don't mind me saying this, Miss Farika, but I think you're a very pretty lady. Would you like to see my lobotomy scar?"

"Inbred dickwhistle slapper!" screamed LaTaurus, as Farika pushed her way past the flirtatious obsessive-compulsive and ran from the room.

**

"So how did group therapy go?" Mara Marhoe inquired, as she lay sideways on her bed, flipping through the pages of a magazine.

Farika collapsed back-first onto her own bed, with her arms straight out to her sides as though she were physically exhausted. She looked up at the cracks running across the ceiling. "Oh, it went just super. Better than I could have ever hoped for. I succeeded in pissing off half the people there, including Nurse Mars."

Mara Marhoe let out a laugh that almost sounded like a witch's cackle and gave Farika a thumb's-up.

"I also seemed to have made enemies with a psycho girl with multiple personalities who wants me dead," said Farika.

"Lucky you," remarked Mara Marhoe. She snickered, smiled and shook her head.

"Oh, but I haven't even told you the best part, yet. I was actually propositioned by a man who had a lobotomy!"

Mara Marhoe closed her magazine and tossed it onto the floor. "If you ask me," she declared, "I think probably half the men in this world could benefit from a good lobotomy. If they aren't thinking about screwing you, they're thinking about how to screw you over. Lobotomies for all, I say. It would make this world a damn better place for all concerned."

"Not all men are bad," protested Farika. "Some can be very kind, caring and gentle."

"Oh yeah? Name one," challenged Mara Marhoe, as she extracted a cigarette from a pack of Viceroy. She lit it and stared at Farika.

Farika at once felt as though her mind was drifting away from her body and her surroundings took on an unreal quality. She could clearly see Mara Marhoe's lips moving, forming words and even appearing to be laughing at certain intervals. However, Farika was deaf to everything that her rotund roommate was saying. The only sound that made its way into her ears was a familiar, yet unknown, man's voice. Starting faint and then gradually growing louder, his words were melodic and haunting as he sang:

Farika, soul of mystical flame,
Farika, omens whisper her name,
Farika, my Farika...

Something caught the corner of Farika's eye. She slowly turned her head and thought she could see the faint, almost transparent, outline of a man standing by the door. He had a strange, golden glow about him and seemed to be beckoning to her in slow motion with his hand as he continued to sing:

Farika, child of silver moonbeams,
Farika, smile of stardust and dreams,
Farika, sweet Farika...

"I'm Lady Bird Johnson and I've come to kill you!" screamed a hysterical, high-pitched voice.

The ghostly, golden form instantly evaporated and was replaced by the startling sight of Zora Zenith. She charged madly into the room with her right hand held high in the air, clutching a pair of scissors.

Farika was gripped by terror and let out a scream as the deranged woman ran towards her, growling like a wild beast. Farika could see a bit of frothy saliva dripping from her lower lip, which gave her the appearance of a rabid dog.

"Die!" screamed Zora Zenith, as she came at Farika with the scissors, in an attempt to stab her.

Farika instinctively rolled out of the way at near-lightning speed and the sharp point of the scissors plunged into her mattress. She screamed again and bolted from the bed.

Zora Zenith let out a wolf-like howl and then began laughing insanely as she pulled the scissors from the mattress, once again raising them high into the air. She turned and was about to give Farika chase when Mara Marhoe lunged at her from behind and knocked her to the floor, trying desperately to wrestle the scissors away from her. Zora lost her grip and the scissors went sliding across the floor until they disappeared into the darkness under Farika's bed.

They struggled and grunted until a small band of nurses and orderlies rushed into the room and broke them up. In less than a minute, Zora Zenith was subdued and strapped to a gurney and rolled away. "You're as good as dead!" she screamed, twisting her head violently from side to side.

Trembling, and with tears in her eyes,, Farika threw her arms around the panting Mara Marhoe. "That was so brave!" she cried. "Thank you for saving my life!"

Mara Marhoe returned the embrace and whispered into her ear, "The only thing that would make this moment more perfect would be four-hundred milligrams of Thorazine."

"Stop that!" shrieked Nurse Mars, running into the room with her cruel eyes blazing. In her hand was a black leather medical bag. "Stop that physical contact at once! Patients are not permitted to engage in sexual acts with each other in Midtown Psychiatric Hospital! We frown upon that sort of lascivious behavior in this institution!"

Farika and Mara Marhoe quickly stepped away from each other.

"I was only thanking her for saving my life," Farika

explained. "If she hadn't..."

"I suggest you watch your Ps and Qs, young lady," remarked Nurse Mars, interrupting Farika in mid-sentence. "You've caused more than enough trouble around here and I won't stand for it! Do you hear me?"

"Yes, I hear you," Farika replied. "I'm not trying to start trouble. Really, I'm not!"

"And you!" Nurse Mars shouted at Mara Marhoe. "Out of this room. Now!" She pointed her finger at the door.

"Screw you!" sneered Mara Marhoe. She crossed her arms in defiance and refused to budge. "I'm not leaving Farika alone in this room with you and your little bag of tricks there. I know what you're up to."

Nurse Mars looked over at Mara Marhoe and grinned. Without saying a word, she opened up her medical bag, extracted her trusty cattle prod, and then zapped the defiant girl on the side of her leg. Mara Marhoe let out a cry of pain as a stinging jolt of electricity surged through her flesh and then she fell to the floor, groaning. Farika gasped at the scene that was unfolding before her eyes and covered her mouth with her hand as if to prevent herself from screaming.

"I'm afraid I didn't hear what you said," Nurse Mars declared to Mara Marhoe as she tapped the side of the cattle prod against the palm of her other hand. "Would you care to repeat it?"

Mara Marhoe clumsily scrambled to her feet and, while rubbing the side of her sore leg, dashed over to the door. Before leaving the room, she turned to Nurse Mars and hissed: "I'll get even with you, Vinegar Tits. Your day will come. Just you wait."

Nurse Mars wasted no time in locking the door after Mara Marhoe exited. With a disciplinarian tone in her voice and the electric cattle prod still in her hand, she informed Farika of her intention to perform a

The Amnesia Girl!

gynecological procedure and then barked out an order to the trembling girl to strip completely naked and lay herself down on her bed. "Spread those legs, bitch, and spread them wide!" she demanded.

As Farika reluctantly removed her clothing, Nurse Mars slipped out of her nurse uniform, revealing a skin-tight red latex catsuit underneath. She once again reached into her black leather medical bag and, this time, pulled out an electric drill to which was attached a twelve-inch black dildo. She plugged the drill into an electric outlet on the wall near Farika's bed and then revved it up, delighting in the look of terror that appeared on Farika's face as the young girl eyed the plastic phallus rapidly rotating before her.

"We're going to have a little party," announced Nurse Mars. "Just the two of us."

A woman's voice suddenly rang out over the loud speaker in the hallway: "Paging Nurse Mars! Paging Nurse Mars! Please report to the nurses' station immediately!"

Nurse Mars frowned with irritation upon hearing her name being paged. She hastily re-dressed, putting her nurse uniform on over her red catsuit. As she packed her cattle prod and drill back into the medical bag, she stated, "You got lucky this time, piglet, but just remember... sooner or later everybody's luck runs out." She headed for the door and then paused and turned her head to look over her shoulder at Farika, who was sitting at the edge of the bed, shivering. "Oh, by the way... I have a little surprise for you, Farika," she said with an evil grin. "Come tomorrow, you'll be strapped to a gurney and taken up to the fifth floor where you will undergo your first of a series of E.C.T. treatments."

"E.C.T.?" asked Farika. A look of fright presented itself on her face. "What is that?"

"Electroconvulsive therapy," replied Nurse Mars.

"Or to put it into simpler terms: shock treatment. Doctor I feels that the use of electric current to stimulate the brain might help to evoke memories that have been lost to amnesia. I must warn you, though. It can be quite a painful experience. Especially without anesthesia."

With a look of satisfaction on her face, Nurse Mars exited the room. Seconds later, a worried Mara Marhoe rushed back in and asked Farika if she were all right.

Farika nodded her head and then covered her naked body with the sheet from her bed and began to weep. "This can't be happening," she sobbed. "This is like some kind of bad dream. This place. These people. They're all insane!"

"Of course they're all insane," replied Mara Marhoe as she lit up a cigarette. "This is an insane asylum!"

"I've got to get out of this place," Farika moaned desperately. "I don't know how. But I've just got to get out of here!"

Chapter Four

The Fall of Freud

"Who are you?" Farika asked the reflection that stared back at her from the mirror. Her eyes were sad, her voice soft and doleful. "Why don't I recognize your face - my face? Where do you come from? What was your life before I woke up here? Why won't you share your secrets with me? I'm you. You're me. When will this mystery unravel? Will it ever unravel?"

Her reflection was joined by the reflection of Mara Marhoe, who stood behind her and spoke to her via the mirror.

"I don't mean to crash your little party," Mara Marhoe interrupted, "but you should take care not to let anyone hear you talking to yourself in the john like that. They might think you're a dice short of a Yahtzee and ship you off to a mental hospital."

Farika smiled slightly and then let out a little laugh.

"Why, that's my dainty Farika! They shall miss thee;

but yet thou shalt have freedom," said Mara Marhoe in a sudden British accent.

"Is that Shakespeare?" asked Farika.

Mara Marhoe twisted her head, looking around the room to make sure that they were alone. Returning to her normal voice, she whispered to Farika, "Christmas came early this year. I have a little surprise for you."

Farika turned away from the mirror.

Mara Marhoe reached into her pocket and pulled something out, which was hidden inside her fist. She held her hand out to Farika and slowly unfolded her fingers to reveal in the palm of her hand a paperclip. "I spotted it on the floor near Doctor Farfle's desk this afternoon during my session with him," she announced. "And when the old quack wasn't looking I nabbed it and stashed it in my pocket." Mara Marhoe grinned with pride.

"It's a paperclip," Farika declared, flatly.

"It's the key that unlocks the door to our freedom," Mara Marhoe responded. "But that isn't all. Santa Claus has been extra generous."

Puzzled, but curious, Farika switched off the lavatory light and followed Mara Marhoe back into their shared bedroom without saying anything. She watched as Mara Marhoe carefully slid her hand between the mattress and box spring of her bed and extracted the pair of scissors which Zora Zenith had tried attacking Farika with earlier in the day.

"That Zora Zenith screwball bestowed a blessing upon us without even realizing it," beamed Mara Marhoe, displaying the scissors and gazing lovingly upon it as though it were treasure. "We're as good as out of this loony-bin!"

She quickly returned the scissors to its hiding spot as a blood-curdling scream permeated the hall and was followed by the sound of running footsteps and excited

The Amnesia Girl!

voices.

Farika and Mara Marhoe hurried to the door and opened it. The scene outside in the hall was utter chaos with staff and patients rushing and shouting.

"What's happening?" asked Mara Marhoe to an unshaven, wheelchair-bound man wearing a blue hospital gown and army boots.

"Viet Cong ambush, soldier," he replied, as he rolled by. "You can't trust Charlie! They've got all sorts of tricks up their sleeves."

Farika recognized one of the faces in the stampeding crowd. It was the hippie girl who had attacked the nurse in the dining room the other day. "Hey!" she called out to her, waving her hand. "What's going on?"

The girl paused and shouted, "It's Mrs. Sylvers! Somehow she managed to get out onto the roof! She's reciting poetry and threatening to jump! Doctor I is up there right now trying to coax her to come back inside."

"Oh my God!" cried Farika. "That poor woman! I hope he saves her."

"They called in the fire department and I heard there's even a news crew outside filming the whole thing. Isn't that far-out? I gotta split before all the windows with the best views are taken!"

Mara Marhoe shut the door and looked at Farika, grinning. "This is our golden opportunity, Farika. It's time we make our move!"

"Our move?" asked an alarmed Farika, . "Do you mean breaking out? Right now?"

The sound of fire truck sirens and horns grew louder as the emergency vehicles approached the Midtown Psychiatric Hospital. The sense of urgency that they conveyed sent chills through Farika's body.

"Unless you want to sit around here waiting for your brain electrocution in the morning... and Zora Zenith's next attempt at killing you," replied Mara Marhoe.

"Next time I might not be around to save you," she added.

Mara Marhoe's words resonated within Farika, filling every fiber of her being with dread. She felt deep down in her heart that Mara Marhoe was right and that Zora Zenith would sooner or later launch another deadly attack upon her. However, she also realized that there existed the chance that she would get caught trying to escape and feared what the repercussions of that action might be.

Farika deliberated for a moment, weighing the pros and cons of the situation, and then made her decision. "Okay," she agreed. "Count me in."

"Good," Mara Marhoe smiled. "It's time for Operation Clip and Snip to go into effect!"

* *

While Farika kept an eye out for staff and other patients, Mara Marhoe crouched down and inserted the mangled paperclip into the keyhole of the door leading to Doctor I's office. She wiggled the steel wire back and forth and up and down, blurting out colorful expletives underneath her breath every so often, as her impatience grew. Tiny beads of perspiration appeared on her forehead and she wiped them away with the back of her hand and then continued trying to pick the lock.

"I've just got to get this door unlocked," she grumbled. "This office has access to the fire escape, which means no bars on the window."

"Someone's coming!" Farika whispered, as the sound of footsteps emerged from around the corner.

Mara Marhoe immediately withdrew the paperclip from the keyhole, and, in the blink of an eye, returned to a standing position and turned around to see who was approaching.

It was a patient who went by the name of Jessica Christ and believed herself to be the daughter of God. Her wrists and ankles were bandaged with white gauze that concealed the wounds she inflicted upon herself during a botched attempt at self-crucifixion.

"Oh, Christ," Mara Marhoe groaned. "What the hell do you want?"

"It's a sin to use my name in vain," replied Jessica Christ. "And what I want is for you to accept me as your Savior so that you, too, will inherit the kingdom of heaven."

"Piss off, Jessica," said Mara Marhoe, rolling the paperclip around in her pocket.

"I will not repay evil with evil," answered Jessica Christ with a gentle smile. "I do not delight in wickedness."

"Don't you have a fig tree or something that you need to go put a curse on?" asked Mara Marhoe with a sneer. "Or maybe some water to turn into wine?"

Jessica Christ cast Mara Marhoe a dispirited expression. "You do weary me with your words, Mara Marhoe. Your Philistine mouth is always opened and speaking against me with a wicked tongue. Sister, why have you forsaken me?"

Mara Marhoe shifted her gaze to Farika and shook her head. "It's always the same old crap with her."

"I am the same yesterday and today and forever!" exclaimed Jessica Christ, quoting Scriptures. "Blessed is the fruit of my womb!"

"Poor Mrs. Sylvers is up on the roof threatening to commit suicide," informed Farika. "She could sure use your divine intervention."

"I will go to her at once and cast out her devils," announced Jessica Christ, gently placing her hand on the top of Farika's head. "Bless you, my disciple." She then nodded her head in Mara Marhoe's direction. "And heed my warning about that one. She will lead you astray, my child. She has an unclean spirit inside of her which needs to be fed."

Mara Marhoe rolled her eyes and groaned.

Farika's attention was suddenly drawn to something bright red on the floor directly in front of Jessica Christ. She lowered her head to look and observed at least half a dozen quarter-sized splatter marks that resembled little ruby-colored pinwheels. She then looked up and saw that blood was oozing from a gaping circular lesion in the palms of Jessica Christ's hands.

"You're bleeding!" Farika exclaimed, pointing to the woman's bloody hands.

"It's a miracle!" Jessica Christ cried out with glee, as she held her hands up to the sky. "Behold the holy wounds of my crucifixion!"

"I've had just about all I can take of this shit," Mara Marhoe snarled. She balled up her hands into tight fists. "Take your goddamned stigmata and piss off!"

With blood still dripping from the wounds in her palms, Jessica Christ made the sign of the cross with her right hand and then scurried down the hall, joyously singing:

"Turn your eyes upon Jessica,
Look full in Her wonderful face,
And all things of earth will grow strangely dim,
In the light of Her glory and grace."

With Jessica Christ gone and the corridor momentarily devoid of any staff or other patients, Mara Marhoe quickly resumed her crouching position with the bent paperclip probing the inside of Doctor I's keyhole. As she attempted, once again, to pick the lock, she breathed a sigh of relief. "That was quick thinking on your part, Farika. I thought that wacko and her burning

The Amnesia Girl!

bush would never leave."

Suddenly, there was a click, and Mara Marhoe turned the knob, incapable of hiding her excited anticipation. The door opened, and the forbidden darkness within the room beckoned. "Praise the Lord!" she sarcastically exclaimed.

Mara Marhoe dashed into the doctor's office, followed closely by Farika. She shut the door and locked it, and then flicked the switch on the wall next to the door. Hanging from the painted, tin-tiled ceiling on a dusty chain, an old brass light fixture with a white, milk glass shade instantly illuminated the room, revealing its contents.

On the wall straight ahead, behind a five-foot-tall ficus tree in a large, white ceramic pot and covered by beige Venetian blinds, was the unbarred window, which lead to the fire escape at the back of the building. Against the wall, to the right, stood an imposing mahogany bookcase filled with a plethora of hardcover volumes on psychiatry and psychology; and positioned near the opposite wall was a large antique desk that was topped with a pile of papers, a souvenir ashtray from a 1971 psychiatric convention, a pipe holder with tobacco humidor, and Doctor I's prized, life-sized, marble bust of Sigmund Freud. Situated at the rear of the desk was a huge, Naugahyde office chair, and against the wall, behind the desk and chair, stood a long cabinet covered by potted ivy plants and a Spanish-style, wrought iron lamp with a gold, velvet shade. A gallery of Doctor I's framed diplomas and achievement awards looked down from the wall above.

Something about the room made Farika feel uneasy. "Let's hurry and get out of here!" she whispered.

"All in good time," Mara Marhoe replied, drawn to the desk, like a moth to a flame. "Let's see what we have here." Spotting a thick journal bound in a royal blue leatherette cover with a lock on the side, she snatched it from the desktop and stuffed it into her back pocket.

"What are you taking that for?" inquired Farika.

"It's Dr. I's treatise, *The Joy of Insanity*. I always like to be insured," replied Mara Marhoe as she sat down in the Naugahyde chair and attempted to pull the desk drawers open. However, to her dismay, she discovered that they were all securely locked. She instinctively inserted her trusty paperclip into the ornate brass escutcheon of the top drawer and, within a few moments, managed to unlock it. She rifled through the drawer and then extracted a brown leather wallet personalized with the initials, "I.I." A look of glee came over her face as she opened it and discovered sixty-nine dollars within its money compartment. She stashed the currency into her pocket and returned the empty wallet to the drawer.

She then withdrew a plastic bottle of piña colada-flavored Emotion Lotion. Upon realizing that it was a sexual lubricant, she quickly tossed it back into the drawer. "Ewww," she blurted out, disgustedly. "That must be what he uses on his thing when he balls Nurse Mars."

She moved on to the next drawer; however, the lock refused to yield as easily as the first one did. She frantically wiggled the paperclip around in the lock while at the same time attempting, in vain, to pull the drawer open. "Damn it!" she grumbled. "I think this thing is stuck." And with that, she yanked on the handle of the obstinate drawer as hard as she could, causing the desk to lurch towards her and the bust of Sigmund Freud to topple. It landed on the floor with a loud, crashing sound and broke into several pieces.

Farika looked horrified.

"Son of a bitch!" growled Mara Marhoe.

The two women made a mad dash for the window;

however, unlike the Venetian blinds, the window refused to open. They tried pushing it up with every bit of their combined strength, but the only thing they accomplished was getting the sash to slide up about two inches, before it got stuck again.

"We need something to pry it open the rest of the way," observed Farika.

"Or just smash it and make a run for it," added Mara Marhoe.

The sound of footsteps materialized outside of the door, followed by a knocking. And then Nurse Mars' voice rang out.

"Ivan? Are you in there?" she inquired, and then knocked again. "I heard a strange noise coming from inside your office. Are you all right?"

Hearing the sound of jingling keys, Mara Marhoe turned to Farika and whispered, "Quickly, hide!"

Farika rushed to find a hiding spot behind the desk while Mara Marhoe switched off the light and fled to the closet, which was next to the door that was now being unlocked.

Just as Mara Marhoe shut the closet door behind her, the door to the office opened and the light clicked back on.

Through the space underneath the desk Farika could see Nurse Mars standing in the doorway, making a visual inspection of the room.

"Hello?" called Nurse Mars, suspiciously.

Farika's heart was beating rapidly, as the adrenaline rushed through her body. It pounded so loudly in her ears that she feared Nurse Mars would hear it from across the room. She held her breath, afraid to breathe, and wished that Nurse Mars would turn and leave.

However, something near the desk caught the nurse's eye and she walked over to where the broken pieces of the bust lay on the floor. She stood silently for a length of time as though studying the chunks of marble for some kind of clue. She then kneeled down to retrieve the Freudian fragments and, while doing so, caught a glimpse of Farika from under the desk. Outraged, Nurse Mars opened her mouth and unleashed a tirade upon Farika.

"What is the meaning of this? And just how in hell's name did you get into this office? This room is off-limits to all patients! Well? I expect an answer!"

Shamefaced, Farika stood up and looked at Nurse Mars, avoiding eye contact. Not a single word did she utter. From out of the corner of her eye, she could see the closet door behind the angry woman slowly opening and Mara Marhoe emerging with her right hand wrapped tightly around the scissors. With the index finger of her other hand over her lips, Mara Marhoe gestured for Farika to keep quiet.

Nurse Mars' face was contorted with rage as she continued giving Farika a tongue-lashing. "You can be rest assured that Doctor I will be informed of this insolent intrusion," she threatened. "And I will personally see to it that maximal disciplinary action is taken to correct your behavior!"

Creeping as silently as a cat, Mara Marhoe took a few steps forward and then suddenly rushed towards Nurse Mars from behind. She wrapped her left arm around the startled nurse's body and, with her right hand, held the pair of scissors firmly to her throat. "The only behavior that's going to get corrected is yours!" she hissed into her ear.

Mara Marhoe then instructed Farika to shut the door and lock it.

"You need to calm down, Mara," said Nurse Mars, speaking each word slowly and carefully. "I know you're experiencing turbulent emotions right now and I want to help you, if you'll let me. But it's imperative that you put your trust in me." She tried to sound as calm as possible, but the nervousness in her voice betrayed her. "You're just having a psychotic episode. Don't do anything you'll regret later."

"Oh, don't you worry, you rancid, old slag," Mara Marhoe replied in a phony British accent. "Slitting your bloody throat is one thing I'd *never* regret doing!"

Farika gasped. "Don't do it!" she cried.

"Turn your head or shut your eyes if the sight of blood makes you queasy!" Mara Marhoe shouted to Farika, pressing the blade of the scissors harder against Nurse Mars' throat.

"You've made your point," quipped Nurse Mars. "Now let me go and I'll see that you're given a strong dose of Thorazine and any high-calorie, dopamine-releasing dessert of your choice."

"Listen, douche bag," snapped Mara Marhoe. "Skewering your nasty neck is the only point I intend to make!"

"Mara, please!" begged Farika desperately. "Don't kill her! We came here to escape from this awful place, not to murder anyone!"

"Listen to your friend," Nurse Mars advised. "She knows what's best for you. Now put down my scissors and..."

"Shut the hell up!" screamed Mara Marhoe wildly. "One more word out of your goddamn mouth and I swear I'll gut you like a pig right here in your precious lover-boy's office. Imagine the look on his face when he sees your intestines spilled out all over his Naugahyde chair!" Mara Marhoe then turned to Farika, who looked horrified and was covering her mouth with her hands. "I don't think it's a coincidence that these scissors - the very same scissors that Zora Zenith tried killing you with - belong to Mars," she said. "In fact, I'd be willing to bet that this noxious nurse here gave them to her as a little present with instructions to kill you!"

"Listen to me, Mara Marhoe," pleaded Nurse Mars, "Your delusions and paranoid thoughts are taking over your mind. You're in grave danger of losing all touch with reality unless you allow me to help you by..."

"I've had enough of you!" screamed Mara Marhoe, pressing the scissors against the nurse's neck even harder until a small droplet of blood dribbled down onto her starched white collar. Turning again to Farika, she wrinkled up her nose and squinted her eyes. "Please, Farika. Let me disembowel this tuna twat. I've been aching to do this to her for years. Pretty please?"

Farika removed her hands from her mouth. "No, it's not right. Besides, they'll send you to the electric chair for murder. And then I won't have anyone. You're the only friend I have. So please don't kill her!"

Mara Marhoe snickered. "They banned the electric chair in New York two years ago, so I'm afraid your point is an invalid one."

"Please, Mara, let's just lock her in the closet and get out of here before Doctor I comes back. If he catches us in here, that'll be the end of us. We'll never get this opportunity to escape again."

A disgusted look formed on Mara Marhoe's face and she let out a loud sigh. "Oh all right, Farika, you win. I'll spare this rotten bitch's life."

Mara Marhoe barked at Nurse Mars to get into the closet and, without hesitation, the frightened nurse obeyed the order. Mara shut the door and asked Farika to unplug the lamp that was sitting on the cabinet behind Doctor I's desk and bring it to her.

After Farika handed her the lamp, she used the scissors to cut off the cord and then tossed the lamp onto the floor. She wrapped one end of the cord several times around the doorknob of the closet and double knotted it. Pulling the cord tight, she then wrapped its other end around the knob of the office door and knotted it securely. "This ought to hold her for awhile," she asserted.

Informing Farika that an idea had popped into her head while hiding inside the closet, Mara Marhoe returned to the desk and grabbed the bottle of Emotion Lotion. She took it over to the window and poured some into the tracks. "If this stuff works on that dried-up old cunt-zilla, it should work on the window," she chortled. She then attempted once again to open the stuck window.

Farika joined her in the effort and, after a few moments, the lubricated lower sash began to slide freely. Without wasting a moment, they climbed out onto the fire escape and hurried down the black metal steps as quickly as their legs could carry them.

The outside air was warmed by the late afternoon sun and filled with diesel exhaust and industrial fumes. But to Farika and Mara Marhoe, it was sweet with the smell of freedom.

They took off like two racehorses bolting out of the starting gate, running down the sidewalk as fast as their feet could carry them and then turning off into a long, litter-strewn alley filled with rusty green dumpsters and intoxicated derelicts. They emerged near a city park, which Mara Marhoe convinced Farika to take a detour through to avoid being spotted by any police cars cruising the streets near the psychiatric hospital. No sooner had the two escaped mental patients started down one of the wooded trails, a rustling noise came from one of the nearby shrubs and a grubby man wearing a trench coat jumped out from behind it, waving a gun in front of them.

"Hand over all your money, as well as your jewelry and any drugs you got on you," the man in the trench coat demanded as he nervously looked around to make sure nobody was approaching.

Mara Marhoe looked at the man's gun and burst into laughter. "That's nothing but a plastic water pistol!" she snorted. "You have got to be the most pathetic excuse for a New York City mugger that I've ever encountered!"

"It's filled with acid," the man threatened, "and unless you and your little lady-friend there want a face full of it, you'd both better be smart and give me all the valuables you got. And be quick about it! I don't have all frigging day!"

"Hey, wait a minute," mused Mara Marhoe, studying the mugger's face. "You look familiar. I know who you are now. I've seen you on the Phil Donahue Show! You're that hermaphrodite, Johnny Waffle, who impregnated himself, aren't you?"

"That's right," smirked the mugger. "Now let's have the money, lady!"

"Sure thing, Johnny. But first, could you please sign my autograph book?" Mara Marhoe reached into her pocket and pulled out the book she had stolen from Doctor I's office. "I've never met anyone famous before, let alone an honest-to-God television personality! I'll bet there's even a Johnny Waffle fan club out there!"

The mugger smiled and looked down. "Well," he began bashfully, "not really. I mean, not yet. Okay, I'll sign your book, since you're a big fan and all. But I'm still going to mug you afterwards. We hermaphrodites have to make a living too, you know."

Without warning, Mara Marhoe swung the book into the mugger's face, breaking his nose. He let out a yell as blood gushed from his nostrils, and then Mara Marhoe planted her foot between his legs with all her might. He fell to the ground, clutching his crotch, and Mara Marhoe immediately pulled the wristwatch from his wrist and deposited it inside her pocket. She and Farika then took off running through the park, looking over their shoulders periodically to make sure the hermaphrodite wasn't in pursuit. When they reached the end of the trail at the other side of the park, they stopped to catch their breath.

"I can't believe you actually mugged a mugger," Farika breathlessly exclaimed.

"Oh, man, that was a real trip," affirmed Mara Marhoe, panting. "I've never given anyone a dick-kick and a cunt-punt all at the same time!"

"I can tell you got a real kick out of it," Farika punned.

Chapter Five

Friends in Low Places

Block after block of brownstone apartment buildings, half-obscured by mountainous piles of garbage bags, seemed to go on forever and then, finally, a bus stop came into view.

Farika and Mara Marhoe sat down on the graffiti-scribbled bench, enjoying the relief from over an hour of walking on the unforgiving pavement. They both removed their shoes and massaged their aching feet while waiting for the bus to arrive.

"You'll dig my friend," Mara Marhoe was saying. "She goes by the name Forrest Lawn. Isn't that wild? She's an actress-model and she's heavily into the New York underground scene. I heard she was even hanging out with the Warhol crowd for a while. We haven't seen each other in a couple years, but she's cool people and I know she'll let us crash at her pad up in Hell's Kitchen."

The bus pulled up, belching out a black cloud of malodorous diesel exhaust. The door opened and a group of people disembarked. Farika and Mara Marhoe climbed aboard, paid their fare, and sat down next to each other.

Farika glanced around the bus, feeling conspicuous and on edge. A matching pair of laughing sailors sat a few seats behind her and across from a young black woman wearing a huge Afro wig and large hoop earrings. There were a couple of middle-aged men garbed in drab business suits with briefcases, a book-reading nun, a mother with a cranky baby, a passed-out Puerto Rican man with a pony-tail, and a gray-haired lady, busy knitting some hideous-looking thing out of multi-colored yarn. Farika pretended she didn't see the yarmulke-wearing man with ringlet sideburns sitting directly across the aisle from her, eyeing her intently while masturbating himself underneath his raincoat.

"Ah, sweet freedom!" sighed Mara Marhoe.

Night was starting to fall and the colorful, blinking neon signs of the pornographic bookstores, x-rated theaters, and hotels advertising monthly, weekly and hourly rates lit up Eighth Avenue like a carnival of sleaze.

The bus pulled up to the stop where Farika and Mara Marhoe got off.

"Her place is just half a block down from here," said Mara Marhoe. "We'll be there in no time."

As they made their way down Eighth Avenue, several heavily made-up women who were obviously ladies of the evening stared at them. An outrageously dressed transvestite flashed them a dirty look as he exited from an adult bookstore with peepshow cubicles, and a blond-haired man wearing a Stetson hat and a bell-bottomed denim outfit sparkling with rhinestones whistled and tried to proposition them.

"This is it!" cried Mara Marhoe excitedly, stopping in front of a decaying brick building with a red and purple neon sign that flashed: *Man-In-The-Moon All-*

Male Massage Parlor. "We finally made it!"

"This couldn't be the right place," protested Farika. "The sign says it's a massage parlor! Are you sure you have the right address?"

Mara Marhoe laughed. "My God, Farika, sometimes you're dense." She pointed up to the second floor. "She lives in a cold-water flat upstairs. Follow me and let me do all the talking."

They ascended a dimly lit, graffitied stairway, that led up to a small landing and a green wooden door that was covered in large stickers depicting erotic Art Nouveau- styled women. On the wall next to the door was an old brass mailbox, upon which was stuck a strip of black plastic embossed with white letters that spelled out: *F.L. Talent Unlimited.*

Mara Marhoe knocked on the door and waited. A few moments later a raspy woman's voice called out from the other side of the door in a heavy Brooklyn accent, "Who the fuck's banging on my door?"

"It's me, Mara Marhoe!"

Close to half a minute passed and then Farika and Mara Marhoe heard the sound of deadbolts sliding and chains rattling as numerous locks on the door were unlocked one-by-one.

The door slowly opened, revealing a groggy-looking woman wearing a kimono with a wild floral print. Her bleached blonde hair was long and unkempt, and she squinted as though the light bulb that barely illuminated the landing brought discomfort to her mascara-smeared eyes.

"Mara Marhoe!" she exclaimed. "I heard through the grapevine that you'd been committed to that nuthouse down in Chelsea again. When the hell did you get out, and who the hell is this?"

"They discharged me this morning," Mara Marhoe fibbed. "And this is my good friend, Farika. We were kind of hoping we could crash here with you for a little while."

"Well, this is your lucky day," declared Forrest Lawn. "My roommate OD'ed last night. She's in New York Presbyterian in a coma, again, so you're more than welcome to crash here." She gestured with her hand for them to come inside.

The inside of the apartment was dark, depressing, and smelled like old clothes and stale incense. Stacks of books and record albums, towering mountains of boxes containing God-knows-what, and two large wardrobe racks crammed with odd clothes, garish stage costumes and feather boas filled up most of the main room. What little space was left over had been furnished with a pair of ratty, old wingback chairs, a tension pole lamp with dented, gold-colored, metal shades, and an inverted pair of wooden crates. One of the crates served as a stand for a small television set with bent rabbit-ear antennas, and the other was used as an end table to hold a black rotary-dial telephone, an ashtray overflowing with cigarette butts, a half-empty bottle of cheap, red wine, and a lava lamp.

A partially-opened door at the far side of the room revealed a grungy bathroom with a rusty, paint-chipped, claw-foot tub that was dimly illuminated by a bare light bulb attached to a wire coming out of the cracked plaster ceiling.

About five feet to the right of the bathroom door, on the same wall, was an archway from which dangled a curtain made entirely of long strands of plastic beads. Peeking through the strands was a small, cluttered galley-style kitchen. Unwashed dishes, pots, and pans rose up from a sink above a curtained storage area, as if in defiance of the bottle of lemon-scented dishwashing detergent that sat on the white-tiled countertop next to the sink, and across them, scurried a cockroach.

As the three women made their way through the cluttered room, they had to carefully maneuver to avoid stepping on clothes, shoes, books of matches, a transistor radio, an almost-empty carton of Virginia Slims cigarettes, and a Styrofoam wig head. Farika couldn't help but notice that the clutter included a number of pornographic magazines that featured on their glossy covers, a naked woman who bore a striking resemblance to the woman in the kimono. She wondered if Mara Marhoe had noticed them as well.

"Welcome to the Ritz, ladies," Forrest Lawn quipped. "I'm proud to say that I furnished this place all by myself. My furniture and decor is all stuff that I found in the trash." As she spoke, she pointed to everything in the room as though she were giving a tour of a grand house. "All these boxes in this room are filled with wonderful items, big and small, that people tossed into garbage cans and dumpsters."

"It's all very nice," proclaimed Farika, pretending to be impressed.

Forrest Lawn stopped pointing. "Just how long were you guys planning to stay, if you don't mind me asking? If you need some bread I might be able to get you jobs as gay masseurs at the all-male massage parlor downstairs. I know the dude who runs the place. But you'd have to dress in drag as men, of course, and change your names to Muscle Mary and Bruce. He *only* hires homosexuals."

"Thank you, ever so much, Forrest Lawn, but you needn't go out of your way to do that," said Mara Marhoe.

"It was very kind of you to offer, though," Farika added, trying to sound as gracious as possible.

"Actually," said Mara Marhoe, "we were hoping we could stay with you for a few days, maybe longer. If you have no objections, of course."

The Amnesia Girl!

"Well, honey," responded Forrest Lawn, "you can stay until Topaz comes out of her coma. I wouldn't mind the company and I could sure use some help with the housework around here. That damn junkie bitch left this place a god-awful mess!"

"How awful!" commiserated Mara Marhoe.

"Isn't it? I'm a woman on the go. My life is devoted entirely to my acting and nude modeling career, and rescuing treasures from the trash! Who the hell has time for housecleaning?"

Mara Marhoe and Farika thanked Forrest Lawn for her hospitality and took turns embracing her.

"One of you ladies can have the guest bedroom," said Forrest Lawn, pointing to a corrugated cardboard refrigerator box lying on its side in the corner of the room. Within it was a pillow and a crumpled blanket. "And the other can sleep in the bathtub. I sleep on the Murphy bed because I'm the queen of this castle."

* *

"Good morning," said Forrest Lawn cheerfully. "And how did my precious little house guests sleep last night?"

"Oh, just wonderful," said Farika, struggling to crawl out of the corrugated cardboard refrigerator box. She stood up and simultaneously massaged her aching lower back and neck with her hands. She then gently rolled her shoulders a few times and slowly twisted from side to side, in an attempt to get the kinks out of her back. "I've never slept in a refrigerator box before."

"You haven't?" Forrest Lawn sounded rather surprised.

Farika shook her head, no.

"Well, I'm so happy that you found my guest bedroom to your liking."

The bathroom door swung open and Mara Marhoe emerged, beaming. "That was the most comfortable bathtub I've ever slept in. It was more comfy than a Ramada Inn. I feel so spoiled!"

After a breakfast consisting of leftover carryout Chinese food, Forrest Lawn announced that she was receiving an important male visitor in an hour. "His name is Jeff," she confided, "and he's from Pennsylvania. He visits me every time he drives into New York City on business. You might say he's a *special* client of mine."

"A client?" inquired Farika, as she began washing the breakfast plates and utensils. "What sort of client?"

"The sort that pays extremely well, my dear. So I'm gonna need the two of you dearies to make yourselves invisible for half an hour while I conduct business. But don't worry, he never stays for more than thirty minutes."

Farika finished washing the dishes. As she dried her hands with a pink and green paisley dishtowel with a hole in it, she asked, "Where are we supposed to go? I don't know my way around here."

"It doesn't make any difference to me where the two of you go, just so long as you go," snapped Forrest Lawn as she brushed her hair. "Take a walk through the Red Light District, do some shoplifting, or go find yourselves a wino in the back alley and rape him for all I care."

"Don't worry, Forrest Lawn," Mara Marhoe responded in a reassuring tone of voice. "We'll split before your client gets here. And I'm sure Farika and I will find something to do to keep ourselves occupied."

"Good, because he doesn't like a live audience."

At that moment there came a loud knock at the front door and a look of panic swept across Forrest Lawn's half-made-up face. She quickly looked up at her plastic

Kit-Kat wall clock with its swinging tail and ridiculous rolling eyes. "It couldn't be him. He's not due for another half hour." She turned her face towards the front door and shouted loudly, "Who is it?"

"It's Jeff," came a muffled reply from the other side of the door, "and I brought the mannequin."

"Oh, shit," Forrest Lawn grumbled under her breath. "He's usually very punctual, but this time the bastard's early." Turning to face Farika and Mara Marhoe, she shooed them out of the kitchen with her hands and whispered, "You two, quickly, go sit outside on the fire escape and keep yourselves quiet until he's gone. Vamoose!"

She sashayed through her hoard of dumpster delights and pulled the Murphy bed down from the wall as Farika and Mara Marhoe dashed to the window and climbed out onto the fire escape.

From outside, Farika and Mara Marhoe could hear the sound of the front door being unlocked and then opened.

"Come on in, Jeff. You're a bit early," they could hear Forrest Lawn say. "I wasn't expecting you for at least another thirty minutes. You'll have to excuse my make-up. I only had time to apply green eye shadow to one eye."

"Don't worry about it, Miss Lawn," Jeff replied. "I think you look even more radiantly beautiful with just one eye made up like that."

"Why, thank you, Jeff. Would you care to sit down?"

"Thank you."

"Are you ready to begin?"

"Oh, yes!"

The strange sounds of moaning and whimpering replaced the conversation between Jeff and Forrest Lawn, and as it continued on for minutes and intensified, Farika's curiosity grew and grew until it finally compelled her to take a peek through the window.

Through the old lace curtains she could make out the sight of a man seated in one of the wingback chairs. Forrest Lawn was standing in front of him, delicately caressing and teasing his face with the pink and green paisley dishtowel, and as she did this, he rubbed his crotch through his trousers.

"Is it damp enough for you?" Forrest Lawn asked.

"Mmm-hmm," he replied.

"And is the odor to your liking?"

"Oh, God, yes!"

Forrest Lawn pulled the towel away from Jeff's face and bitch-slapped him with it several times and he cried out in ecstasy, "Yes! Yes! Yes!" She then took the towel and violently pushed it up into his face, covering his nose and mouth so he couldn't breathe. "I could kill you with this dishtowel," she told him in a vicious tone of voice, "just as easily as I could kill a housefly."

Jeff let out a bizarre squealing sound and jumped to his feet, still rubbing his crotch. "It's time," he exclaimed excitedly. "And remember, you're not to look. Not even a little peek until I've finished!"

"Don't worry, Jeff," Forrest Lawn said, shaking her head. "I know how you like it."

Jeff quickly disrobed; tossing his clothes onto the clutter that covered the floor, and made a beeline straight to the Murphy bed where the mannequin was lying. "It's time for the voice!" he cried. "And make sure you turn your back and don't look at me!"

Forrest Lawn obediently turned her back to Jeff as he eagerly climbed on top of the plastic woman, fondled its breasts, and humped it.

"Ooh, give it to me, Daddy. Insert your love-biscuit inside my oven," purred Forrest Lawn, speaking for the mannequin. "Ohhhh, you make me feel so lusty. I love it

The Amnesia Girl!

when you pump my cha-cha with your big purple mushroom. Oh, do it harder, Jeff. No one tickles my taco like your Mister Winky does. Your genitals are so golden!"

"Yes! Yes! Don't stop!" cried Jeff. "I need to hear more dirty talk!"

"Oh, that's it, Daddy," Forrest Lawn continued. "You're so naughty. Rub that throbbing sperm-slinger all over my hoochie-coochie. Mmmm, I'm your love-slave. I'm your Venus. Ooh-la-la. Launch that pocket rocket! Glaze my doughnut!"

"Ahhhhh!" screamed Jeff as his eyes twirled. "I'm reaching the point of no return! Here I come! Don't look at me! Oh, Mother Mary! I'm about to achieve an orgasm!" His words gave way to fast and furious heavy breathing followed by a primeval cry of, "Eeeeeeaaaaaaah!" which was then followed by a minute of dog-like panting.

Farika watched in horror as Jeff dismounted the mannequin, which was now all wet and glistening from his perspiration, drool and other bodily fluids, and carried it with him to the bathroom. She saw him shut the door and could hear the sound of the shower running. The sudden mental impression of Jeff and the sexually violated mannequin bathing together made her left eye twitch.

She gazed over at Mara Marhoe, who was busy fondling her pendulous bosoms through her blouse.

"Ooooh," Mara Marhoe purred. "Acts of perversion make my nipples hard!"

Farika peeked through the window again. She could see Forrest Lawn wrapped in her kimono and smoking a cigarette as she walked over to the television set. Its knob made a loud clicking sound as she turned it on. Moments later, after its tubes warmed up, the articulate and nondescript voice of a male newscaster spilled out of it and found its way into Farika's ears, filling her with great alarm.

"Good Morning, Manhattan. Topping today's news stories, the NYPD is on the lookout for two women who escaped from the Midtown Psychiatric Hospital yesterday. It is not clear at this time how the two patients broke out of the facility, but there are unconfirmed reports that a nurse working at the hospital was attacked. The two women have been identified as Mara Marhoe - a patient with a multitude of mental disorders, too numerous to list, and a mysterious amnesiac known only by the name of Farika. Anyone knowing the whereabouts of these two escapees is urged to contact the NYPD immediately!"

Forrest Lawn gasped and rushed over to the window to confront Mara Marhoe and Farika. She looked bug-eyed and her face was drained of color. "What the fuck is all this shit? You told me you got discharged from that goddamn hospital yesterday. You didn't tell me you broke out! Oh, man, this just changes everything. I can't have two escaped mental patients staying here!" she exclaimed.

"There's no need for you to panic," Mara Marhoe tried to reassure her.

"No need for me to panic? Are you putting me on? They were just reporting about your escape on the morning news and the fuzz is looking all over the city for you! You have to realize that this kind of thing is bad for my career. Plus, I can get into big trouble harboring fugitives. I really must insist that the two of you leave my beautiful apartment at once!"

"I understand how you feel," Mara Marhoe put her arm around Farika, who was now trembling. "But my friend here just can't go back to that horrible hospital. Her life is in great danger there! You have to believe me, Forrest Lawn. Please, for Farika's sake, let us hide out here until the coast is clear. We won't get in your way. I promise."

Forrest Lawn shook her head. "I'm sorry, Mara Marhoe. That is out of the question. However, you and I have been friends for a long time and I do owe you a favor for helping me to dispose of the you-know-what. So I am going to call my dear friend, Madame Contessa Cherie, and arrange for you and your friend to stay at her mansion. She owes ME a favor so I know she'll agree to it."

"Madame Contessa Cherie?" questioned Mara Marhoe.

"Yes, you remember her, don't you? She was a big star on Broadway back in the 1920s and now she runs that funky discotheque, the Castle de Sade. It's all the rage!"

"Yes, I remember her. But doesn't she live in San Francisco?" asked Mara Marhoe.

Forrest Lawn nodded her head.

"San Francisco?" echoed Farika. "California is thousands of miles from New York City and we don't have much money. How are we going to get there?"

"You could hijack a plane at gunpoint," suggested Forrest Lawn. "Everybody's hijacking planes these days. Even the Manson family planned a hijacking in order to free Charlie."

"But we don't have a gun," Mara Marhoe pointed out.

"Well," suggested Forrest Lawn, "in that case I guess you'll just have to hitchhike your way to San Francisco. Everybody hitchhikes these days. And I'm sure it'll be a great adventure for you. Jeff is heading back to Pennsylvania today and I'll ask him to give you a ride. *Bon voyage!*"

Chapter Six

An Emotional Wreck

The westbound traffic heading into the Lincoln Tunnel was bumper-to-bumper and extended for as far as the eye could see. The sound of beeping horns and angry motorists shouting obscenities from their rolled-down windows seemed to ricochet against the tile-covered walls and ceiling, and echo chaotically. The noise was juxtaposed by a row of lights on each side of the long passage that cast a silent and eerie glow.

"I heard they want to raise the toll to one dollar next year," remarked Jeff, sounding disgusted. He briefly turned his eyes away from the long, creeping trail of red brake lights that stretched out ahead to look at Farika, who was sitting next to him in the front passenger seat. "It's goddamn highway robbery if you ask me."

He impatiently began banging his fist on the horn and yelled out the driver's window of his yellow Mercedes Benz for everyone to get their asses moving. The driver of a mustard-colored taxicab in front of him stuck his head out of his window and bellowed back at Jeff to shut the hell up and called him a "shit-head." Jeff retorted by flipping the cabbie his middle finger.

Turning back to Farika, he whined, "It's always been fifty cents to take the Lincoln Tunnel into New York, ever since they built this goddamn thing back in the Thirties. And now they want to double it! And for what? For a mile and a half of this aggravation?"

Farika did not reply, nor did she make eye contact with Jeff. Her mind was too cluttered with unanswered questions and filled with dancing images of pink and green paisleys.

"How long will it take for us to get to Pennsylvania?" asked Mara Marhoe from the back seat.

"About an hour and a half," replied Jeff. "If we ever get out of this damn tunnel. And then it's another hour to my destination."

"That's a long drive," observed Mara Marhoe. "If you put this mannequin in the trunk I could stretch out my legs and take a nap."

"Molly always sits in the back seat," Jeff retorted, sounding slightly miffed. "Except on special occasions when she gets to ride up front with me. So just forget it."

Mara Marhoe frowned, then turned her head and stared out the window at nothing in particular.

After a long wait, the traffic began to move at an almost normal pace and the sounds of honking horns and irate voices ceased. When the yellow Mercedes Benz reached the middle of the tunnel, Jeff remarked about being in the belly of the beast and welcomed his two passengers to New Jersey.

As they traversed the Garden State, the urban grime and congestion gave way to tree-lined suburban subdivisions, which eventually gave way to quaint rural villages, dairy farms, and hilly woodlands.

Jeff turned on the car radio to a Top 40 station and

lit a cigarette. "You look like a couple of hip girls to me," he remarked, as the news reported a shootout between the Los Angeles police and the Symbionese Liberation Army. "I've got some joints in the glove compartment. Acapulco gold – the best in all the land. Feel like getting stoned?"

"No thank you," Farika, politely responded.

"Okay. Well, if grass isn't your thing, how about some speed or acid?"

"I'll take some Thorazine, please," Mara Marhoe requested, holding out her hand.

"Thorazine?" Jeff asked, taken aback. "That's a weird scene. I've got uppers, downers, hallucinogens, and a ten-pound bag of cocaine. But no Thorazine. Sorry."

As they drove on, Farika felt herself growing increasingly sleepy. Surrendering to her drowsiness, she closed her eyes and allowed herself to drift off. She dreamed about persons and places that seemed hauntingly familiar, yet were shrouded in mystery.

In her dream, a man was attaching a strange device to her head and reassuring her that there would be no pain. His words, however, did little to console her fear. He then told her it was time for him to switch on the dream machine and a loud buzzing sound filled her head.

"Pennsylvania state line!" shouted Jeff.

Waking abruptly from her dream, Farika opened her eyes and saw a large "Pennsylvania Welcomes You" sign fly past her window. She yawned as Mara Marhoe sang along to a song that was playing on the car radio.

Please make this recording number one or maybe two,
I spent my whole life praying this very song would get to you.

The Amnesia Girl!

> *This song I give to you*
> *From West of Jupiter above*
> *Its message rings clear and true*
> *The time has come for love.*
> *Please make this recording number one or maybe two,*
> *I spent my whole life praying this very song would get to you.*
> *Let my song shine like a star*
> *And play it on the Top Ten radio.*
> *The music is from my heart,*
> *The lyrics are from my soul.*
> *Please make this recording number one or maybe two,*
> *I spent my whole life praying this very song would get to you.*
> *After hearing this song of mine*
> *You may dig the groovy sound you heard.*
> *But play it once again*
> *And just listen to the words...*

As the song faded out, a disc jockey announced in an overly excited voice, "Moving up the pop charts to the lucky number thirteen position, that was 'Play It on the Radio' - the latest far-out hit single by Leopard Man and the Heavenly Blue!" He let out a long, loud howl, then continued with, "Can you dig it, baby? I know I can! And I'll keep playing it on the radio, right here on the howlin' Werewolf Wayne show as long as you keep phoning in those requests. And now, for your listening pleasure, here's a commercial..."

Jeff switched off the radio.

"Don't turn it off!" implored Mara Marhoe. "I wanted to hear the commercial."

"Screw the commercial!" Jeff interjected. Turning to Farika, he placed his right hand on her left thigh and gave it a squeeze. "How about a blow job, baby?"

"How about you go screw yourself!" shouted Mara Marhoe from the back seat.

"I wasn't talking to you," Jeff replied. "But don't get all bent out of shape. I'll let the two of you take turns blowing me. I got nothing against fat chicks."

Farika was frozen with fear.

"Who the hell do you think you are talking to us like we were a couple of cheap hookers? You stupid fucking pig!" Mara Marhoe yelled. At that moment she saw Jeff's hand on Farika's thigh, creeping its way up towards her crotch. "And you'd better get your goddamn putrid hand off of her!" she added. "Or you'll be sorry."

"Shut up!" yelled Jeff. "I'll say and do whatever the hell I please. And you're the one who's stupid if you thought this was going to be a free ride. I've got news for you, chubby; there's no such thing as a free ride in this world."

"Please," begged Farika. "Just stop the car and let us out."

Jeff laughed. "Not until after you've paid the toll. And the toll booth is in my pants!"

Mara Marhoe leaned over the back of Jeff's seat and started slapping and punching his arm in an attempt to get him to remove his hand from Farika.

The car started to swerve.

"I thought sniffing dishtowels and balling plastic ladies were more your speed, you freak," Mara Marhoe taunted. "Bet you can't get it up if anybody watches while you make a sickening asshole out of yourself. Isn't that right, freak?"

Clenching his teeth, Jeff angrily elbowed Mara Marhoe's arm and flew into a maniacal rage. Steering with only his left hand, he reached under his seat with his other hand and extracted a hypodermic syringe. He announced that it contained enough heroin to kill five people and threatened to inject Farika with it if she didn't comply with his demand for her to perform oral sex on him.

Fearing for her friend's life, Mara Marhoe instinctively yanked the mannequin's left arm off its body and began swinging it at the back of Jeff's head with all of her might.

Jeff let out a grunt as the hard plastic arm made impact with his head, blow after blow. He dropped the syringe on the seat and then his other hand dropped from the steering wheel and he slumped forward. Bright red streams of blood trickled from his battered head.

The Mercedes Benz swerved out of control and Farika and Mara Marhoe screamed in unison as it crashed through a guard rail and smashed into a tree at the edge of a forest in what appeared to be the middle of nowhere.

* *

Farika's eyelids slowly opened as she came to. Through the cracked glass of the windshield, she could see steam pouring out from underneath the crumpled hood. The air around her was infused with the smells of gasoline and burnt rubber, and a constant hissing sound came from the front of the mangled vehicle.

She turned her head to the left and let out a scream at the sight of the blood-splattered mannequin arm resting on the driver's seat. There was no sign of Jeff.

"Oh, good, you're finally up," she heard Mara Marhoe say from somewhere outside of the wrecked car. "I didn't want to disturb your beauty sleep. Come on out here and give me a hand with something."

Farika opened the passenger door and exited the car. She looked around but didn't see Mara Marhoe.

"Over here!" Mara shouted.

Fighting off a slight attack of dizziness, Farika walked around to the other side of the car and found Mara Marhoe dragging Jeff's body away from the opened driver's side door. His head was bloodied and he appeared to be lifeless.

"Oh, my God!" screamed Farika. "You killed him! You bashed his brains in with a mannequin!"

"Just the arm," Mara Marhoe corrected, calmly and unaffected. "Besides, I don't think he's dead. He's probably just out cold."

Farika looked closely at Jeff, inspecting him for any sign of life. "It doesn't look like he's breathing. I think he's dead! Oh, my God! What are we going to do?"

"Calm down, Farika. You freak out over every little thing," pointed out Mara Marhoe. "Help me get his body into the trunk. Well, just don't stand there gawking like some sort of spaz. Give me a hand!"

"Oh my God, how can you remain so calm, cool, and collected? Don't you realize you just murdered a man, and in cold blood I might add?"

Mara Marhoe rolled her eyes and continued dragging Jeff's body towards the rear of his Mercedes. "Big deal," she said, stopping momentarily to catch her breath and wipe the perspiration away from her forehead. "Even if he *is* dead, the creep had it coming. He tried to rape you. Or did you forget that? And besides, what sort of man performs sex acts with a department store dummy?"

"We should call for some help," Farika suggested, desperation seeping into her voice. "Maybe there's a house somewhere around here with a telephone we could use."

"Use your head, Farika! What are the cops going to do if we call them? Hmmm? Well, I'll tell you what they're going to do. They're going to arrest us for murder."

"But I'm not the one who killed him."

"It doesn't matter. You'll be charged as an accessory and they'll ship you right back to Midtown. Or some place even worse. Is that what you want? Is it?"

"This can't be happening," moaned Farika. "I must be having a bad dream or an hallucination of some sort. Maybe Nurse Mars... "

"Nurse Mars!" Mara Marhoe interjected. "I don't ever want to hear that name again. As far as I'm concerned Mars is nothing but a four-letter word. Now, snap out of it and give me a hand!" She let Jeff's legs drop to the ground and placed her hands upon her hips. "Do I have to do all the hard work by myself? I thought we were in this thing together."

"We are, but I never agreed to be involved in murder," replied Farika, as she reluctantly took hold of one of Jeff's ankles.

Mara Marhoe grabbed Jeff's other ankle and the two women dragged him the rest of the way to the back of the car. Mara Marhoe retrieved the keys from the car's ignition and then unlocked the trunk, which popped open, ready and waiting for its cargo.

As she helped her friend pull Jeff up from the ground and deposit him inside the trunk, Farika felt like her mind and body were floating in a dream. The situation had lost all sense of reality for her and she felt, and hoped, that at any minute she would awaken and find herself in her own bed, in her own home, wherever that might be.

Mara Marhoe was about to shut the trunk when Jeff stirred slightly and groaned.

"He's alive!" exclaimed Farika, as a feeling of relief flowed through her.

"In that case," declared Mara Marhoe, "he's going to need some company for when he wakes up." She went into the car and retrieved the one-armed mannequin from the back seat. She tossed the plastic woman on top of Jeff and then threw the car keys into the trunk, alongside them, and slammed the lid shut.

"It's going to be dark soon," she mentioned to Farika.

Chapter Seven

An Unbalanced Diet

Farika and Mara Marhoe made their way back up to the highway and, without uttering a word to each other, walked alongside the guardrail until the wreckage of Jeff's car was far behind them and out of their view. They stuck out their thumbs and waited patiently as car after car and truck after truck whizzed past them.

Mara Marhoe finally broke the silence. "It's too bad that weirdo back there didn't have more money in his wallet. We could've taken a train the rest of the way instead of having to thumb a ride."

Farika did not reply.

The minutes stretched into five minutes short of an hour. Finally, a car slowed down, and then pulled over onto the shoulder of the highway, about twenty-five feet up ahead of the two hitchhikers. It was a 1955 Rambler American station wagon that had clearly seen better days. All but one of its dirty whitewall tires were missing their hubcaps, and an array of dents, pitted paint and rust spots covered its exterior of faded salmon pink like a rash. The driver was a middle-aged, stubble-faced man whose soiled denim overalls gave him the appearance of a farmer. He leaned over to the passenger side, and rolled down the window.

"Are you two wimmin' okay?" he asked with a bit of a twang in his voice. "I saw your vee-hicle down the road a-ways. It looks like it's out of commission. Ya'll need me to drive you ladies to the hospital or somethin'?"

Before Farika had a chance to say anything, Mara Marhoe quickly blurted out, "NO hospitals!"

The man squinted his right eye at her.

"We're fine," she continued, "really, we're just fine."

"No broken bones. Not even a scratch," Farika added.

"We just need to get to San Francisco," pleaded Mara Marhoe. "It's a matter of life and death!"

"Well, in that case," said the man, as his eyes grew wider, "ya'll had better hop in!"

Farika and Mara Marhoe looked over at each other and each gave a slight nod of approval. They thanked the man, who had introduced himself as Freddie, and climbed into the back seat of the station wagon and looked around. The floor was strewn with odd bits and pieces of litter, including: a broken wristwatch, a length of greasy rope, a pair of men's glasses with a cracked lens, some tattered bits of old clothing, and a woman's black pump that was badly scuffed and missing part of its heel. The seats were ripped and covered in dark brownish stains, and from them emanated a repulsive smell. Farika felt overcome by nausea and asked if she could roll down her window.

Eyeing Farika from his rear view mirror, Freddie grinned and nodded his head. "Ain't never been to Californy myself," he declared as he drove, seemingly oblivious to the shaking and rattling of the car. "In fact, I ain't never been out of this here county. Ain't that a hoot? So what's the rush to get to San Francisco, if ya'll don't mind me askin'. I'm just tryin' to make friendly conversation."

"Uh, it's our grandmother," Farika lied. "She's extremely ill. On her death bed as a matter of fact."

"That's right," agreed Mara Marhoe. Her voice turned sorrowful and she pretended to hold back her tears. "I'm afraid she doesn't have much time. We promised Grandma that we'd visit her one last time before she, you know, buys the farm."

"Oh, I bought a farm too!" the grubby man behind the wheel quipped. "Bought it close to forty years ago after they sent me home from the war. It's about ten miles down the highway. Ever since my wife, Ovaria, God rest her soul, got called home to be with Jesus, it's just been me and my daughter living out there. Say, I got me an idea! Why don't you let me take you girls back to the house for supper? You both look like you could use some home cookin' and I just know my daughter will love you."

"Thank you, but I'm afraid we're really not very hungry," said Farika, "and besides..."

"Speak for yourself, Farika," Mara Marhoe interrupted, frowning disapprovingly. She rubbed her hand over her belly. "I'm starving!"

"Besides," Farika continued, returning an equally disapproving frown to her travel companion, "my friend and I really have no time to spare."

"Your friend?" Freddie inquired, suspiciously, as he once again eyed Farika from his rearview mirror. "I thought ya'll said that you were kin."

"Uhh, we're sisters from different fathers," said Mara Marhoe.

"And mothers," added Farika.

The driver squinted his right eye for a moment and then he stated, "My daughter, her name is Lorelei, she's been ill. Poor little thing, she hardly ever gets out of the house anymore, let alone get out of bed in her condition. She don't get many visitors up at the house. But she shore loves visitors when she does get 'um. The doctors, they don't know what's wrong with her. Been that way ever since her poor mama exited this world. I pray every day for that child, that the good Lord'll see fit to heal what's ailin' her. She's all the kin I got left." He began to weep.

"Well, maybe a quick bite to eat wouldn't be such a bad idea," uttered Farika, feeling sorry for Freddie.

Mara Marhoe smiled in anticipation of a hot meal.

The station wagon exited the highway and turned off onto a rural road dotted with a few sagging barns, a ramshackle trailer or two, a run-down motel, and a small Art Deco-styled brick diner, in front of which stood an old man in a cowboy hat and a woman dressed in a long, floral-print, cotton frock. She was short and frail and dwarfed by a huge, red bouffant hairdo. They waved at the Rambler as it passed by them, then the cowboy took the woman by her arm and they disappeared into the diner.

After a while, the pavement, and what little signs of civilization there were, came to a sudden end, and the road transformed into a long stretch of noisy, loose gravel as the setting sun transformed the afternoon into dusk.

"We're almost there," Freddie grinned. "It's just another mile or so down the road, and the last house on the left."

Within a few minutes, a white clapboard farmhouse slowly came into view. It was old, dilapidated and partially shaded by a large, half-dead tree that stood in the center of the small front yard. Its porch, with its crooked wooden spindles and broken gingerbread accents, sagged forlornly. A door, with a ripped screen, banged back and forth in the breeze. Some of the windows were boarded up, as if to conceal some dark terrible secret, and there were a few areas on the side of the building where the clapboards were missing. The property surrounding the house was littered with garbage and junk, including: stacks of old tires, the rusted remains of ancient automobiles and farm equipment, and odd pieces of discarded furniture that were warped and stripped naked by years of exposure to the elements.

For some odd reason, the sight of the old wooden chairs, and dressers without drawers, reminded Farika of the sun-bleached bones of dead things that she had once seen, but from where, she couldn't recall. *Perhaps it was in a book or on a postcard*, she thought to herself. The sight of them made her feel uneasy.

Behind the house stood the rotting remains of a paint-peeling barn, and acres of farmland, overrun by weeds and the withered corpses of shrubs, that had succumbed to some long-ago drought. The land, and the house upon which it stood, looked as if neither had been in use for decades.

"Home sweet home," Freddie announced, almost singing out his words as he turned left and pulled into the weedy, dirt driveway.

Farika gulped. "This is where you live?"

"Yep," Freddie replied, sounding proud. "Just me and Lorelei. She's just gonna love you." He parked the rattling car, which was now smoking from underneath the hood, alongside the house and everybody got out.

As the man stepped up onto the rickety front porch and fumbled for the key to unlock the front door Farika nervously whispered into Mara Marhoe's ear, "I think I'm the one who's going to need some Thorazine before this night is through. Just look at this place. It looks like an abandoned house. Like something out of a bad horror movie. I don't have a good feeling about this."

"Oh, stop being such a snob," snapped Mara Marhoe. "This is how the backbone of America lives! I wonder if he's got any apple pie?"

Freddie opened the front door, stepped inside the dark house, and, with a wooden match, lit an old-fashioned kerosene lamp. "Poppa's home, Lorelei!" he called out. "And I brought us some pretty girls for supper!" Receiving no reply, he turned to Farika and Mara Marhoe and smiled. "She's probably taking a nap. Now you sweet things go sit down there in the front parlor and make yourselves comfy while I go and fetch her."

"Now this is what I call down-home, country hospitality!" Mara Marhoe whispered into Farika's ear.

Freddie ushered his guests into a musty-smelling room, set the lamp down on a coffee table that possessed a crackled leather top, and waited for the two women to sit down. He lit a few candles for additional light and then cranked up an old Victrola, which stood in one corner of the room near a rocking chair, upon which sat an old doll with missing eyes and a tattered dress. As a dusty 78-rpm record spun around, filling the air with some scratchy forgotten tune from the nineteen-thirties, Freddie politely excused himself and, with one of the flickering candles to guide him, left the room.

Mara Marhoe's stomach made a growling sound. "I could sure go for some apple pie. Couldn't you?"

Farika shrugged her shoulders and gazed at her surroundings. The dimly-lit parlor was filled with worn-out furniture that was as rickety as the front porch and appeared to date back to the Depression era. Every side of the musty-smelling room was covered in brown and yellow floral wallpaper that was stained and peeling away from the walls. Rotting lace curtains hung in front of a tall boarded-up window, matching the rotting lace doilies that covered the surfaces of every table as well as the tops of the sofa and chairs.

"I don't think Freddie ever mentioned apple pie," responded Farika, "or even what was on the dinner menu."

"I'm sure whatever it is, it's going to be good and tasty," Mara Marhoe replied, licking her lips and salivating at the thought of a hot meal filling her empty stomach. "All-natural, home-grown and nutritious. That's what people in the country eat, you know. They don't live on Screaming Yellow Zonkers."

By now the song had reached its end, leaving only the repetitious sound of crackles and hisses as the black shellac disc continued to spin around and around on the record player until it finally slowed down and came to a stop. Silence filled the room.

As the minutes slowly passed, Farika grew concerned. After a quarter of an hour, she mentioned to Mara Marhoe, who was beginning to doze off, "What happened to Freddie? He's been gone for quite some time, and I haven't heard a sound."

Mara Marhoe called out, "Freddie! Do you need any help fixing supper?"

There was no reply. Only silence.

"I'd be happy to help you set the table!" Farika called out.

Still, there was no reply.

Farika was beginning to have misgivings about accepting the ride from Freddie and accepting his invitation to supper. She couldn't quite put her finger on it, but something about this situation was making her feel ill at ease. She looked over at Mara Marhoe and studied her facial expressions and movements for any sort of clue that might indicate she was experiencing the same misgivings. However, as hard as Farika tried to read her body language, she was unable to determine with any amount of certainty if Mara Marhoe was feeling disquieted or just empty-bellied.

As more time passed, Farika started to ponder whether or not she and Mara Marhoe should venture out of the parlor in search of Freddie. *Could he have somehow become ill or injured, and needed help?* Farika wondered. The thought of just fleeing from the house also crossed her mind, but then she realized that it had grown dark outside and that she and Mara Marhoe were miles from the main highway. She eventually decided that the most logical thing to do was to simply wait for her peculiar host to return and announce that supper was ready.

Farika's thoughts were interrupted by what sounded like the giggle of a little girl floating out of the next room. "Hello?" she called out. "Is that you, Lorelei?"

There was another minute of strange silence and then another girlish giggle.

"Lorelei!" Mara Marhoe called out. "Where is your father?"

From the other room the childish voice spoke. "Will you come and play with me? We always play a game before we eat. It makes supper more fun."

Mara Marhoe looked perplexed. "What the hell?"

The little girl voice let out another giggle, then shouted angrily in a slightly deeper voice, "If you don't play with me, I'll have to be a bad little girl!"

Suddenly, a door burst open, revealing a man on roller-skates. He was wearing a girl's pink party dress with a white sash tied into a bow at the front, and his knees were covered by kneepads. Obscuring his face was a plastic Betty Boop mask, and in his hands was a chainsaw covered with what appeared to be dried splatters of blood. "It's my party and I'll kill if I want to!" he yelled, in a demented little girl voice, just before pulling on the starter handle and activating the chainsaw.

Farika and Mara Marhoe screamed and immediately bolted from their seats. They ran to the front door, but discovered that it was locked and they were unable to get out. They heard the chainsaw revving and turned to see the man rolling towards them at a high rate of speed. He was waving the chainsaw in the air and giggling madly.

Mara Marhoe picked up a small wooden chair that was close at hand and threw it into his path. It halted the deranged man momentarily, allowing the two terrified women enough time to flee down the hallway and into a small candle-lit bedroom. Without a moment's hesitation, they slammed the door shut and locked it. Their hearts were racing.

"Oh, my God!" Farika cried. "That man's insane! How are we going to get out of here?!"

"Look!" exclaimed Mara Marhoe, pointing to a small bed against the wall. Its patchwork quilt was draped over what appeared to be the body of a sleeping child. She grabbed the top of the quilt and pulled it down, exposing the skeleton of a little girl. Attached to the top of her skull was a blonde pig-tailed wig, and grotesque red lips had been painted onto the areas above and below her rows of rotting teeth.

Before either of the women could react to this latest horrifying sight, there came a loud roar of the chainsaw and splintered pieces of wood began flying into the air as the power tool's bar and chain sliced through the locked door.

"I take back what I said about down-home country hospitality," growled Mara Marhoe.

Within a matter of moments, a large opening had been cut out of the door and the chainsaw-wielding madman roller-skated into the bedroom. He shifted his gaze to the skeleton on the bed and began speaking to it in a soft and loving voice. "As soon as I butcher these two hogs," he cooed, "I'll fix us both a nice stew for supper. You won't be hungry for long, Lorelei."

Mara Marhoe grabbed the skull, made a pitching windup like a baseball player, and then threw it at the deranged man. It hit him on the forehead and knocked off the Betty Boop mask, revealing his face.

"Oh, my God, it's Freddie!" screamed Farika.

The skull landed on the floor next to the plastic mask, which prompted Freddie to instantly drop the chainsaw and fall to his knees. After retrieving the skull, he cradled it in his arms as if it were a baby. "Lorelei, my sweet Lorelei," he crooned to the skull as tears welled up in his eyes. "Don't cry. Poppa's here and he ain't gonna let anybody hurt you ever again."

While Freddie was momentarily preoccupied with the skull, caressing it and singing, "Bye, baby bunting, Poppa's gone a-hunting," Farika and Mara Marhoe fled from the bedroom and back into the hall. "Let's try this room!" shouted Mara Marhoe as she opened a door on the wall to her left. Farika followed her, and she and Mara Marhoe found themselves in the kitchen.

They both spotted a back door at the rear of the room, next to a pale green Wedgewood cook stove from the nineteen-thirties. They immediately darted towards it, running past an old wooden table upon which sat a kerosene lamp on a lace tablecloth. But no sooner did they reach the door, did they realize that, like the front door, it, too, was locked and offered them no escape from Freddie's house of horror.

Mara yelled at Farika to start looking in the cupboards and drawers for meat cleavers or anything else that they could use as a weapon with which to protect themselves, and then she and Farika quickly began opening cupboard doors and pulling out drawers in a frantic search for such items.

The sound of the chainsaw filled the kitchen as Freddie skated into the room, once again wearing the Betty Boop mask over his face and waving his power tool in the air. "Sooo-weee!" he shouted at Mara Marhoe. "I'm gonna slice you like a spiral-cut ham!"

Finding a large iron skillet on the stovetop, Mara Marhoe picked it up and flung it at Freddie while Farika bombarded him with Mason jars, and a drawer full of flatware and miscellaneous kitchen utensils. He raised his arms to shield his face from the barrage, and, in doing so, accidentally rammed the nose of the chainsaw's bar into one of the hand-hewn wooden beams, which ran across the kitchen's ceiling. The chain broke, and, within one-tenth of one second, it flew into Freddie's head, rendering him unconscious. He collapsed upon the kitchen floor, and, except for the furious spinning of his eight roller-skate wheels, he lay completely motionless. A stream of blood ran out from the sides of the cracked Betty Boop mask.

Overcome with feelings of joy and relief, Farika and Mara Marhoe embraced each other and, with tears in their eyes, began to laugh.

"This nightmare is over," pronounced Mara Marhoe with a smile. "You don't have to worry about that flesh-eating, roller derby reject any more."

"Look!" shouted Farika, excitedly. "Keys!" She pointed down to a silver-colored ball chain around Freddie's neck that had fallen out of the top of his pink party dress when he hit the floor. Attached to it were several old skeleton keys and a pair of more modern-looking keys, which appeared to be the type used for an automobile.

"We're as good as out of here!" exclaimed Mara Marhoe joyously, as she knelt down beside Freddie and tried removing the chain with the keys from his neck.

"And we can take that old jalopy of his, too. I wonder if it'll make it all the way to San Francisco."

Suddenly, Mara Marhoe yelled out in terror and Farika saw that Freddie had grabbed her by the wrist. Mara Marhoe struggled to free herself but the cannibal refused to release his grip on her.

Farika rushed over and kicked him between the legs as hard as she could. He yelped with pain, but still refused to let go of Mara Marhoe. Farika delivered another blow to his crotch with the heel of her shoe, then another one, and another one until he finally relinquished his hold.

Mara Marhoe ripped the chain from his neck and, in less than a minute, had the front door of the house unlocked and wide open.

As they fled from the house, Farika looked back to make sure that Freddie hadn't returned to his feet and was roller-skating after them. She could see that he was still on the floor, but was weak and struggling to get up. He grabbed onto the lace tablecloth for support, but yanked it down instead, along with the kerosene lamp, which crashed to the floor and burst into flames. Within a matter of moments, the kitchen was engulfed with flames, and thick, black smoke began pouring out of the room and into the hallway.

After several attempts at getting the engine to turn over, Mara Marhoe finally succeeded in starting up the Rambler American station wagon. With a badly-shaken Farika sitting in the passenger seat, she backed the car out of the driveway, and then tore out down the unpaved road, kicking up loose gravel and dust. From the rear view mirror, she could see Freddie's house burning like a beacon in the night.

"It looks like Freddie's dead," commented Mara Marhoe, as the reflection of the bright flames flickered in her eyes.

"Freddie's dead?" asked Farika, turning her head to take a look at the orange glow that danced in the darkness behind them.

"That's what I said," Mara Marhoe replied.

As they sped past the small Art Deco-styled brick diner on their way back to the main highway, the old man with the cowboy hat and the redhead with the colossal coiffure emerged from the building and waved goodbye to them.

Chapter Eight

Spaced Out

The sudden flashing lights and wailing sounds of a police siren startled Farika and filled her with an overwhelming feeling of panic. As the wailing grew louder, her panic level intensified and her heartbeat increased. Images of being questioned, arrested, and then sent back to the Midtown Psychiatric Hospital, where Nurse Mars and Zora Zenith would be eagerly awaiting her return with scissors in hand, flashed through her mind like a bad slideshow.

"Oh shit!" yelled Mara Marhoe, looking up at the rear-view mirror. "We've got pigs up our ass!"

"What are we going to do?" cried Farika, turning her head over her left shoulder to get a look at the quickly-approaching squad car.

Mara Marhoe thought for a few seconds and then replied. "I could floor it and try to ditch them. Or pull over so we could jump out of the car and make a run for it. Or I could grab the pig's gun while you distract him with your bare breasts and then we could lock him in the trunk of his car like we did to Jeff."

Farika felt her entire body going numb.

Mara Marhoe put on the car's right turn signal and was about to pull over onto the shoulder of the highway when the police car changed lanes and zoomed past the Rambler on the left, apparently in pursuit of a different vehicle. As its flashing lights disappeared into the darkness, and its blaring siren gradually faded out, Farika and Mara Marhoe breathed a sigh a relief.

After stopping at a 24-hour gas station to fill up the tank, purchase some snacks, and use the ladies' room, Mara Marhoe and Farika returned to the station wagon.

Mara Marhoe inserted the key into the ignition and turned it; however, the car refused to start. She pumped the gas pedal and tried the ignition again, but no sound came from the engine. It was dead. A string of obscenities that would have undoubtedly brought a blush to the cheeks of a drunken sailor or a road-weary truck driver flowed from her mouth. She then gave the ignition another turn -- this time the engine started.

Another sigh of relief was breathed.

After merging back onto the highway, Mara Marhoe lit up a cigarette and took a deep drag on it. "It must be weird having amnesia," she remarked to Farika. "I've never not known who I was, although sometimes I wish I could forget. You must feel that your entire past is like some sort of Agatha Christie mystery. I read somewhere that she had amnesia, too. Well, at least that's what two of her quack shrinks claimed, after she disappeared for ten days and then showed up at some hotel registered under the name of her husband's mistress. But everyone else said it was just a big put-on - a publicity stunt to get people to buy more of her books. Nobody really knows for sure. You're the amnesiac. What do you think?"

Farika cleared her throat. "I hope you don't think I'm

being too nosy by asking you something," she began.

"By asking me what?" asked Mara Marhoe.

"Well, you and I have become really good friends," Farika continued, awkwardly. "But, when it comes right down to it, I really don't know very much about you. Actually, I don't know anything about you at all. And I've been, you know, sort of curious. I've been, uh, well, I've been wondering how you ended up in the psychiatric hospital."

Mara Marhoe's silence and lack of eye contact made Farika feel extremely uneasy and she wondered if perhaps it would have been better had she not inquired. "If you'd rather not talk about it, that's fine," Farika hastily added. "It's really none of my business anyway."

A few more moments passed before Mara Marhoe broke her silence. "I used to share a walk-up in Greenwich Village with a university student named Paisley Pendleton," she began. "Let me tell you, Farika, this girl possessed the face and body of a goddess. I can only describe her as shockingly beautiful... almost as beautiful as you. Paisley was my best friend and confidante, as well as an extremely gifted artist. I first met her at an art gallery on LaGuardia Place, where she was displaying some of her work and I knew instantly that she was different from anyone else I had ever met. Paisley sculpted religious statues out of bowel movements that she found in Central Park, and once a month she would create these breathtaking portraits of great social import using her own menstrual blood. It was like love at first sight."

"Bowel movements?" Farika asked, incredulously.

"Yes," replied Mara Marhoe. "You know, dog shit. It was truly an ingenious concept. Anyway, Paisley and I lived together for two years, six months and three days. And then, as fate would have it, I arrived home early one day from my part-time job at the S and M Green Stamp redemption center and saw the prosthetic leg."

"The prosthetic leg?"

"There was a prosthetic leg leaning against the wall in the hallway outside of Paisley's bedroom," Mara Marhoe explained, with a sudden bleak tone overpowering her voice. "It belonged to a one-legged novelist named Donatello DeNucci who Paisley was having a secret love affair with. You see, they had dated for a while and then broke up almost a year before I had met her. She had always told me how much she despised him." Mara Marhoe's lower lip began to tremble. "I opened the bedroom door and there they were, together, in bed, and sixty-nining! Well, I just freaked out."

"What happened next?"

"I picked up the prosthetic leg and began beating Paisley and Donatello with it. They kept screaming and begging me to stop, but I continued beating them with that goddamn thing. I think I might have knocked out a couple of Donatello's teeth. And I hungered so badly to kill both of them. Oh, you have no idea how badly! But then I looked into Paisley's eyes, and even though I felt so betrayed and filled with rage, I just couldn't bring myself to do it. So I bolted from the bedroom, and all I can remember after that is running through the whole apartment screaming hysterically and smashing every single one of Paisley's bowel movement sculptures with the artificial leg until, finally, the police showed up and wrestled me to the ground and put me in handcuffs. They dragged me off, and, after being given a thorough mental evaluation, I ended up back in the Midtown Psychiatric Hospital. And, to add even more insult to injury, that DeNucci bastard wrote a book about the whole incident, which made the *New York Times* best-seller list."

"Oh, my God!" exclaimed Farika. "That's so awful."

Mara Marhoe's glum expression suddenly lit up, as a

smile formed on her lips. "Oh, it's not all that bad. If they hadn't committed me, I would have never met you," she pointed out.

The clock on the dashboard revealed that it was quarter after one in the morning when Mara Marhoe pulled into a brightly-lit truck stop outside of Youngstown, Ohio. She parked the car and then let out a long yawn as she stretched her arms. "I'm too beat to do any more driving," she stated. "Let's sleep here for the night, and then grab a bite to eat in the morning before we hit the road again." She climbed into the back seat and sprawled out. "Good night, Farika, and pleasant dreams."

Bidding her friend goodnight, Farika curled up into a fetal position on the front seat. She shut her eyes, and within minutes she was fast asleep. However, her dreams were anything but pleasant.

* *

Farika awoke abruptly with the morning sun in her eyes and the sound of diesel truck engines in her ears. Yawning, she looked at the clock on the dashboard to check the time and found it odd that it said 1:18. *I couldn't have slept until afternoon*, she thought. She turned her head and saw Mara Marhoe lying across the back seat and beginning to stir from her peaceful slumber.

"Ugh, that sun is so damn bright!" whined Mara Marhoe, as she rubbed the sleep away from her eyes. "And this damn backseat is lumpy and full of springs. It's nowhere near as comfortable as Forrest Lawn's bathtub. What the hell time is it anyway?"

"According to the clock, it's eighteen minutes after one. But it hasn't moved since I woke up. I think it stopped."

"Screw the clock. I'm feeling ravenous!" Mara Marhoe exclaimed, stretching her arms. "I don't know about you, but I'm in the mood for something exotic... like spaghetti. Let's go get some breakfast!"

Farika followed her friend across the parking lot to the truck stop. After freshening themselves up in the restroom, they promptly proceeded to the snack bar, where they purchased two lunch meat sandwiches encased in clear plastic wrap, a bag of nacho cheese-flavored tortilla chips, and two bottles of soda from the vending machines up front. They returned to Freddie's station wagon with the food, and as they consumed their meals, they made conversation about the horrific events from the previous day, as well as the sanctuary that awaited them in the far-off city by the bay.

"It's time to hit the road again," announced Mara Marhoe gleefully, as she swallowed the last bite of her sandwich. She crumpled up the plastic wrap and tossed it into the backseat to join the other bits of litter on the floor. "San Francisco, here we come!" She inserted the key into the ignition and turned it, but nothing happened. She tried it again and again, but still the engine refused to start. The car was dead.

"What's wrong with the car?" asked Farika, with a tortilla chip in her mouth.

"I don't know," Mara Marhoe replied, as she tried the ignition again. "This goddamn piece of crap is as dead as that cross-dressing, chainsaw-wielding, freak show who tried to eat us for supper." She climbed out of the car, opened up the hood, and wiggled all the wires and hoses before instructing Farika to try starting it. But her efforts were all in vain.

"You son of a bitch!" Mara Marhoe yelled at the car. "You worthless piece of shit!"

In an attempt to further vent her pent-up frustration, she angrily kicked one of the whitewall tires of the car, causing its hubcap to dislodge and fall onto her other foot. She screamed out in pain and grabbed her injured foot in an attempt to subdue the pain.

Farika got out of the car and rushed over to inspect her friend's foot. "Are you all right?" she asked.

"No!" shrieked Mara Marhoe. "I'm not all right!" With a growl, she picked up the hubcap and forcefully flung it, like a huge aluminum Frisbee, against the window of the driver's side door. However, instead of smashing through it in a dramatic display of exploding glass fragments, it impacted the window and then rebounded, hitting Mara Marhoe in the breast. "Owwww!" she screamed. "I just got hit in the tit by that piece of shit!"

As she massaged her sore breast, a tomato-red Volkswagen Super Beetle pulled up alongside the station wagon. The driver, a curly-haired young man with a Fu Manchu mustache, popped his head out of his rolled-down window.

"Car trouble?" he asked.

"Yes," Mara Marhoe replied. "I can't get this old clunker to start. I don't know what's wrong with it. It just seems to be dead."

"Hmmm, it could be your battery or alternator, maybe a shot solenoid or even a bad ignition switch," the man said. "It could be any number of things. Would you like me to take a look under the hood?"

Having nothing to lose, Mara Marhoe and Farika gave him the green light to proceed and then stood and watched intently as the Good Samaritan poked around under the hood of the inoperative Rambler. After a ten-minute inspection, the man slammed the hood shut, shook his head and broke the bad news to them.

"It looks like you've got a broken timing chain," he said. "I'm afraid you'll need to have it towed to a garage."

"Screw that," snarled Mara Marhoe. "We don't have the time or the money to get it fixed. But we need to get to San Francisco as quickly as possible. So I guess it's time for us to thumb a ride again."

"I just hope we can get there before our dear old grandmother climbs the stairway to heaven," said Farika, displaying a sad face.

The man looked puzzled. "Your grandmother's attending a Led Zeppelin concert?"

"No," corrected Mara Marhoe. "Before she takes a permanent vacation."

"She's moving to Florida?"

"No," Mara Marhoe tried again. "Before she cashes in her chips."

"She's going to Las Vegas?"

"Oh, Christ," Mara Marhoe groaned. "Before she kicks the oxygen habit! Before she pushes up daisies! Before she checks into the Horizontal Hilton! Before she..."

"Ah," said the man, nodding his head. "You mean before she dies! I understand."

"Good," Mara Marhoe replied. "I was beginning to run out of euphemisms."

"I make it a rule never to pick up hitchhikers," said the man, as he started back to his car. "However, I'd be willing to make an exception in this case, seeing that your car bit the dust, stranding you ladies, and with a dying grandmother to boot! I'm heading out west, to Roswell, New Mexico, to be exact. You can ride with me as far as Cheyenne; that's as far as I go on 80 before I turn off onto 25."

Farika and Mara Marhoe thanked him and climbed into the back seat of his Super Beetle.

As he pulled out of the truck stop parking lot, the driver introduced himself as Scott Javelin, and proudly added that he was the founder and sole member of a

UFO research group called A.S.T.R.A.L. He went on to explain that the name of the group was actually an acronym for the American Society To Research Alien Life-forms.

"I know a couple of people back in New York who claim to be alien life-forms," mentioned Mara Marhoe.

"Really?" Scott asked as his eyes lit up. "My group and I would very much love to speak with them and gain a few insights. How can we make contact with these intergalactic visitors? Would it be possible for you to arrange a meeting?"

"It might be somewhat difficult," said Mara Marhoe, gazing out the car window at the passing scenery. "They're both inpatients at a lunatic asylum."

"Oh, I see," acknowledged Scott, sounding a bit disappointed. "That's indeed a shame, yet, at the same time, hardly atypical of this planet of narrow-minded Earthlings. Instead of opening our hearts and our minds to our extra-terrestrial brothers and sisters, we choose to label them as crazy and lock them away simply because of our primitive fear of the unknown. And it's a crying shame, really, because there's so much we can learn from them: like how to levitate, how to travel back and forth through time, and how to communicate telepathically."

For the next two hours, the UFO enthusiast rambled on, non-stop, about flying saucers and alien technology, cattle mutilations, the recent sightings of red luminous spheres over Australia, the interbreeding of humans with extra-terrestrials to produce a hybrid race of intellectually superior beings, and the strange and mysterious goings on at a United States Air Force facility in Nevada known as Area 51.

"That's the secret location where our military brought the wreckage from the saucer that crashed in Roswell back in '47," explained Scott Javelin.

The Amnesia Girl!

"According to eyewitness reports, there were two extra-terrestrial occupants inside the spaceship - one dead and one that was barely alive. These outer-space beings were also taken to Area 51 to be studied by doctors and scientists. The entire event was covered up by the U.S. government, of course, and the Air Force fabricated a phony story about a weather balloon in order to throw the public off the track!"

After stopping to fill up with gas, the trio was back on the highway and Scott Javelin was going on about more cases of flying saucer sightings, politicians who were actually reptilian spacemen posing as humans, and Dwight D. Eisenhower's 1954 visit to Edwards Air Force base supposedly to meet with space aliens on a diplomatic mission to Earth. Occasionally, he would toss out a question to Farika and Mara Marhoe, inquiring as to what their opinions were on different matters relating to space aliens. However, almost immediately after each question was posed, and before either of his two passengers could answer them, his rambling would resume.

He also shared some of his strange theories pertaining to government conspiracies -- one being that the CIA assassinated John F. Kennedy because he was on the verge of discovering the truth about UFOs. Another, even more far-fetched sounding one, concerned the American government abducting citizens with psychic abilities and secretly sending them to a top secret colony on the planet Mars. He then announced that, for his self-protection against the government's mysterious "men in black," as well as any hostile alien forces he might encounter during his travels, he had invented a special ray gun which emitted a numbing beam of laser light that produced a temporary state of paralysis, giving him enough time to escape from their evil clutches. He had yet to try it out, of course, but was convinced of its effectiveness, just the same.

Mara Marhoe inconspicuously leaned over towards Farika and whispered into her ear. "I'm beginning to think that you and I aren't the only ones who escaped from a mental hospital." She smiled, seeing Farika grinning and struggling to keep from letting out a chuckle.

The rambling from the driver's seat now extended to Javelin's childhood fascination with Space Patrol, the numerous UFO conventions he attended throughout the country, and how he founded his one-man A.S.T.R.A.L. group. He also mentioned that he was currently working on a book that detailed a bizarre personal encounter with extra-terrestrials that he claimed to have experienced in 1969, after being beamed aboard an alien spaceship.

"I was put into a state of suspended animation," he asserted, "stripped totally naked, and given an embarrassing rectal examination by a lizard-headed space traveler. He had these huge black eyes and wore a glowing silver uniform."

In an attempt to redirect the conversation to a subject less otherworldly, Farika asked Scott Javelin if he were married or had a girlfriend.

"Absolutely not!" he replied. "Women are a huge hindrance in my field of research. I have no time to waste on wining and dining female earthlings when, beyond our galaxy, there are worlds of advanced civilizations waiting to be discovered and explored."

"What good is a world of advanced civilization, if it's a world without love?" asked Farika.

"Or sex!" Mara Marhoe added, with a grin.

"I'm a virgin," confided Scott Javelin. He gazed at Farika from his rear-view mirror. "Aren't you?"

"I don't know," replied Farika. "I'd have to check."

As they passed a large sign welcoming them to Indiana, the sky, which had been bright and sunny back

The Amnesia Girl!

in Ohio, was now growing obscured by dark, threatening clouds.

"It looks like we might run into some inclement weather up ahead," Scott Javelin announced. "I'd better turn on the radio to get an update on the current atmospheric conditions."

He switched on the car radio, and snippets of country-western music, gospel singing, and advertising jingles hiccuped from the built-in speakers as he rotated the tuning dial, in search of a local weather report. He finally stopped on an AM station that was broadcasting the news. "Hopefully, they'll give the weather," he said.

The voice of a newscaster was jabbering about the latest on the Watergate hearings, which was followed by a report on the energy crisis, and then an update on the continuing Patty Hearst saga.

A few raindrops appeared on the windshield, and, as the sky grew even darker, the radio station crackled with a bit of electrical interference from a distant discharge of lightning.

"Turning now to regional news," said the newscaster, "a Pennsylvania youth pastor was brutally assaulted and robbed after picking up two female assailants posing as hitchhikers along Interstate 80 yesterday. Investigators, in cooperation with the Pennsylvania State Police, have put out an all-points bulletin for the apprehension of the hitchhiking duo, which are described as unbalanced and extremely dangerous. They are also advising motorists against giving rides to strangers. The victim of the attack, Mister Jeffrey Piggist of Manson Heights, described his painful ordeal..."

"I was on my way to the church," Jeff told the reporter in a shaken voice, "when I happened to spot these two young women thumbing for a ride. Of course, being the concerned citizen that I am, as well as a member of the League of Americans for Decency, I felt it was my duty to help these poor ladies in distress and protect them. I mean, after all, we're living in the 70s, and these are dangerous times. There are predatory perverts prowling the highways and byways of this great nation of ours! Anyway, I'm sure you can just imagine my shock and utter disgust when these girls - especially the one who was garbed in obesity - started making lewd sexual advances towards me! I mean, who knows what sort of disgusting venereal diseases they could have been carrying, as they were obviously women of extremely loose morals."

"The nerve!" shouted Mara Marhoe.

Farika immediately responded with the sound of, "Shhhhh."

"And can you tell us what happened next, Mister Piggist?" the reporter asked.

"Well," Jeff began, "I explained to them that I was a faithful, happily married husband and a God-fearing Republican... and that's when they attacked me. They knocked me out cold, stole my hard-earned money, and locked me in the trunk of my car, leaving me for dead. That's the thanks you get for helping people these days."

The newscaster continued on with the report. "Officials are looking into a possible connection between the two suspects in yesterday's incident and the recent escape of two female patients from a New York City mental hospital as the descriptions of the women in both cases are strikingly similar. A generous cash reward is being offered by the League of Americans for Decency for any information leading to the arrest of these two wanted fugitives..."

Mara Marhoe's face was flushed with anger. "Why, that lying son of a bitch!" she bellowed, as she transformed her hands into claws. "That mannequin-molesting bastard! On his way to church, my ass! I

The Amnesia Girl!

should have killed that sexual dysfuntionalist when I had the chance!"

"Mara Marhoe!" gasped Farika, nodding her head in the direction of the driver.

"Oh, shit," said Mara Marhoe, snapping out of her fit of rage and realizing that the flying saucer enthusiast was within earshot. Her tone of voice suddenly switched from outrage to an uneasy calmness. "What I meant was, if I were one of those two women I would have wanted to kill that pervert for saying all those lies about me on the radio."

Farika flashed her a look that was an amalgamation of her anger and astonishment.

Scott Javelin's face was expressionless as his gaze remained fixed on the road ahead. Several minutes passed without any conversation or weather report and then he announced that the lunch hour was rapidly approaching and complained that his stomach was growling from lack of nourishment. He turned off at the next exit, and pulled up in front of an old roadside diner in front of which stood, like silent sentries, a pair of gas pumps. Between them was a towering, artificial palm tree with plastic leaves that seemed to gently dance in response to the wind and lightly falling rain. A large sun-bleached sign on the top of the building spelled out: *Ali Baba Diner and Gas Oasis*.

Scott Javelin parked the car and quickly got out. "Come on, girls!" he called, as he gestured with his hand for them to accompany him. "Lunch is on me!"

Farika and Mara Marhoe exited the vehicle and followed him into the diner through a keyhole-shaped glass door, upon which hung a sign that announced, "Sorry, We're Open." Glimpsing the unusually worded sign as she passed through the entrance, Farika thought, *that can't be a good omen.*

Inside, she and her companions were greeted in a

small, smoke-filled vestibule by a dark-complexioned man sitting at a small counter behind a cash register. He was dressed in a floor-length white robe and smoking a hookah water pipe. Covering the top of his head was a multi-colored turban.

Scott immediately inquired where the location of the men's restroom was and the man in the turban handed him a key attached to a large wooden key chain in the shape of a genie lamp and, in a heavy, Middle-Eastern accent, explained that the doors to the washrooms were outside at the back of the building. Scott thanked him, and then asked Farika and Mara Marhoe to get a booth where the three of them could dine, while he "performed his duty" in the "little boy's room." He politely excused himself and, after promising to return in a few minutes, left the diner with the key in his hand.

Farika and Mara Marhoe picked a booth by the window, and proceeded to walk over to it.

The interior of the diner, which was painted in an alarmingly bright color scheme of purple, pink, and tangerine-orange, appeared to be deserted except for an elderly Arabic man with a scraggly white beard, who sat at a red booth at the far end, unhurriedly crumbling saltine crackers into a bowl of curried lentil bean soup. An old Seeburg Select-o-matic jukebox in the corner was playing a song called *West of Jupiter*.

Ooh, west of Jupiter, so far away,
Greatness is the destiny of future days.
So don't be afraid of the ones who come to help,
They might know a way to save you from yourself.
West of Jupiter
West of Jupiter
Look to the star of many colors bright
Like neon flashing in the night.
We're a tyro galaxy with more learning to be done,

The Amnesia Girl!

> *2099 with an electric sun.*
> *Celestial beings from another star,*
> *Don't run, they've traveled light years far.*
> *When they come, don't hesitate to communicate,*
> *Knowledge grows in different ways.*
> *West of Jupiter*
> *West of Jupiter*
> *West of Jupiter...*

The two women sat down, across from each other, and Mara Marhoe grabbed one of the two plastic-coated menus that were lying on top of the table and opened it up. She licked her lips in anticipation of a free hot meal to pacify the hunger pangs that tormented her empty stomach.

"I'm starving," she moaned, as she browsed the list of available dishes. "The Muhammad and Cheese Melt sounds tasty, but then so does the Chicken Allah King. Hmmm, maybe I'll get myself a couple of Sheik Kebabs with a Djinn and Tonic to help calm my nerves after what we went through yesterday. Wasn't that insane?" She placed the menu down and looked across the table at Farika. "Have you decided yet what you're going to order?"

Unbeknownst to Mara Marhoe, Farika hadn't looked at her menu. Nor was her mind on food. Instead, she was gazing out the window at the darkening sky and looking worried. "Something about this situation just doesn't feel right," she said, sounding ominous.

"Oh, here we go again," Mara Marhoe grumbled, rolling her eyes.

"Didn't you find it a bit odd how Scott Javelin suddenly decided to stop here for lunch after he heard Jeff on that news report talking about being attacked and you opening your big mouth without thinking, almost letting it slip that you and I are the two women the police are looking for?" asked Farika.

"It's too bad today isn't Wednesday," said Mara Marhoe, browsing through the menu again and ignoring Farika's question. "It says here that the Hump Day special is Camelback Burgers with Sultan's Harem Secret Sauce."

"I don't know about you, but I find it odd," Farika continued, despite Mara Marhoe's indifference. "Very odd. I have a feeling that there's more to it than just coincidence. I have a feeling that he's on to us."

"Hmmm, what do you suppose they put in that Secret Sauce?" asked Mara Marhoe, suddenly wrinkling up her nose as though a slew of disturbing possibilities were running through her mind.

Before Farika had the chance to reply to Mara Marhoe and tell her that the mystery ingredients of the Sultan's Harem Secret Sauce were the least of her concerns at the moment, the man with the multi-colored turban hurried over to their booth with a distressed look upon his face.

"A thousand pardons," he said. "I gave to your husband the key to the ladies' toilet by mistake. Here is key to the men's toilet." He placed a key upon the table, which, like the one he had given to Scott Javelin, was attached to a large wooden key chain in the shape of a genie lamp, but with an "M" written on it. He bowed his head apologetically.

Farika looked at Mara Marhoe, smiled, and then let out a little chuckle.

Mara Marhoe exploded with riotous laughter, which caused the old man in the back to look up from his bowl of soup and stare at her. "Our husband? That space cadet? You're putting us on, right?"

"A thousand pardons," said the man in the turban.

After her adrenalized snickering subsided, Mara Marhoe stood up and announced that she would go outside and bring the correct restroom key to Scott Javelin while Farika looked over the menu and decided what to order for lunch. She snatched up the key from the table and trotted out of the diner.

Despite her lack of an appetite, Farika picked up the menu that was in front of her and began to browse through it. She soon found herself also wondering about the contents of the Secret Sauce. But, before her imagination could run wild, a visibly upset Mara Marhoe burst into the diner, yelling wildly and startling the old man who was sipping on his soup. His body jolted and he spilled some curried lentil beans into his lap.

"Humping whore!" he yelled at her, as he picked the lentils from his trousers. He then unleashed a steady barrage of insults and obscenities in a foreign language.

Mara Marhoe rushed back to the booth where her friend was sitting. Breathlessly, she explained that when she went around to the rear of the building in search of Scott Javelin, she made the startling discovery that he was inside a telephone booth engaged in a conversation with someone. As she drew nearer to him, she overheard what he was saying from the other side of the folding glass door; he was reporting to the police the whereabouts of the two escaped mental patients who attacked the man in Pennsylvania. And, as if that wasn't bad enough, he was also making an inquiry about collecting the cash reward for turning them in.

"He's a goddamn bounty hunter!" exclaimed Mara Marhoe in a near state of hyperventilation. "My woman's intuition about him was right on the money! We've got to get the hell out of here right now!"

They made a quick dash towards the exit, passing by the red booth where sat the old man, who, by now, was reeking of curry and lentils. He angrily made an obscene gesture at them and hurled his spoon in their direction.

As they fled from the diner into the misty rain, Scott Javelin was rounding the corner of the building and spotted the escaping women running past the gas pumps and plastic palm tree.

"Hey!" he shouted to them. "Where are you going? Come back here!"

Farika and Mara Marhoe ignored him and continued to dart across the parking lot in the direction of a cornfield that seemed to stretch across the landscape to the dark and distant horizon. Scott Javelin gave chase and shouted for the two women to stop. However, they continued running and even stepped up their pace. He then threatened to blast them with a paralyzing beam from his ray gun if they didn't immediately stop and surrender themselves into his custody. But, his words were paid no heed.

Just as she and Mara Marhoe were within a few feet of the cornfield, Farika suddenly experienced an odd sensation. It could only be described as an intense, vibrating chill that struck her in her lower back, then quickly spread throughout the rest of her body. Her legs came to an abrupt halt as everything went numb, and then, unable to move or even stand, she collapsed onto the ground alongside Mara Marhoe, who also appeared to be rendered incapable of physical movement. All physical sensation was now replaced by an icy wave of emotions that surged through her inner core like a terrible tsunami. She felt overpowered by a sense of helplessness and trapped in a web of trepidation spun by the uncertainty of her fate. There was also a bit of resentment towards Mara Marhoe for her refusal to give credence to Farika's suspicions about Scott Javelin's dubious intentions. And in addition to all of the above, astonishment had a firm grip on her for, right up until the very moment the paralyzing beam struck her, she had dismissed the idea of a ray gun as nothing more than

The Amnesia Girl!

the fantastical and semi-entertaining ramblings of an eccentric.

Prior to this implausible predicament, which Farika was sure she would have seen as farcical had the magnitude of its gravity not been so great, she had come to rely on Mara Marhoe to help her out of a jam, albeit it was Mara Marhoe who got her into the jams in the first place. However, the despairing sight of her friend on the ground and every bit as helpless as she was, dashed every iota of hope for rescue that existed within her.

Although unable to use their arms and legs, Farika and Mara Marhoe found that they were still able to open their mouths and scream, which they did, and quite loudly.

Scott Javelin caught up with them and stopped, momentarily, to catch his breath. "I warned you silly girls that my ray gun would be deployed if you continued running," he declared, with an I-told-you-so tone in his voice. "This is nobody's fault but your own!"

At that moment, the turban-topped, hookah-smoking man from the diner's vestibule emerged from the keyhole-shaped door of the building and ran out into the parking lot with his eyes widened into two dark brown saucers. "What goes on here?" he yelled, waving his arms frantically. "You cannot be doing this sort of thing in front of my Ali Baba Diner and Gas Oasis! I thank you veddy much to be returning my bathroom keys and going away, right now! If you do not, I shall summon my wife from the goat stable. She has a black belt!"

Without so much as a moment's hesitation, Scott Javelin aimed his ray gun at the arm-waving man and pulled the trigger, releasing a bright beam of silvery-blue-colored light from the corkscrew-shaped nozzle at the end of the bizarre device.

"Aaaaah! I curse you, infidel!" the man underneath the multi-colored turban cried, as the paralysis-producing beam struck him in the center of his chest. Overcome by numbness, his white-robed body instantly fell to the ground like a bundle of wrinkled bed

sheets, and a sinister imprecation came forth from his lips. "May the ticks from ninety-nine camels burrow deeply within your testicles!"

"Help me! I can't move my body!" cried Farika, terrified. "I feel like I'm paralyzed!"

"I can't move either!" Mara Marhoe cried in response. "This day isn't going exactly as I had planned!"

"Relax," Scott Javelin uttered as he crouched down and reinserted the ray gun into a hidden compartment within the thick, square heel of his brown, imitation suede leather platform shoe. "The incapacitating numbness is temporary and won't leave any permanent neurological side effects. There's nothing to fret about. In fact, it should wear off before the police arrive to collect you. But if you try to make another run for it, I'll have no choice but to zap you again. So don't make it necessary for me to do that."

Using both hands, he grasped a wrist of each of the recumbent women and began dragging their limp bodies back across the rain-dampened asphalt of the parking lot in the direction of his Super Beetle. "There's a generous reward being offered for your capture," he maintained. "With all that money I'll finally be able to purchase all the materials necessary to build my very own interplanetary space vehicle and explore the Pleiades!"

"You interplanetary imbecile!" Mara Marhoe screamed at Scott Javelin. "You freaky, flying saucer fuck-up! Just wait until I get my hands on you! You'll be seeing the stars all right... constellations!"

"Calm down," Scott ordered. "There's no point in getting yourself all worked up. The best thing for you to do, Miss Marhoe, is to simply accept your situation as it is." He smiled strangely, and his eyes suddenly looked ablaze with madness. "In time you will find joy in knowing that in the larger scheme of things, you, and your friend here, have contributed one small step towards mankind's giant leap into the final frontier of outer space!"

"My foot is going to take a giant leap right up your asshole!" Mara Marhoe angrily yelled. "I guarantee there's a one-way ticket to the moon waiting for you!"

"Now, now," uttered Scott Javelin. "There's no need to get belligerent."

He opened the door of his car, took Farika in his arms, then propped her up in the backseat, and strapped her in securely with the seat belt. He next turned to Mara Marhoe, who was still lying helplessly on the asphalt, glaring up at him. "You're next," he informed her. "All that reward money will be well worth the hernia I'll probably get trying to lift you."

"I'll give you more than a hernia!" Mara Marhoe threatened. "I'll give you a Tabasco sauce enema after I eunuch-ate you!"

Unfazed by her threat of violence, Scott Javelin responded with an amused grin. "You can run your mouth off all you like. But whether you like it or not, your running days are over!"

Chapter Nine

Warped Minds

A steady armada of expletives and threats of bodily harm launched from Mara Marhoe's mouth as Scott Javelin struggled to lift her corpulent frame from the ground and deposit said corpulent frame inside his Volkswagen Super Beetle. He grunted and groaned with great exertion, stopping every now and then to catch his breath and revitalize himself. He toiled away with unwavering determination, oblivious to the black van that pulled up in front of the gas pumps, and the woman with long black braids wearing tinted, aviator-style glasses who emerged from its driver-side door.

She stood in silence for a few moments, intently watching Scott Javelin's unfruitful and somewhat amusing attempts at hoisting the hefty woman, and listening to the screams and cries for help that issued forth from Farika. Finally, the woman with the tinted glasses took several steps towards the Super Beetle and then stopped. She placed her hands upon her denim-covered hips and yelled, "Hey! You over there! What the hell are you doing to those two women?"

Scott Javelin looked up, startled to see the woman standing less than ten feet away from him. "I don't believe this is any business of yours," he snapped petulantly. "Be on your way, madam."

"The emancipation of women from the clutches of male dominance *is* my business!" she asserted.

"Help us, please!" cried Farika, from the back seat of the car. "This man is trying to kidnap us!"

"He immobilized us with some kind of futuristic stun gun!" Mara Marhoe added. "He's out of his mind!"

"I am most certainly not!" Scott Javelin protested, appearing miffed. "I'll have you know that I am very much in control of my faculties, unlike you and your partner in crime. What was the name of that mental hospital you escaped from in New York?"

"Fatima!" thundered the man in the turban, who was still lying on the ground near the door of the diner, but beginning to regain a bit of movement in his arms and legs as the paralyzing beam slowly began to wear off. "Put on your veil and come at once to help your husband! And bring your black belt! I command you!"

The woman with the tinted glasses turned her face in the direction of Fatima's husband, and let out a gasp of revulsion. Her face flushed with rage as she yelled, "Here's a news flash for you, Farook! A wife is not a man's personal property, or servant to wait on him hand and foot! How dare you bark out orders to a woman like she was a trained dog, you scum-sucking, male chauvinist pig!"

"A thousand pardons," replied the man with the turban.

Scott Javelin was eyeing the woman carefully. "Hey, wait a minute," A look of recognition swept across his face. "I know who you are! I've seen you before on television, on the news. You're that militant women's libber from that radical anti-penis organization. You're Valerian Kiwanis!"

"How very astute of you," the braided-haired woman remarked in a condescending tone of voice. "For a man!"

As the temporary effect of the paralyzing laser beam slowly lost its grip over Farika's body, she could feel her numb extremities gradually warming up and returning to life. She slowly wiggled her fingers and toes, and from the open car door she could see Mara Marhoe also beginning to stir, ever so slightly.

"Listen, Miss Kiwanis," Scott Javelin began.

"That's *Ms.* Kiwanis to you!" hissed Valerian.

"Fine. *Ms.* Kiwanis. Not that this is any of your business, but these two girls are escapees from a lunatic asylum who attacked a defenseless man in Pennsylvania - a youth pastor!"

"He was a perverted pig and a rapist!" yelled Mara Marhoe. "I should have rammed that mannequin right up his rectum!"

"Right on, my sisters!" cheered Valerian, applauding.

"These 'sisters' as you call them are wanted by the police and extremely dangerous!" Scott Javelin continued. "I've risked my life to apprehend them and I intend to turn them over to the authorities who'll be here very shortly. Now, if you'll stop interfering where you are neither wanted or needed, I suggest we disengage from this conversation and you hop back onto your broomstick and buzz off!"

"No man with a penis dictates to me!" growled Valerian. "I am woman! Hear me roar!"

At that moment, Farika spotted Scott Javelin reaching down to extract the ray gun from inside the heel of his shoe.

The Amnesia Girl!

"Valerian! Watch out!" she cried. "He has a gun inside the heel of his shoe! He'll paralyze you with it!"

Within a matter of seconds, Scott had pushed a secret button on the front of his shoe that was disguised to look like an ordinary grommet. It automatically opened the hidden compartment where the ray gun was concealed. He grabbed hold of the device and, with his index finger poised on the trigger, quickly sprung up and took aim at Valerian -- only to discover that she, too, had a gun in her hand, and its barrel was pointing straight at him. Before he could react, she squeezed the trigger and fired off a bullet that hit the corkscrew-shaped tip of his gun, knocking it out of his hand. It flew through the air a number of feet before falling upon the pavement and breaking apart.

"You broke my gun!" Scott Javelin cried out in anguish, his eyes fixed upon his wrecked weapon.

Valerian smiled and took aim at Scott Javelin's crotch. "I've got three more bullets in this gun," she informed him. "One for your wang and two for your nuts. Now strip off all your clothes and run into that cornfield or my itchy trigger finger will be glad to give you an all-expense paid sex change – courtesy of Smith and Wesson!"

"Yeah!" yelled Mara Marhoe, excitedly. "Do it! Do it! Blow his balls off!"

"Oh, my God!" screamed Farika, shutting her eyes tightly. "I can't watch!"

A horrified expression came over Scott Javelin's face, quickly replaced by one of priggishness. "I beg your pardon," he told Valerian indignantly. "I will do nothing of the sort! This is well beneath my dignity. I'm a man of principle! I'm a man of science!"

"The choice is yours, Mister Science," advised Valerian. "You've got three seconds to decide the fate of your family jewels. One Mississippi...two Mississippi..."

"Very well," Scott Javelin grumbled. "I'll remove my clothes and expose myself to the elements to appease your twisted brain. Just don't riddle my genitalia with bullet holes! That's all I beg of you!"

"Hurry up!" shouted Valerian, as the pleading man unbuttoned his shirt. "I don't have all day to wait. Now unzip those pants and throw them over here! Good boy. Now your underpants, and don't forget the shoes and the socks. Hurry up, you worthless sac of seminal fluid!"

Scott Javelin hastily removed the last article of clothing from his body and, with his hands covering his private parts, stood like a nude statue in the rain as Valerian eyed him up and down. Embarrassment shaded his cheeks with a reddish hue and his face grimaced with humiliation and ire. His pale and nearly hairless physique gently trembled as the biting raindrops relentlessly pummeled his exposed flesh.

"How does it feel to be a piece of meat?" Valerian sneered. " How does it feel to be put in your place by a woman? Ewwww. The very sight of you sickens me. Now start running before I shoot off that pathetic-looking genital of yours!"

Scott Javelin gasped and took off running into the cornfield as the air rang with Valerian's vicious laughter. "Beam me up, mothership!" he cried, frantically waving his arms to the battalion of gray clouds that slowly floated overhead.

"It's a sad world we live in when there's no honor among the insane," Mara Marhoe bemoaned.

"How true," replied Valerian, nodding her head in agreement.

Two shots rang out and Farika felt the Volkswagen suddenly drop down on one side as the air rushed out of the bullet holes in the tires. She opened her eyes and was greeted by the sight of a grinning Valerian blowing the smoke away from the tip of her gun.

"It pays to take precautions," she admonished, while returning the warm gun to the black leather ankle holster hidden under her bell-bottomed jeans.

By now, the paralyzing effects of the flying-saucer fanatic's ray gun had all but completely worn off, and Farika stumbled out of the incapacitated car into the rain. Her body felt weak, yet liberated, and the sensation of cool droplets of water dancing upon her face not only felt refreshing, but also filled her with a short-lived feeling of serenity and renewal.

Valerian Kiwanis was in the midst of helping Mara Marhoe to her feet and the man in the turban was struggling to crawl back into the diner when the dreaded sound of police sirens began to wail from somewhere off in the distance, gradually increasing in volume.

"Pigs!" cried Mara Marhoe. "We need to get the hell out of here and fast!"

"Quick!" shouted Valerian. "Get into my van and hide in the back! It's time for us to blow this scene!"

The sound of the sirens grew louder by the moment.

Valerian's foot floored the accelerator pedal and the van took off with a loud screech, leaving a black trail of burned rubber on the pavement of the parking lot. Like a deranged rodeo cowgirl, she emitted an excited "woo-hooo!" and then held up her right hand in a fist and trumpeted, "Vagina power!"

"Right on!" Mara Marhoe cheered gleefully from the back of the van. "Right on!"

* *

Farika stared out the window of the van at the seemingly endless procession of wooden telephone poles, ramshackle barns, and isolated farmhouses that went by as the distance that safely separated her from the nightmare of the psychiatric hospital slowly, but steadily, widened with each revolution of the tires. She shifted her gaze to a passing flock of birds and wondered where they were heading and if they, like her, wondered and worried about what would be awaiting them when they arrived at their destination.

Her attention was suddenly drawn to the multicolored arc of a rainbow that formed in the sky over a farmer's field and she realized the rain had stopped. She marveled at its beauty, feeling quite sure that she had seen numerous rainbows before, but unable to determine where or when. Convincing herself that its colored bands were some kind of lucky sign, she crossed her fingers and silently made a wish for a full recovery from her amnesia. The rainbow seemed to shimmer for an instant and then faded from view, replaced once again by the telephone poles, barns and farmhouses.

Farika closed her eyes and savored the silence that filled the van now that Mara Marhoe's constant rambling about the degenerate Jeff and his mannequin, the freaky Freddie and his chainsaw, and the spaced-out, flying-saucer man had finally, and mercifully, ceased after she exhausted herself to the point of slumber. The only sounds she now emitted were infrequent stomach rumblings and an occasional, dog-like, snore.

Suddenly, within Farika's mind, disjointed bits and pieces of thoughts that had been floating about freely, like flotsam after a ship wreck, briefly assembled to form a jigsaw puzzle piece of a lost memory that was as fleeting as the green metal sign that crept into view outside the van window, announcing *CHICAGO 45 MILES*, and then, in an instant, rushed by and was gone.

"Who is that faceless man and why does he keep haunting me?" Farika asked herself aloud, but in a barely audible whisper, as she pondered the mysterious mental image that had a certain familiarity attached to it, but still made no sense. The inability to answer her own question filled her with a new frustration. With each passing day, her desire to regain her forgotten memories and lost identity grew, as did a sense of dread over what her reinstated memories might reveal.

At that moment, Valerian turned her head sharply, whipping the air with one of her long black ropes of braided hair and made eye contact with Farika. "Men are nothing but pigs!" she suddenly blurted out, shattering the fragile stillness of the approaching evening and leaving Farika feeling somewhat startled. "P-I-G-S, pigs!"

Mara Marhoe roused from her nap with a quick, snorting sound and Valerian returned her head to its original position, enabling her to once again keep her eyes on the road ahead.

"Disgusting pigs!" agreed Mara Marhoe with her eyes half open and nodding her sleepy head. "I've always thought the world would be a much better place if it were run by women. The problem with men is that they let their baloney pony do the thinking for them!"

"What on earth is a baloney pony?" asked Farika, looking puzzled.

Mara Marhoe rolled her eyes as if annoyed by Farika's ignorance. "You know," she encouraged. "A putz!"

Farika continued to look baffled and then Valerian burst out into laughter.

"If you require a more scientific definition," Valerian began, turning her head once again to look at Farika, before continuing, "it's the fleshy peninsula that dangles between a guy's legs and causes a brain malfunction that makes him believe he's the superior sex."

Mara Marhoe joined Valerian in laughter, then explained, "You'll have to excuse my friend, Farika. She's suffering from a nasty bout of amnesia and most of her mind has evaporated into thin air. She has no memories of fleshy peninsulas!"

"You're putting me on, right?" asked Valerian as she eyed Farika curiously in the rear-view mirror. Observing the nodding of Farika's head and the expression of sincerity that exhibited itself within the contours of Farika's lovely, but saddened face, she added, "Wow. If I couldn't remember any of my past, I'd be constantly wondering, who am I? Where do I come from? But I'll bet you a man is somehow responsible for it. They always are!"

Valerian's words resonated within Farika's soul as they echoed strangely inside her head. *"Who am I? Where do I come from? Who am I? Where do I come from?"*

"But it's probably just as well," Valerian responded. "Penises aren't good for anything. They aren't even necessary anymore for propagating the human race! Did you know that? It's true! Males are completely useless and obsolete!"

After a moment or two, the echoes inside Farika's head faded away into silence, like the end of a song when the grooves on a record run out. She thought it to be quite a curious thing and began to ponder its meaning. However, she soon chased it from her mind, as it only left her feeling even more confused than before. She re-focused her mind on Valerian's odd comment pertaining to the obsoleteness of males.

"I don't understand how such a thing would be possible," Farika said with a frown. "I might have amnesia, but I haven't forgotten the basics of the birds and the bees. You don't have to be an expert in biology to know that it takes both sexes to make a baby. I mean, it's just common sense!"

Valerian immediately erupted into a laughing fit, which seemed rather derisive to Farika and left her

The Amnesia Girl!

feeling slightly affronted.

"Obviously," said Valerian, struggling to subdue her laughter so she could speak, "you've never heard of parthenogenesis!"

"Partheno what?"

"It's a term that combines the Greek *parthenos*, which means 'virgin,' and *genesis*, which, of course, means 'creation.' It basically means asexual reproduction. Or, in other words, a female's ability to self-conceive."

Valerian looked up into the rearview mirror and cracked an amused smile in response to the puzzled look she observed upon Farika's face. She went on to explain that there existed a number of female animals and insects in the wild that were perfectly able to reproduce without the need for a male, and delightedly spoke of scientists working on ways to create artificial sperm from a woman's own bone marrow that would allow her to have a child without the need of fertilization by a male. "And the best part of parthenogensis," she declared, as her voice grew even more jubilant, "is that the babies conceived through this method will *always* be born female!"

"Mmmmm," purred Mara Marhoe dreamily. "All this sex talk is giving me a major craving for Coney Island hot dogs with tons of sauerkraut and mustard, and foot-long chili cheese dogs too. Yummmm!"

"How vomitory!" replied Valerian, wrinkling up her nose in disgust. "Hot dogs are absolutely revolting. I've never had the desire to ingest any sort of phallic food whatsoever. It would be like self-rape!"

"Wow!" exclaimed Mara Marhoe. "I never thought of it like that before. It sure is food for thought." She then burst out into laughter and poked Farika in the arm with her elbow. "Ha ha! Get it, Farika? Food for thought!"

Farika let out a small and weary-sounding groan. Her eyes turned upward and her mouth formed into a crooked grin. "Yes," she responded, unenthusiastically. "I get it."

At that moment, the deeply nasal and pompously-affected voice of a male newscaster emanated from the dashboard's radio and Valerian turned up the volume to enable her two passengers in the backseat to hear the news broadcast.

"Topping today's news stories," began the newscaster. "President Nixon vowed not to step down from the nation's highest office under any circumstance despite Congress' action last week to begin impeachment proceedings against him. India detonated its first nuclear bomb in an underground test, which immediately drew criticism from anti-nuclear activist groups around the world. In the Middle East, Syrian and Israeli tanks and artillery battled on Mount Hermon and along the Golan Heights front today for the sixty-eighth straight day, with no end in sight to the fighting. And in Vietnam, Communist forces, supported by artillery and backed by at least five tanks, overran three government outposts, seized a nearby village, and threatened the town of Ben Cat in the heart of the Iron Triangle. Five thousand government troops and one hundred armored vehicles have been dispatched to the area. Elsewhere in South Vietnam, widespread fighting was reported from the Quang Tri province in the north to the Mekong Delta in the south."

"There wouldn't be any wars if men didn't have penises!" Valerian angrily screamed at the radio. "There isn't one goddamn problem in this screwed-up world that men aren't directly responsible for: atomic bombs, concentration camps, mass murder, police brutality, corrupt governments, assassinations, the Spanish Inquisition, the rape and exploitation of women and children, uncomfortable shoes, and badly-designed kitchens. You name it, and goddamn men are to blame."

"And us women are the ones who always end up getting the shitty end of the stick because of them!" Mara Marhoe exhorted.

"Exactly!" agreed Valerian, nodding her head. "It's time for females from every corner of the globe to unite in sisterhood and rise up against the scourge of maleness! To save the world from testosterone-driven destruction, we have no other alternative, but to overthrow every male-dominated government that exists, implement mass castrations, and ultimately bring about the elimination of all men from the planet. It's all outlined in the *WARP Manifesto*."

"The *WARP Manifesto*?" echoed Farika, looking rather bemused. "What is that?"

Valerian explained that WARP stood for Women Against Repugnant Penises. "The manifesto," she stated, "is a twenty-one-page pamphlet that I wrote and self-published. It's a comprehensive handbook for the women's revolution. There's a box filled with them in the back of the van. Take one and read it. I'm going to be distributing them at the bra-burning rally in Omaha tomorrow and you can help me hand them out if you like."

"Sure!" said Mara Marhoe eagerly.

Valerian Kiwanis smiled and made a thumbs-up gesture. "For the sake of mothers, daughters, sisters and grandmothers everywhere, the time has come for women to WARP the world!"

Farika retrieved two copies of Valerian's manifesto from a large cardboard box and handed one to Mara Marhoe, who eagerly flipped through the pages, feasting her eyes upon its printed contents. She returned to her seat with the copy she had taken for herself and opened it to the first page...

THE WARP MANIFESTO

Part 1: Men Are Shit
Part 2: The World is Shit and Men Made it That Way
Part 3: The Fallacy of the Phallus
Part 4: The Fallopian Chronicles (or God Has a Vagina)
Part 5: 101 Methods of Torture and Execution for Rapist Pigs
Part 6: Obliteration of the Patriarchy
Part 7: Ovaries Belong in the Oval Office
Part 8: The Ferocious Female (Embrace Your Inner Bitch-Goddess)
Part 9: The Self-Conceiving Woman
Part 10: The Fundamentals of a Warped World

As Farika perused Valerian's preposterous agenda, she was ambivalent whether to be amused or alarmed by the absurdities printed on its pages. Halfway through it, she began to seriously question the sanity of the woman who had penned its contents. However, she felt it to be in her best interest to refrain from discussing Ms. Kiwanis' state of mental health within earshot of her.

A cold chill ran up Farika's spine as her eyes scanned the words on the last page of the manifesto, which ominously recapitulated:

In summary, the only viable solution available to women for permanently ridding the world of all military conflicts, acts of rape, wife abuse, and other despicable destructive male behavior, is the immediate mass extermination and disposal of the male human pig. WARP views this course of action as vital to the health, safety and survival of womankind and Mother Earth,

Herself.

WARP also proposes that in the interest of gender cleansing, all males be required by law to undergo an evaluation to determine whether or not they are worthy to continue breathing. Those who fail will be placed in high-security detainment camps to await the termination of their wretched existence. However, the males who prove to be top physical specimens will be spared execution, at the discretion of a female council, of course, only so they can be exploited as beasts of burden, and naturally without pay or benefits of any kind. The law of the land shall require them to wear shock collars at all times and to be confined to cages with electrified locks when not in use.

Some of the males that will be permitted to live will be exhibited in zoos for entertainment purposes, while others will be donated to laboratories for medical research. The remaining males will be forced to assume the subservient roles of household domestics, punching bags and pets. Those who dare to rebel or escape shall be hunted down like rabid dogs and shot on sight.

In closing: Females of the world – mothers, grandmothers, daughters, sisters – must unite as one and, via our collective woman power, obliterate the cancerous growth otherwise known as repugnant penis-bearers. Only then can this world truly evolve into a harmonious and nurturing haven of peace and beauty. The phallus is dead. Long live the Feminine Divine!

"I'm certainly all for women's equality," said Farika, "but with all due respect, Valerian, your manifesto sounds a little bit extreme to me."

Mara Marhoe beamed. "I think it sounds fantastic! Count me in!"

"It's no more extreme than the way the human female has been continually used and abused, and exploited by the male of the species for eons," Valerian challenged, looking at Farika's reflection in her rear view mirror. "It's time we rise up and turn the tables on them. It's a man's world no more!"

As the van approached the Illinois state line, the highway traffic suddenly doubled in volume and a light drizzle began to streak the windshield.

"We'll be in the Windy City in no time," announced Valerian, as she turned a knob to activate the wipers. "My friend, Brenda Rhinestone, lives in a secret underground bunker behind an abandoned World War II munitions factory on the North Side. She won't mind if the three of us crash at her place for the night."

"Are you sure?" asked Farika. "Mara Marhoe and I wouldn't want to be an imposition or anything. After all, your friend doesn't know us. We could always sleep here in the van if you think..."

"Don't be ridiculous!" Valerian interrupted, laughing. "Once Brenda hears how the two of you clobbered that perverted penisaurus with his own mannequin and locked him inside the trunk of that bourgeois car of his, she'll welcome you both as sisters-in-arms! She and I go back a long way. Like me, she's a woman of power, principle, and great intellect. And, believe me, she rallies for her cause! However, there might be some people who'd regard her political views as... shall we say, ultra-unorthodox?"

"Welcome to Illinois," intoned the middle-aged toll collector with the misaligned glass eye, as he counted out the change that Valerian had dumped into the palm of his hand. After depositing the coins in his drawer, he looked up and flashed Valerian an impish grin and then winked his one good eye at her. "I wouldn't mind giving a foxy lady like you a private, guided tour of the city, if you dig what I'm saying. I know a funky little place downtown that whips up a mean Harvey Wallbanger. I get off in less than an hour... work, I mean. Maybe we could, ya know, hook up and..."

"Up yours," Valerian blurted out in disgust, casting a contemptuous look towards the man in the tollbooth. She rolled up her window and pushed down upon the accelerator pedal with her foot, causing the van to screech loudly as it tore out onto the Chicago Skyway.

"The average male, as you've just witnessed, is a pathetic, biologically-inferior creature with a propensity for self-destruction," began Valerian, "whereas the so-called 'fairer sex' tends to think and operate on a higher psychological level. That's one of the reasons women across the industrialized world outlive men. It's a proven fact! And, unlike the female of the species, who vibrate on a higher frequency, the average male has barely reached the halfway point on the evolutionary scale between Homo erectus and Homo sapiens."

"I used to know a couple of homos back in New York: Claudio and his boyfriend Ambrose. Man, they were a real trip!" Mara Marhoe reminisced. "Claudio was an anal retentive fashionista who always wore a floor-length fox coat with a funky black wool beret. He did ladies' hairdos for a living. You know, a hairdresser. And he'd always be waving around this ridiculously long cigarette holder with little rhinestones on the end! Ambrose used to perform in a drag show at some gay dive bar on Christopher Street. His stage name was Ambrosia and he was as queer as a three-dollar bill for Jackie Kennedy Onassis. I mean right down to dressing up in a pink Chanel suit and pillbox hat. Anyway, to make a long story short, Claudio met a tragic end when the bottom of his fur coat got caught in the escalator at Bloomingdale's. It wasn't a pretty sight. Poor Ambrose was never the same after that. He quit the drag show, shaved his head, and joined some weird, underground cult in New Jersey called the Order of the Divine Ferret, or something like that. And he was never, ever seen again."

"Don't be so ignorant!" Farika upbraided her. "She said Homo *sapiens*, not homosexuals. There's a difference."

"Oh, really? And what makes you such an expert on 'homos' all of a sudden, Miss Professor Marvel?" Mara Marhoe tauntingly inquired. "Have you come out of the closet as some sort of sexual intellectual? Maybe you could teach Masters and Johnson a thing or two, do you suppose? I'm sure their knowledge would be *greatly* enriched by a bustling neurotic brain such as yours."

"Thank you for that keen observation, Doctor Marhoe, PhD.," Farika replied sarcastically, clapping her hands in mock applause. "I wasn't aware you were such an expert on the bustling brains of neurotics. But then, that hardly comes as a surprise given that you're by far the most neurotic person I know!"

"Ladies! Ladies!" shouted Valerian. "We need to stop fighting amongst ourselves and join together in sisterhood! Remember, united we stand; divided we fall. And let us not forget who the true enemy is: the sperm-slinger!"

The first shadows of evening were beginning to fall as the van crossed a bridge over the murky Calumet River. Moments later, the Skyway curved to the right and looming on the horizon in a brown, dreamy haze was the imposing skyline of Chicago.

"I'm so hungry, I could eat a reticulated giraffe and still have room for dessert!"exclaimed Mara Marhoe, as she examined the black void of space within a box of crispy, light butter-glazed popcorn. "All right, who the hell ate all the Screaming Yellow Zonkers?"

"You did," replied Farika, looking out the window at the passing scenery. "Along with the rest of the nacho chips, a bag of pretzel twists, two Twinkies, my Bit-O-

Honey bar I was saving for later, and a stale Scooter Pie that rolled out from underneath your seat."

"Well, I need nourishment," Mara Marhoe whined. "I can literally feel myself wasting away. I'll be nothing but skin and bones by the time we get to San Francisco and I'll have to buy myself all new bras."

"A bra," clarified Valerian, "is nothing more than a cross-your-heart straightjacket that suppresses a woman's body, mind and spirit, and symbolizes her centuries-long enslavement to a nipple-sucking, patriarchal society! Burn your bra, sister, and let the flames of freedom melt away your shackles and emasculate all men!"

"But, if I go bra-less, my boobs will hang down to my belly button and bounce all over the place," complained Mara Marhoe, cupping her bosoms with her hands.

"You gotta let it all hang out, baby, if you truly wish to be liberated," explained Valerian, as she merged onto the Dan Ryan Expressway. "A free breast equals a free mind!"

Within a short matter of time, both sides of the expressway became lined with towering housing projects – some with broken windows and walls defaced by spray paint. The graffiti and traffic increased simultaneously, and the cluster of downtown skyscrapers, like great monolithic beasts of concrete and glass, emerged from their toxic shroud and steadily advanced in size as the van drew nearer to the heart of the city.

What sort of woman lives in an underground bunker? Farika pondered, feeling as though she were gradually being swallowed up by the prodigious megalopolis that was now enveloping the van. She also thought how odd it was that Chicago would be nicknamed "the Windy City" when it looked to be most calm to her. *The calm before the storm*, she thought, half with whimsy and half with dread. And then, all at once, a strange, yet familiar, voice inside her head whispered: *It's an ill wind that blows no one any good.* And the goose bumps sprung up on her arms.

Chapter Ten

Tales from the Fuhrerbunker

"I really don't understand why we have to wear these ridiculous blindfolds over our eyes," Farika mildly protested in a tone of bewilderment, as she waited with Mara Marhoe and Valerian outside the entrance to Brenda Rhinestone's underground bunker.

"I think it's kind of exciting," Mara Marhoe was heard to say. "I feel like a contestant on a TV game show."

"The kind of game show where you win a one-way trip to Hell," Farika muttered to herself, underneath her breath.

Valerian, sensing Farika's anxiety, told her not to worry and assured her that the blindfolding of all guests before arriving at the bunker, as well as after leaving it, was standard protocol because the bunker was classified as a 'Top Secret' location.

Farika then heard the sliding of a bolt, immediately followed by the squeaking of rusted hinges, and then, what sounded to be a steel hatch door being thrown open. She was promptly escorted down a narrow flight of metal stairs that echoed with each step. It reminded her of the fire escape outside the window of Doctor I's office in the Midtown Psychiatric Hospital, not only because they both produced a similar sound, but also at the bottom of each awaited a world of uncertainty.

Halfway down the stairs, Farika was overcome with a great unease, and began to wonder what new web of madness she had unwittingly allowed herself to get tangled up in this time. It would not be long before she found out.

After reaching the bottom, Farika heard the sound of another metal door opening. All at once, her ears were assaulted by a blast of marching band music, the wild barking of dogs, and a deep female voice that said, "*Willkommen in meinem Zuhause.*"

Farika suddenly felt hands at the back of her head undoing the blindfold. The sensation startled her at first, and then filled her with a sense of relief since it meant that her vision would no longer be obscured. The blindfold was yanked away, taking the darkness with it, and a glaring light invaded her eyes, causing her to squint.

As her eyes adjusted to the brightness that surrounded her, they became focused upon the extraordinary sight of a young woman sitting in a motorized wheelchair and dressed in a men's brown, World War II Nazi uniform complete with black leather jack boots and a red armband which bore the insignia of a swastika. She wore a cervical collar around her neck, and her blonde hair had been cropped into a short, almost crew cut, hairstyle. Her dark brown eyebrows were tweezed pencil thin, which gave her somewhat of a surreal appearance, and in the area between her upper lip and nose she sported a black toothbrush mustache that was held on with some sort of adhesive. Had it not been for her false eyelashes, black eyeliner and blood red lipstick, she could have easily been mistaken for a man.

Immediately, Farika fearfully backed away as two large, spike-collared German shepherd dogs began charging towards her, growling and snarling in a most unfriendly manner. White, frothy saliva dripped ominously from their bared fangs and onto the gray concrete floor where they formed little horrifying puddles. Like their mistress, both dogs were each clad in a brown Nazi uniform adorned with a red swastika band that wrapped around their midsections.

Much to Farika's relief, the matching pair of canines immediately stopped in their tracks and obediently assumed a sitting position upon hearing the woman in the wheelchair bark out in a feigned German accent: "Halt, Heinrich! Halt, Himmler!"

With the threat of attack diverted, Farika tried her best to appear nonchalant. However, the look of consternation that manifested upon her face ultimately betrayed her. "Those two dogs... they're... they're wearing Nazi uniforms!" she exclaimed in astonishment.

"Why, yes!" the woman in the wheelchair gloatingly smiled. "I made them myself, a few years ago, in a Socialist sewing circle that I belonged to. Personally, I've never been an advocate for any sort of indecency, and I find a dog without a uniform is nothing less than obscene. Don't you?"

"Brenda!" Valerian cried out, as she removed her glasses and laid her eyes upon her wheelchair-bound friend. Her face wore a look of shock and surprise. "What on earth happened to you? What's the deal with the wheelchair and the neck brace?"

"I'm in this sorry state all because of my desire for that goddamn Reuben," Brenda Rhinestone explained. But before she could proceed with her story, Valerian's face contorted in a maniacal manner and she flew into a fit of rage.

"I swear to God, I will single-handedly butcher that abusive piece of scum!" Valerian screamed. "Where is this fucking Reuben? Give me his address right now! When I get my hands on him I'm going to uproot his penis! It's time to put WARP into action and strike a blow for uterus unity the world over!"

"Calm down, sister," Brenda Rhinestone coolly answered, as she lit up an imported German cigarette. She took a long drag and then exhaled. "It's only a goddamn Reuben sandwich I'm talking about."

Valerian appeared to be startled by this new revelation. "A what?"

"Allow me to explain. I had this urge for a Reuben sandwich, so I stopped at a Jewish deli down on North Clark Street to buy one. And when I came out of the place I was jumped by a herd of hostile yentas. They kicked and beat me senseless, Val, and one even tried to choke me to death with her babushka."

Valerian let out a gasp.

"It's not so bad," Brenda continued. "The doctor said I should be out of this chair and goose-stepping again in no time! At least it hasn't prevented me from working on my contribution to society."

"Your contribution to society?" asked Farika, displaying a quizzical expression.

A smile stretched across Brenda Rhinestone's face. She promptly reached up and gave a tug on a red, tasseled cord hanging from the ceiling, which caused a pair of red, crushed-velvet drapes to draw back, revealing a monstrous life-like mechanical replica of Adolf Hitler. It stood close to six feet tall and was dressed in a brown World War II Nazi Party uniform complete with a red swastika armband, a brown wool gabardine visor cap, and a pair of calf-high jackboots.

The Amnesia Girl!

Farika gasped loudly as she laid her eyes upon the horrifying contraption before her. However, the sound of her sudden deep intake of air was drowned out by Brenda Rhinestone's fevered cry of "*Sieg heil!*" as she gave a Nazi salute to her creation.

"Far out!" exclaimed Mara Marhoe, looking astonished.

"What the hell is it?" asked Valerian, fearlessly stepping forward to get a closer look.

"Behold the future!" Brenda Rhinestone cried out with mad glee. "What you see standing in front of you is a Fuhrer-bot prototype in the final stage of completion. I call him 'Adolf-2' and he's the fruit of my labor, my pride and joy. He's the result of more than a decade's worth of blood, sweat and tears, painstaking trial and error, and unwavering devotion to the new Master Plan. I constructed him with only the finest of space-age alloys and polymers. All his parts are German-made, naturally, and he contains the most technologically advanced robotic internal workings known to modern science! He's operated by remote control and he possesses the capability of developing artificial intelligence. He's nearly indistinguishable from the original human Fuhrer, wouldn't you say? He's the perfect man!"

"You didn't give this freaky thing a penis, did you?" Valerian asked concernedly, as she crouched down to closely inspect the Fuhrer-bot's slightly bulging crotch.

Brenda Rhinestone's eyes lit up and she grinned. "Rest assured, *Liebling*, that I designed Adolf-2 to be anatomically correct, as well as fully functional, in every possible way." She then closed her eyes as if enraptured and licked her lips.

"Big mistake!" proclaimed Valerian, frowning and shaking her head in disgust. "Penises bring nothing but trouble."

"With my trusty Fuhrer-bot by my side, programmed to obey my every command, I, Brenda Rhinestone, shall succeed where the first Hitler left off in achieving world domination! Soon my vision of a master race of Fuhrer-bots shall be brought to life and I shall reign supreme as Fuhreress of the unparalleled Fourth Reich!"

With the push of a button, Brenda Rhinestone put her motorized wheelchair into drive and led her guests into a large museum-like room that was filled to near-capacity with almost every sort of German World War II military memorabilia imaginable.

Housed in glass display cases were Luftwaffe daggers, pistols, and a plethora of Iron Crosses, German Crosses, Hitler Youth Proficiency badges, and assorted war merit medals. Shelves and tabletops spilled over with dusty collections of World War II gas masks, ammunition pouches, combat helmets, officers' visor caps, National Eagle paperweights, and Third Reich beer steins. There were also numerous reproductions of Adolf Hitler's pre-war watercolor artwork, and framed photographs and postcards of various concentration camps – one of which tastelessly punned: *Having a gas at Auschwitz! Wish you were here!*

Across the room, and tucked away in a shadowy corner, a large hardcover edition of Hitler's *Mein Kampf* dominated a small antique side table with turned legs. Atop two nearby faux marble pedestals that flanked a life-size oil painting of the uniformed Fascist dictator surrounded by an ornate gilded frame, rested a pair of large bronze busts: one of which depicted an eerily smiling Eva Braun, and the other, a lurid likeness of the Fuhrer himself, which gazed down from its base with an unrelenting scowl.

"Wow!" Mara Marhoe blurted out, appearing to be strangely entranced by the extraordinary multitude of militaria and curious objets d'art that pervaded the room.

The Amnesia Girl!

"This sure is one hell of a freaky scene!"

Brenda Rhinestone thanked her and then once again set her wheelchair into motion and led her guests into an adjacent dining room where they were seated at a long table draped with a Nazi flag that served as a tablecloth. Upon the center of the table sat a silver-plated platter containing a dozen liver dumplings, which Brenda called *Leberknodl*.

"This was Adolf Hitler's favorite meal in the whole world to eat," she explained with a gleam in her eyes. "And even though the Fuhrer converted to a vegetarian diet during the war, he was known to give in to his cravings for liver dumplings every now and then."

Inches away from the platter of dumplings sat a large Blue Danube tureen upon a white linen doily. Brenda removed the lid and began to ladle out heaping helpings of its mysterious contents into four soup bowls decorated with the same blue floral pattern as the tureen, taking great care not to spill a single drop. An odd and faintly fishy redolence escaped from the uncovered tureen and wafted through the air, eventually finding its way into Farika's nostrils and prompting her to make an inquiry.

Brenda Rhinestone let out a gasp. "Have you never partaken of turtle soup before?" she asked Farika. A look of surprise overtook her face as Farika shook her head from left to right, indicating she had not. "I use only the finest Lake Michigan turtles in my soup, I'll have you know. And I catch each and every one by hand! I'm quite a turtle-wrangler if I do say so myself."

Gazing nervously at the bowl of turtle soup that her hostess had placed before her, Farika asked if turtle soup was another of Adolf Hitler's favorites.

"Certainly not, Fraulein Farika!" snapped Brenda Rhinestone with sudden indignation. "Everybody knows it was Eva Braun's favorite!"

Valerian, in amusement, emitted a minuscule chuckle, which was followed by a snort and a giggle from Mara Marhoe.

Brenda Rhinestone then grimaced at Farika. "Everybody... except, of course, the dregs of society!"

Feeling somewhat downtrodden by her hostess' remark, Farika proceeded to nibble at her meal in silence, finding the unusual fare to be not quite as unpleasant as she had anticipated. The continuous German military marches playing in the background on a reel-to-reel tape player were wearing on her nerves; however, Mara Marhoe's rhythmic masticatory sounds from the opposite side of the table did provide somewhat of a welcome distraction from the nerve-wracking bickering between Brenda Rhinestone and Valerian over Aryan torture techniques.

Immediately following dessert, which consisted of blueberry streusel scones and chocolate éclairs decorated with little frosted swastikas, Brenda Rhinestone, being the quintessential Nazi hostess that she was, produced a tarnished antique tea tray upon which sat an elegant cut-crystal decanter and four stemmed glasses.

"Peppermint Schnapps for all!" she declared, almost as if shouting out an order, and began pouring the liqueur into the glasses. She then raised her glass high into the air. "A toast... to the revolution!"

Not wishing to be perceived as impolite, Farika raised her glass up and toasted with the others. Unsure if she had ever consumed alcohol in her forgotten past or what effect it might have on her, she closed her eyes and braced herself for the worst and then took a sip of the clear liquid, which filled her mouth with the startling minty flavor of a candy cane.

Several glasses of Peppermint Schnapps later, Farika felt overcome by a rush of giddiness. Her eyelids started to grow heavier with each sip that she took and it soon became an effort for her to simply keep them open. Her insides had gone all tingly and pleasantly warm, but soon a fuzzy numbness wrapped itself around her like a fleece blanket and to it she willingly surrendered herself. The incessant sound of the marching band mercifully faded away as she drifted off into a dreamy peppermint slumber.

* *

It was at some unknown hour during the dead of night and in the middle of a most peculiar and disturbing erotic nightmare involving Adolf Hitler when Farika was rudely awakened from her sleep by the unpleasant sensation of something cold furiously squeezing the nipples of her bare breasts. Startled, she popped open her eyelids to find that she had somehow ended up on a waterbed in a dimly-lit and unfamiliar room, devoid of all clothing except for a pair of panties. And, to her absolute horror, she discovered that lying next to her, with its mechanical fingers firmly clamped onto her tender teats, was Adolf-2, the Fuhrer-bot. It was clad only in crotchless lederhosen and in an obvious heightened state of sexual arousal.

Farika's brain reeled with confusion and for several seconds she was unsure if she were still dreaming or perhaps experiencing some horrible hallucinatory state of mind brought on by the quantity of Schnapps she had consumed earlier.

The metallic hands of the libidinous mechanical monstrosity proceeded to squeeze Farika's nipples harder, causing her to experience a sharp pinching pain and the realization that what was happening to her was neither nightmare nor side-effect of the liqueur. Struggling to free herself from the Fuhrer-bot's grasp, she screamed for help as loudly as she could.

The electronic eyes of the artificial man flashed rapidly with an eerie red glow and the unsettling sound of heavy breathing issued forth from its synthetic elastic lips. Its foot-long polystyrene phallus stood fully erect and pulsated in quite a shocking manner. "Naughty Fraulein," it said in a robotic voice. Its words were monotonous and spoken with a German-sounding accent.

Farika screamed again and commenced to fight off her assailant. However, the harder she struggled to free herself from the robot's grip, the more aroused it became until it blurted out, "You will suck my swastika!"

Farika's screams and cries for help echoed throughout the dank confines of the bunker and woke Heinrich and Himmler from their sleep and set them to barking. With their pointed ears standing at attention, they barreled into her room, their toenails clicking against the cement floor. Seconds later they were followed by a stunned Mara Marhoe, who exclaimed, "Holy crap! I must be freaking out! Oh, God, I need some Thorazine!"

"Help me, Mara!" Farika pleaded. "Get this horrible thing off of me!"

Mara Marhoe rushed to the waterbed, which by now was sloshing from side to side, and attempted to pull the Fuhrer-bot away from her frightened friend; however, she found that her strength was no match for the determined robot. With its eyes flashing even brighter and faster than before, it positioned itself above Farika's squirming body and attempted to mount her.

"I don't see an off switch!" shouted Mara Marhoe frantically. "How do you shut down this crazy thing?"

"I don't know!" screamed Farika. "But do something! Anything! Quick!"

Mara Marhoe ran from the room and then returned

The Amnesia Girl!

straight away with the empty decanter of Peppermint Schnapps, which she promptly smashed over the robot's chromium cranium. But her efforts to stop it were to no avail. If anything, they enraged the robotic rapist, prompting it to fire off a round of dart-like objects from the excretory orifice of its alimentary canal in Mara Marhoe's direction. Narrowly missing her, the projectiles struck the cinderblock wall behind her and detonated into little fireballs of smoke and sparks.

Awakened by the commotion, Valerian dashed into the room to see what was the matter, followed by Brenda Rhinestone in her motorized wheelchair. Both women were instantly taken aback by what they saw.

A look of outrage took over Brenda's face as she gazed upon the sight of her crazed creation in the near act of copulation with Farika on the churning waterbed. "*Ach mein Gott!*" she shrieked. "What is the meaning of this obscene act? This is an outrage! Stop it, Fraulein! Stop this distasteful display at once!"

"Your Fuhrer-bot is out of control!" Mara Marhoe shouted. "I tried to stop it from attacking her but the goddamn thing tried to kill me with some sort of rectal rockets!"

"Only I possess the power to control him," Brenda Rhinestone said avowedly, as she pressed a red plastic button marked with a swastika on a shiny metal panel located on the right side of her wheelchair. "Fuhrer-bot, halt!" she shouted several times in rapid succession.

However, much to her surprise and to Farika's dismay, the mechanical maniac continued its assault upon its helpless victim, whose screams had now increased by a noticeable amount of decibels.

After half a dozen frantic and failed attempts to deactivate the robot, Brenda's face grew pale with trepidation. "The brain plastic control must have malfunctioned," she conjectured. "He's so turned on that

I can't turn him off!"

"Leave it to me," advised Valerian, extracting her handgun from the pocket of her terrycloth bathrobe, which sported an embroidered Venus symbol. "When it comes to turning men off, I know just how to do it!"

"Put that ridiculous gun away!" commanded Brenda Rhinestone. "Mere bullets cannot stop a military marvel like my Fuhrer-bot. I designed him to be impervious to all manner of weaponry, including machine guns, grenades, bazookas, and even atomic bombs. He's an unstoppable machine of death. Heil Hitler!"

"We'll see about that when I blow off his goddamn penis," retorted Valerian as she took aim at the robot's member.

"No!" roared Brenda Rhinestone. "Not the penis! I forbid you to shoot the penis! It took me almost two years to perfect it!"

"Be careful, Valerian!" Mara Marhoe cried. "You might accidentally hit Farika!"

"Don't you worry about a thing," said Valerian with an air of confidence. "This sister is a bull's-eye shot!" And with that being said, she squeezed the trigger and a deafening shot rang out.

In the blink of an eye the bullet from Valerian's gun flew past the humping Fuhrer-bot, missing its intended target by a good six inches, and ricocheted off the cinderblock wall behind the dark walnut headboard with built-in shelves and attached mirror in the center. It rebounded off the opposite wall and eventually shot through the waterbed, creating a spectacular geyser that gushed from the bullet hole in the vinyl mattress straight up to the ceiling.

As two hundred and fifty gallons of cold water rained down, thoroughly drenching Farika and Adolf-2, there suddenly came from within the robot a loud, zapping sound, followed by an even louder crackle and finally a tremendous pop. Its blinking red eyes went black and from its open mouth emerged a puff of smoke that filled the room with an odor of melted rubber and burnt wires. Short-circuited by the copious amount of water, the Fuhrer-bot released its grip on Farika and she immediately bolted from the rapidly draining bed.

"I just hate a man that smokes after sex," sneered Valerian.

"My crowning achievement! My splendid creation!" cried Brenda Rhinestone as she inspected the Fuhrer-bot's smoldering chassis. "My life's work is down the drain!" Angrily pointing her finger at Farika, she growled, "And all because of this, this subversive interloper! This shameless harlot! This impudent, shortsighted coquette!"

Mara Marhoe threw her arms around Farika's trembling torso and bestowed upon her a consoling hug. "My poor little muffin," she said in a strange, infantile voice. "It's all my fault. If I hadn't gotten up to use the latrine down the hall I would have been here to stop that raunchy robot from violating your wholesomeness. Looks like I'm going to have to start retaining my fluids from now on."

"My Fuhrer-bot is the one who's been violated!" charged Brenda Rhinestone emphatically. "This odious tryst is not only appalling, it's downright treasonous! I was his creatress and paramour. I should have been the one to initiate him into the world of carnal pleasures!" With a loud grunt she leapt from the wheelchair and threw herself upon the floor, banging her forehead repeatedly on the concrete. "*Aus der Traum*! My dream for a Master Race is over! I've lost the will to live!"

"I warned you about penises," Valerian gloated to Brenda Rhinestone. "You gotta nip those things in the bud, *Schatzi*!"

* *

As the nightmarish remnants of the wee hours retreated, dawn marched in, bringing with it a breakfast consisting of tepid tea, cold cereal, and even colder glares from the self-proclaimed Fuhreress herself, who sat at the head of the table with the top half of her banged-up head wrapped like a mummy in a white gauze bandage. Her faithful canine Gestapo sat beside her, wearing their uniforms and eyeing her bunker guests with suspicion.

The morning meal was eaten with haste; however, for Farika and Mara Marhoe the minutes seemed to drag into agonizing hours for Brenda Rhinestone sat glaring at them the entire time in silence, fuming and spinning one of her German SS daggers in ominous clockwise circles upon the tabletop.

Valerian looked down at her wristwatch and then broke the uncomfortable quietude by announcing that the time had arrived for her and her two travel companions to hit the road. She explained that the drive to Omaha was seven hours long and it was her desire to arrive on time for the bra-burning rally. A round of swift farewells ensued, which were followed by blindfolds, the resounding ascension of metal stairs, and the angry clunk of a heavy hatch door slamming shut.

With two bruised bosoms as souvenirs and one new psychologically damaging experience to add to her ever-increasing collection of mental traumas, Farika was all too glad to feel the gentle rays of morning light caress her face as she resurfaced from the bunker, leaving behind the peculiar Brenda Rhinestone and her anomalous underground world.

Chapter Eleven

WARP Versus FRUMP

It was mid-afternoon when Valerian Kiwanis, Farika and Mara Marhoe arrived at the bra-burning rally in Omaha. Armed with copies of the *WARP Manifesto* in hand, they exited the van and joined a crowd of several hundred women who had assembled around a small stage decorated with helium-filled balloons and brightly-colored banners printed with catchy slogans that advocated equal rights for women, expressed anti-patriarchal sentiments, and celebrated mammary glands and reproductive orifices.

Vendors strolled through the bell-bottomed and mini-skirted multitudes, hawking such must-have items as "The Breast is Yet to Come" tee-shirts and black coffin-shaped pins that proclaimed "Better Buried Than Married" in red letters that resembled dripping blood. The air was filled with hoopla, anticipation, and the fragrant smoke of incense and marijuana joints.

Farika gazed curiously upon the sights surrounding

her and noticed that a television news crew was on the scene, eagerly interviewing a leather-clad, blonde-haired woman holding a dog leash attached to a collared man who was down on all fours. After firing off a round of probing questions, the reporter held his microphone out in front of the man's muzzled mouth to record his reply for posterity. The man immediately looked up at his mistress, panted a few times, and then barked like a crazed cocker spaniel. His mistress petted the top of his head and smiled into the camera.

Farika then heard the amplified tapping of a microphone and looked over to the stage to see what was happening. At center stage stood a woman who was donned from head to toe in a Statue of Liberty costume and bearing a toilet plunger in place of a torch. Her right hand was placed over her heart and with unrestrained patriotic fervor she belted out an a capella rendition of *America* with slightly revamped lyrics:

> *"My country 'tis of thee,*
> *Land of indignity,*
> *Of thee we sing;*
> *Land where our mothers cried,*
> *Land where our sisters died,*
> *We burn our bras with pride;*
> *Let freedom ring!"*

Energized with exhilaration, Valerian began clapping wildly and shouted out, "Tell it like it is, sister! Woman power!"

She then turned to Farika and Mara Marhoe and emitted a sigh of contentment. "That was incredibly uplifting," she commented, while wiping away a small tear of joy from her left eye. "All right, ladies. It's time we started handing out these copies of my manifesto."

"I'm sorry, Valerian," Farika apologized, having a

change of heart. "I can't, in good conscience, hand these out."

"What's bugging you, Farika?" asked Valerian. "Do you have a hang-up?"

"I guess so," replied Farika, "if that's what you want to call it. The truth is, as bad as men can be, I just don't believe that female domination is the answer. I'm sorry. I just don't share your vision of some utopian Amazon society that exterminates most of the men on the planet and keeps the rest in cages like animals."

"But they *are* animals!" Valerian retorted. "You poor misguided woman. You've been so brainwashed by the patriarchal propaganda machine that you can't see things like they really are!"

"I can see things just fine," replied Farika, feeling somewhat aggrieved. "If you really want to know the truth, Valerian, it's you and your insane friend, Brenda Rhinestone, who are the ones with the distorted vision."

"Oh really?" challenged Valerian, sounding both flabbergasted and peeved. "Well, if that isn't the thanks I get for giving you a ride and rescuing you, not once, but twice! How about showing a little gratitude?"

"I'm very grateful for all that you've done," said Farika. "Truly I am! But I just can't participate in something I don't believe in. Please understand."

"Oh, I understand all right! How does it feel to be a traitor to your own kind?" Valerian asked viciously. "The only thing lower than a male chauvinist pig is a pig sympathizer! Don't you realize that all you're doing is enabling rape and female genocide with your unwillingness to help the cause? If you aren't with us, then you're against us. You don't deserve to have ovaries!"

Mara Marhoe glared at Farika. "Don't turn this scene into a bummer, Farika," she stressed, in an attempt to diffuse the rapidly building tension between Farika and

Valerian. "Just keep your cool and hand out some of these stupid fliers. It's not a big deal. We owe it to Valerian for all that she's done for us."

"I'm sorry," Farika said to Mara Marhoe, who was beginning to look a bit worried. "I just can't be a part of this. It's madness."

"Madness is it?" snapped Valerian. "I'll show you how mad I can really get!"

Valerian was deathly silent for several seconds and, if looks could kill, her eyes would certainly have rendered Farika as dead as a doornail. And then, much to Farika's horror and to Mara Marhoe's ire, Valerian reached down and withdrew her gun from its black leather ankle holster and promptly aimed it at Farika's chest.

"I've had just about all I can take of your bullshit!" Valerian growled, her index finger caressing the trigger of the gun. "If you think your boobies are sore now, just wait until my bullets kiss your nipples!"

Farika gasped, unsure if she should scream for help, run for her life, or try to reason with her gun-toting adversary.

At that moment, someone in the crowd shouted in a high-pitched voice that rang out like an alarm: "Philistina Savage!" All heads immediately turned in the direction of a tall, matronly woman with mouse-gray hair, which was worn in a tight bun at the back of her head. Her larger-than-average frame was covered by a dowdy white blouse with a ruffled collar and matching ruffled sleeves, which was neatly tucked into a long, white skirt. Strapped across her upper torso was a fake bare breast upon which was attached a plastic nursing baby. Her white, imitation-snakeskin, orthopedic pumps click-clacked ominously as she forced her way onto the stage, underscored by the sound of booing women. Her left hand was wrapped around the handle of a black iron skillet.

Mara Marhoe asked Valerian who the woman on the stage was and why were all the bra-burners booing her. Valerian replied that the unwelcome guest was none other than Philistina Savage – the infamous ultra-conservative opponent of the Women's Lib movement and founder of FRUMP. Before Mara Marhoe could ask what that was, Valerian explained in a tone of disgust and loathing that FRUMP was an acronym for Females Rank Under Male Predominance. She then continued to expound that, as the name implied, it was a contemptible organization whose main objective was to keep women "under the thumbs of male chauvinist pigs."

Philistina grabbed the microphone, raised her skillet to the sky, and proceeded to address the booing crowd. "Ladies! Ladies!" she bellowed in a deep voice. "Stop all this bra-burning nonsense at once! Accept that a woman's place is in the home, and more specifically, in the kitchen and in the bedroom. God made the female inferior to the male by design. It says so in the Bible! We women were put on this earth to bake gingersnap cookies and crochet lace doilies. Our roles are to give birth to precious little children and to do all that we can to serve and please our men, who are the dominant gender of our species!"

The booing from the crowd now increased to an almost deafening roar and women began pelting the stage with brassieres, tampons, and just about anything they could retrieve from the numerous trash receptacles, which dotted the rally site.

In defiance, Philistina shook her skillet at the crowd and increased the decibels of her voice. "Ladies, your misguided demands for women's equality will ultimately unravel the fibers of the nuclear family!" she shouted. "Don't you realize women's lib will turn your daughters into axe-wielding lesbians?"

Valerian's face turned red with rage and she slid the gun back into its holster. "Hold these for me," she said, depositing her stack of mimeographed *WARP Manifesto* copies into Mara Marhoe's upturned hands, along with her fringed leather purse. "There's some urgent business that I need to attend to!"

As she pushed her way through the crowd of booing women to get to the stage, Valerian growled, "Ooh that rancid old bitch. Let me at her!"

Within a matter of seconds she was on the trash-strewn stage, ready to confront her adversary and the kitchen implement. She yanked the microphone out of Philistina's hand and threw it to the floor as the phrase "traitorous twat" exploded from her lips like a smoldering cannonball. She then made a fist with her right hand and delivered one, single, violent punch to Philistina's stomach. The unexpected blow knocked the wind out of Philistina and she fell to the floor with a painful gasp, clutching her belly with her large, manly hands. This caused Valerian's mouth to stretch into a crooked smile of satisfaction and she brushed her hands together a few times as though she were ridding them of loose dirt.

Feeling that her mission had been successfully accomplished, Valerian turned away from the FRUMP founder, who lay crumpled on the floor like a large pile of aprons and diapers waiting to be laundered, and began to walk towards the stage steps. Her smile grew wider as the booing from the crowd metamorphosed into loud cheering, and Valerian balled up her hand into a fist and raised her arm straight up to the sky.

Without warning, Philistina retaliated with a surprise attack, lunging at Valerian from behind, and the two women fell to the floor of the stage, slapping, punching and kicking each other in a spectacular catfight. To the delight of the crowd, Valerian ripped the plastic baby

The Amnesia Girl!

away from Philistina's strapped-on artificial breast. Philistina screamed, "Disgusting harlot! Feminist heathen! I want my child back!"

Without hesitation Valerian pulled the plastic baby's head off, causing milk to spill out of the doll's body. As some of it splashed onto her legs and feet, her face contorted with disgust at the sight of the milk, and she exclaimed, "Oh, my God, you sickening twisted bitch!"

Philistina attempted, in vain, to grab the plastic baby, and, once again, demanded its return.

Valerian yelled, "Time to play fetch, Fido!" She then tossed the head into the crowd of wildly cheering women, who immediately scrambled for it. A husky female voice from the crowd blurted out, "Wrap it in a bra and burn it!"

"You dirty dyke!" screamed Philistina, as she began striking Valerian's body with her iron skillet. "You Godless, muff-diving strumpet!"

"You male-chauvinist-pig enabler!" Valerian screamed back as she repeatedly struck Philistina over the head with the decapitated plastic baby. "I'm gonna shove this goddamn doll right up your vagina!"

The two women traded blows and kicks, and, during the struggle, Valerian grabbed hold of her enemy's hair bun and ripped it from her head, revealing the balding head of a man. A look of shock bloomed across her face as she stared down at the sweaty, disheveled wig in her hand, and then looked up at the shrieking Philistina, who was frantically trying to cover her predominantly hairless head with her hands.

"Oh my God, you're not a woman!" screamed Valerian. "You're a man! A filthy, sperm-producing *man*!" She picked up the microphone, turned to the mob of women and yelled, "Look what we have here, sisters! Philistina Savage, the supreme suppressor of all womankind, is actually a possessor of a repugnant penis! Let's fry this fake!"

The rally escalated into a scene of pandemonium. Howls and boos resounded throughout the crowd, followed by screams of "Burn him at the stake! Burn him at the stake!" Working themselves into frenzy, the crazed bra-burners descended upon the stage. A gunshot rang out and the ensuing chaos afforded Farika and Mara Marhoe an opportunity to escape.

Mara Marhoe tossed her copies of Valerian's manifesto onto the ground and turned to Farika. "That's our cue to split," she advised, plunging her hand into the fringed purse entrusted to her safekeeping and retrieved the keys to the van.

"What are you doing?" Farika asked.

"You and I are getting our asses into this four-speed, magical carriage before it changes back into a pumpkin, and then we're getting the hell out of here while we've got the chance! Didn't you hear that gunshot? Valerian's either dead or she's about to get busted for murder. But either way, she's not going to need this van anymore. Now let's bolt before the fuzz arrives and we all get busted!"

Mara Marhoe and Farika quickly climbed into the van, with Mara Marhoe strapping herself into the driver's seat. Fifteen seconds later, the fleeing pair were back on the road heading westbound and the pandemonium of the ill-fated bra-burning rally was but a diminishing reflection in the rear-view mirror.

The seemingly endless stretch of flat and uninteresting landscape that lay to the west of Omaha gradually transformed itself into graceful rolling hills of green until all at once a wall of snow-capped mountains rose up from the horizon into the bluest sky Farika had ever laid her eyes upon. Feeling almost overwhelmed by the majestic sight unfolding before her, like a full-color travel brochure, Farika basked in its splendor and anticipated the wondrous things that she felt surely awaited her and Mara Marhoe in this new picture-postcard environment.

* *

It was somewhere outside of Salt Lake City when Farika and Mara Marhoe passed a glum-appearing trio of nuns in full habits standing on the side of the highway next to an old Chevrolet Belair with a raised hood and steaming radiator. The tallest of the three nuns waved her hand and held up a large piece of cardboard upon which was hand-written: SACRAMENTO.

"Those poor nuns back there look like their car broke down," remarked Farika, turning her head to look out the back window. "We ought to go back and help them."

"Not a chance," blurted Mara Marhoe, her gaze fixed firmly on the road ahead. "Let someone else stop and help them. Nuns give me the creeps."

"I checked the map and Sacramento is on the way to San Francisco. Let's be nice and give them a ride."

"No!" snapped Mara Marhoe. "Forget it! I make it a policy never to pick up hitchhikers. It's dangerous."

"But you and I are hitch-hikers," Farika pointed out.

"Not anymore, Farika. We've got ourselves this shag-carpeted breadbox on wheels. Plus there's enough money in Valerian's purse to buy enough gas and oil and Screaming Yellow Zonkers to get us all the way to San Francisco. No more thumbing for us, baby!"

"But they're nuns in need," Farika protested, looking woebegone.

"For the final time, no! I'm not going to stop for them! Nuns give me hives. Besides, there's three of them and bad luck always comes in threes."

"Oh, please!" Farika begged. "Let's go back and

help them. We just can't leave them there like that. Don't you have any compassion?"

Mara Marhoe's face suddenly took on an angry reddish color and she dug her fingernails into the imitation leather padding on the steering wheel. From her mouth came a thunderous and maniacal howling sound and she slammed on the brakes, nearly causing Farika to be ejected from her seat. Checking the rear-view mirror for traffic, she threw the van into reverse and, driving along the shoulder of the highway, backed it up until she was within twenty feet of the disabled Belair. "Happy now?" she growled through her clenched teeth.

As the elated nuns grabbed their suitcases and trotted over towards the van, Farika flashed Mara Marhoe a smile of gratitude. "I've got a feeling that your good deed won't go unrewarded."

"The good Lord has answered our prayers," the nun with the sign declared jubilantly as she climbed into the back of the van, carrying an acoustic guitar and a small plaid suitcase. Smiling, she introduced herself as Sister Ramada and made a mysterious holy gesture with her right hand, then proclaimed, "May God bless you for your unselfish act of kindness!"

An older nun with a stern-looking face followed her into the van, nodded her head and introduced herself as Sister Imperious. She was a gaunt woman with thick eyebrows, thin lips, and a pasty complexion. From a mole on her pointed chin grew a solitary gray hair of considerable length.

The third and final nun to board the van wore a pair of dark, tinted glasses and was abnormally small, standing roughly three feet tall. She sat down without speaking a word, and Sister Ramada introduced her as Sister Magdalena.

"Sister Magdalena, as you might have noticed, is a

dwarf!" explained Sister Ramada, excitedly. Her voice then grew solemn. "She suffers from a rare and dangerous condition, which requires special treatment from Father Penetralia at the Church of the Perpetual Exemption in Sacramento. That's where we were heading before our car broke down. I only pray that we arrive at our destination before it's too late for her. You see, her sickness grows more serious with each passing hour and Father Penetralia is the only priest specially trained and appointed by the Church to deal with such cases."

"I hope it's nothing contagious," worried Mara Marhoe as she steered the van back onto the highway.

"You have nothing to fear, my child," Sister Imperious reassured her. "Sister's ailment is more of a spiritual nature, which often manifests itself in physical disturbances."

"A spiritual nature?" echoed Farika. "Physical disturbances?"

"Yes," answered Sister Imperious, rather coldly. "Our Sister Magdalena is possessed and has been ever since that fateful day she found the evil Scrabble board down in the basement of the convent. Before bursting into flames, it spelled out the name of the demon which now resides within her tiny body and torments her relentlessly."

"Oh, this is just splendid," observed Mara Marhoe to Farika in a sarcastic tone of voice to which Farika had, by now, grown rather accustomed. "As if we didn't have enough to worry about already, now we've got a goddamn demonic dwarf on our hands."

At that moment, the melodic sound of an A minor 7th chord rang throughout the confines of the van as Sister Ramada strummed out a funky reggae beat on the strings of her musical instrument.

Much to Farika's delight, and to Mara Marhoe's

irritation, all three nuns threw their heads back and joyously broke out into song. The words they sang were:

Father Glory tell me the story
Of the cosmic nun who hijacked the sun
Star-bright halo, blessed and wise
Stained glass eyes reveal her disguise
Love is growing thin
In this world of sin
Trapped in hell's embrace
Truth is the savior that falls from grace
Father Glory in purgatory
Say a prayer for me and set my soul free
Absolve me with your electron gun
Bless the star explosion nun on the run
Time is running out
For this world, no doubt
As the end draws near
Truth is the only thing that we fear.

No sooner had the nuns reached the end of their song, than an outpouring of obscenities in a deep and growling voice blared from Sister Magdalena's mouth. Her facial features appeared painfully contorted and exhibited a slight greenish tint. As she began to levitate from her seat, her dark, tinted glasses flew off her face, revealing a frightful pair of bloodshot, white eyeballs, devoid of irises and pupils.

As the other nuns struggled to restrain her from levitating any higher, Sister Magdalena bellowed out something in a Latin tongue that caused the entire van to vibrate and the hairs on Farika's arms to stand straight up. A thick spray of yellowish-green projectile vomit then flew out of her mouth and into Mara Marhoe's hair, and in a strained, gurgling voice, she immediately began to mumble the lyrics to *Jesus Christ Superstar* in

The Amnesia Girl!

reverse.

"You little son of a bitch!" cried Mara Marhoe as she swerved the van onto the shoulder of the highway and stepped down on the brake pedal. "That's it," she announced, turning her head in the direction of the trio of nuns behind her. "The three of you... out... now!"

As the nuns collected their belongings and prepared to disembark from the van, a State Trooper rapped loudly upon the driver's side window with his knuckles, startling both Mara Marhoe and Farika.

"Where the hell did he come from?" Mara Marhoe asked Farika in a low whisper.

Farika, whose panic had drained the color from her face, whispered back in a shaky voice," I don't know. I was so distracted by the demonically-possessed nun, that I didn't notice him pulling up behind us and getting out of his car."

The State Trooper once again banged his knuckles against the window; this time with more force. His face was beginning to show signs of irritability.

Displaying a fake smile and exerting every effort to make herself to appear calm and unfazed, Mara Marhoe rolled down her window. "Good afternoon, officer. What seems to be the trouble?"

"Are you aware that your left brake light is out?" the State Trooper inquired, craning his neck to get a look inside the van.

"Oh dear," replied Mara Marhoe, feigning concern. "I wasn't aware of that at all! Thank you for letting me know about it. I'll be sure to stop at the next service station and get that fixed!"

"What on earth is that ungodly smell?" he asked, wrinkling up his nose in disgust.

"Oh, one of the nuns in the back, uh, got a little carsick," explained Mara Marhoe, wiping the Satanic slime from the back of her head with her hand.

The State Trooper again craned his neck to peer into the van. "Are you aware," he continued, "that the maximum speed limit on this highway is fifty-five and you were driving thirty miles an hour over that? And are you also aware that you failed to deploy your turn signal when you changed lanes and that it's illegal to park on the shoulder of the highway except in cases of emergencies? I'll need to see your driver's license and registration, Miss."

A sinking feeling came over Farika as she watched Mara Marhoe reach into Valerian's fringed purse and pull out a yellow wet-look wallet from which she extracted Valerian's driver's license. Her sinking feeling quickly metamorphosed into full-blown nausea as her friend handed the laminated card over to the State Trooper who looked at the photo that was on it and then studied Mara Marhoe's face suspiciously.

"This is your van and you're the person to whom this license was issued?" he asked, his voice laced with skepticism.

"Yes," Mara Marhoe affirmed, still smiling. "My name is Valerian Kiwanis. Just like it says there on the driver's license."

"You don't look one bit like the woman whose photo is on this license," challenged the officer.

"Oh," said Mara Marhoe with a slight and very out-of-character giggle. "Well, you see, officer, I decided to change my hair color. Redheads have much more fun, they say. And I'm living proof of that! And I've been on a weight-gain diet for the past year. I must have put on at least a hundred pounds. Thank you for noticing!"

Looking clearly unconvinced by Mara Marhoe's fabricated story, the State Trooper cautiously placed one hand over the service pistol on his black leather belt and firmly demanded that she immediately step out of the vehicle.

Mara Marhoe turned and looked at Farika, the smile upon her face rapidly diminishing. "I guess this is the end of the line," she intoned glumly. "Oh, well. It was fun while it lasted."

At that moment, Sister Ramada opened the back door and stepped out with her suitcase and guitar in hand, followed by the other nuns with their baggage. Humming *Dominique* in unison, they turned and started to walk away from the van.

"Hey!" shouted the agitated State Trooper. "Where do you think the three of you are off to? I'm not falling for the old fake-nun-routine again. Get back into the vehicle immediately or you'll all be placed under arrest!"

Sister Magdalena's Lilliputian body began quivering uncontrollably, as though she were having a seizure of some sort. A ferocious demonic growl burst forth from her mouth and she made a quick lunge at the State Trooper, latched onto his leg, and sunk her teeth deep into his thigh.

The sudden attack and agonizing pain caught him off-guard. He lost his footing and fell backwards onto the ground with the crazed dwarf still affixed to his limb. Grimacing from the pain, he let out a thunderous man-scream and cried, "Get her off of me or I'll shoot her!"

Sister Ramada and Sister Imperious rushed to the fallen officer's aid and attempted to pull the possessed woman away from him. However, their efforts were all for naught as Sister Magdalena, who seemed to have developed superhuman powers, refused to release him from her hellish grip and bit down on his thigh even more viciously.

"I command you to release this man at once!" cried Sister Imperious. "Depart this innocent woman's body now! Hear me, unclean spirit! Return at once to the fiery pit of Hell from whence you came! The power of Christ compels you! The power of Christ compels you!"

To Sister Imperious' dismay, her desperate attempt at driving out the evil entity yielded no success. It did, however, anger the demon that dwelled within the possessed nun.

Sister Magdalena growled even louder and what appeared to be a black, serpent-like tongue darted in and out of her mouth. She then swung her arm and struck Sister Imperious across the belly with the back of her hand. The blow caused the fragile woman to fly through the air a distance of ten feet before landing upon the ground, where she lay groaning and in a state of semi-consciousness.

Horrified, Sister Ramada dropped to her knees, made the sign of the cross, and immediately began uttering prayers.

Laughing maniacally, the dwarf then reached between the State Trooper's legs and, using her fingers like a vice grip, clamped down upon his helpless testicles, mercilessly squeezing and twisting them with all her might. Debilitated by the excruciating pain, he cried out wildly until the agonizing torture grew too much for him to bear, and he passed out on the spot.

Without hesitation, Mara Marhoe floored the accelerator pedal and the van took off with a loud screech, leaving the nuns and the out-of-commission State Trooper behind in a small cloud of dust. "I'd sell me soul for some Thorazine right now!" she spoke in a mock British Cockney accent.

"Be careful what you wish for," Farika warned.

Chapter Twelve

Molotov Cocktails and Pink Champagne

The sight of a green, reflective, aluminum sign welcoming them to the state of California, as well as to Sierra County, filled Farika with a tingle of delight and prompted an unbridled howl of glee to emerge from the mouth of Mara Marhoe. And, as the wheels of the van propelled them farther into the mountainous and pine-covered terrain of the Golden State, the scenic vistas that unfolded before their weary eyes seemed not only to be filled with an almost otherworldly beauty, but with a promise of the proverbial silver lining.

"Welcome to paradise!" enthused Mara Marhoe.

Three and one half hours later, while refueling the van at a service station somewhere in a less-than-posh section of Oakland, paradise was superseded by the sounds of tambourines and marching feet as an angry multitude of afro-wigged protesters flooded the street, chanting: "Tighten up your wigs, and death to the pigs!"

"Oh, my God!" shrieked Farika, looking rather

alarmed, as she gazed out the passenger window at the unsettling scene taking place within a stone's throw of the van. "What on earth is going on here?"

"Oh, wow! This is far out!" exclaimed Mara Marhoe with delight, as she eagerly surveyed the marching militants. She smiled, and the pupils of her eyes became dilated. "It's the Afro Power black radical group! Fasten your seat belts! It looks like there's going to be a riot!"

As the chanting demonstrators drew nearer with fists held high in the air, their unified voices grew louder and bolder. "Tighten up your wigs, and death to the pigs! Tighten up your wigs, and death to the pigs!"

The wailing of police sirens sprung up from all directions and rapidly grew louder, integrating with the chanting of the crowd. Within a matter of moments, law enforcement officers decked out in full riot gear and carrying transparent polycarbonate shields confronted the angry mob. A violent melee broke out and quickly escalated into chaos as white clouds of blinding tear gas and the swinging of billy clubs responded to the hurling of bottles, bricks and rocks. An airborne length of metal pipe made impact with the windshield of the van, cracking the glass with a loud explosive sound and eliciting a terror-filled scream from Farika's lungs.

Without hesitation, Mara Marhoe started up the engine and floored the accelerator pedal. The van took off like a flash with the nozzle of the gas pump still inside the gas tank. The hose snapped under the pressure and gallons of gasoline began spilling out onto the ground, forming a sizable puddle.

As Mara Marhoe and Farika sped away to safety, a Molotov cocktail tossed by one of the rioters crashed to the gasoline-soaked cement, instantly igniting the spilled fuel. The resulting explosion created a huge fireball, which shook the ground like a small earthquake. As the fire burned furiously, a large black cloud of billowing smoke ascended into the sky above Oakland like a small mushroom cloud, and then, suddenly, a massive flock of screeching seagulls appeared, seemingly from out of nowhere. They circled the flame-engulfed gas station for a few seconds and then swooped down from the sky, attacking police and protesters alike.

Farika's heart pounded with excitement as the van made its way onto the San Francisco-Oakland Bay Bridge and began its trek across the windy, white-capped bay that separated the cities of San Francisco and Oakland. Upon entering a tunnel on Yerba Buena Island, a vivid memory of her excursion through New York's Lincoln Tunnel in Jeffery Piggist's yellow Mercedes Benz flashed through Farika's mind. It dissipated, like vapor in the sun, when, less than ten seconds later, the van emerged from the west end of the tunnel, affording Farika's eyes a breathtaking view of San Francisco, which was now just minutes away.

A sprawling cluster of white and gray skyscrapers stood like a fogbound citadel of dreams, and, to Farika, the image felt both welcoming and imposing. Dominating the city's skyline was the newly-constructed Transamerica building, which pierced the cloud-dotted sky with its 212-foot aluminum spire like a towering ancient Egyptian pyramid. In Farika's imagination, it served to guard the mysteries of the enchanted kingdom that surrounded it.

> *"O, stay and hear, your true love's coming,*
> *That can sing both high and low.*
> *Trip no further, pretty sweeting;*
> *Journeys end in lovers meeting."*

Farika snapped out of her short-lived daydream and turned to Mara Marhoe, who was preoccupied humming along to a song on the radio. "Aren't those verses from

William Shakespeare's *Twelfth Night*?" she asked.

"No," replied Mara Marhoe, slightly irritated. "That's the new hit single by the English glitter rock band, The Andromeda Space Station. As soon as we get settled in at Madame Contessa Cherie's place, I'm going to go right out to a record store and shoplift the 45." She continued humming along to the music.

"I'm not talking about the song on the radio," Farika clarified. "I was referring to those lines of Shakespeare that you just recited a minute ago."

"I have no idea what the hell you're talking about," Mara Marhoe protested indignantly. "I didn't recite anything by Willie Wiggledagger."

"Yes you did!" Farika insisted. "I heard you say it. 'Journeys end in lovers meeting'."

"You," Mara Marhoe began sharply, "are imagining things; lots of things. It's all in your head, love!" She then shook her head, perplexed, and let out a long and loud sigh. "Oh, man. Don't get unhinged on me now. Maybe the Contessa can arrange to get you some Librium or something."

Farika gazed out in silence at the water and began to wonder if perhaps she had simply imagined the whole thing, after all. Mulling it over, she could not recall the voice she heard actually being Mara Marhoe's. On the other hand, it seemed too external to be one of her own thoughts rambling through her brain. The more she pondered it, the more of an enigma it became. If Mara Marhoe had not recited the lines, and if they were not the product of her own mind, then from where did they come? Why was she the only one who heard them? And what did it all mean? Farika felt incapable of providing herself with any answers whatsoever; yet, the Shakespearean verses she had either heard or imagined seemed, in a most curious way, to make perfect sense.

Arriving in San Francisco, Mara Marhoe exited

Interstate 80 and, carefully following the detailed driving instructions provided to her by her friend, Forrest Lawn, promptly became lost in the heart of the city's Financial District.

Whilst she and Farika waited at the intersection of California and Montgomery Streets for a red light to change to green, a burgundy-colored late model Chrysler New Yorker pulled up alongside the van in the left turning lane. The driver, a middle-aged banker type in a three-piece, pinstriped suit, rolled down his passenger window and shouted over to Mara Marhoe: "Hey, lady!" Do you know you got a ripped-off gas pump hose hanging out from your gas tank?"

"Mind your own damn business, you pervert!" Mara Marhoe replied. She then turned to Farika, who was attempting to smooth out and decipher a crumpled Coca-Cola-stained street map. "Some of these San Franciscans are pretty forward, aren't they?"

Driving westbound on California Street, Mara Marhoe and Farika eventually made their way across the bustling city to the affluent neighborhood of Pacific Heights, where gentle sloping streets lined with regal homes of old-world elegance afforded them panoramic views of San Francisco Bay and the Golden Gate Bridge.

"This must be the place," declared Mara Marhoe, stopping the van in front of an ornate gate of iron scrollwork. Behind it stood the white brick, Greek Revival-styled mansion belonging to silent film actress, Madame Contessa Cherie.

Standing three-stories high, with four fluted Corinthian columns supporting a balustered balcony projecting from the third-floor, the sprawling nineteenth-century structure was every bit as imposing as it was in need of tender loving care. The paint on the tall wooden window frames was peeling away in a number of spots and a long, jagged crack ran lengthwise through the mortar between the bricks on the left side of the building's facade. The small front yard appeared to have been neglected for quite some time with its landscaping consisting mainly of overgrown yucca plants, a tangle of odd-looking flowering weeds, and patches of lifeless blades of once-green grass.

"Do you suppose it's haunted?" wondered Farika, gazing up at the mansion.

Mara Marhoe pushed open the gate, which let out a loud squeak, and the two women made their way towards the house.

A pair of growling stone lions sporting fangs and strange bird-like wings were perched like silent sentries at the bottom of the slightly-crooked front steps that lead up to a tall dark walnut door decorated with intricately carved panels and a grotesque iron knocker in the shape of a snake-haired Gorgon's face.

Reaching for the knocker, Mara Marhoe remarked jokingly, "Whatever you do, Farika, don't look at its face. You might turn to stone!" However, before she could place her hand upon the knocker's metal ring, the front door opened with a slow and almost painful-sounding creaking.

Standing in the doorway was a lanky, middle-aged man dressed in an old-fashioned, dark gray chauffeur's uniform, which was comprised of a double-breasted coat that had a fold-down collar and two vertical rows of silver buttons, and matching jodhpurs, which were tucked neatly into a pair of high black leather boots. His hands were encased in black kidskin riding gloves, and sitting upon his completely bald head was a dark gray eight-point cap with a shiny, black visor, upon which rested a pair of dark, tinted goggles.

Without a word, he gave Mara Marhoe the once-over and then proceeded to give Farika a quick visual inspection. As he sneered with revulsion, his retracted upper lip revealed a gold-plated canine tooth and caused a two-inch diagonal scar on his left cheek to wrinkle up in an uncanny manner -- which seemed to fascinate Mara Marhoe, while at the same time bringing Farika a feeling of uneasiness.

He threw the door wide open and, in a deep, and almost menacing, voice, spoke. "Come inside. Madame has been waiting for you."

With a sigh of relief at finally reaching her destination, along with a slight amount of trepidation, Farika followed Mara Marhoe into the old mansion, which was stuffed with copious amounts of Art Deco-styled furniture from a bygone era and ancient Egyptian-themed statuary and paintings. Heavy floor-length draperies of crushed velvet with pleated swag valances covered all the windows, blocking out the light of day as well as the outside world. Farika couldn't help but feel that she was walking through a museum rather than someone's house.

"Dig this decked-out crash pad!" Mara Marhoe whispered to Farika, taking in the opulence of the mansion's interior as they trailed the scar-faced man who led them through a purple parlor containing an antique harpsichord bedecked by a gold-plated candelabrum with twinkling crystal prisms. Across the room stood a massive fireplace with a black marble mantelpiece supported by a pair of enormous gargoyles.

Knocking upon a red door at the end of an elongated hallway filled with dozens of old framed movie posters and autographed black and white photos of actors and actresses whose faces and names Farika did not recognize, the man wearing the driver's uniform called out, "Excuse me, Madame. Your house guests from the East Coast have arrived."

A slightly raspy and older-sounding female voice

responded from the other side of the door. "How *marvelous!* Show them in at once, Draco!"

The unsmiling man promptly opened the door and ushered Farika and Mara Marhoe into a hazy, dimly-lit room where they were greeted by the whirring of a running movie projector and the unexpected sight of an old film from the silent-movie era playing upon a large screen attached to a wall adorned with black and pink flocked velvet wallpaper. The exaggerated expressions of faces from the past with ghostly-white complexions and heavy black eyeliner flickered eerily on the screen as their darkened lips moved without sound.

A Tiparillo-smoking woman wearing a marabou-trimmed caftan and earrings of dangling rhinestone clusters that sparkled like miniature versions of the imposing cut-crystal chandeliers that hung from the mansion's high ceilings of ornate plaster, rose from her gold, velvet lounger and sashayed over to greet Farika and Mara Marhoe. She was buxom and swivel-hipped, and appeared to be in her mid-seventies. Her hair was platinum blonde and worn in a Marcel wave, reminiscent of the Roaring Twenties. Her lips were painted an indecent shade of red and upon her cheeks was affixed a heart-shaped beauty mark, which was small and black, but somewhat outrageous in appearance, nonetheless.

Even in the low lighting of the room, Farika could see that the wrinkled skin of the woman's face and neck was heavily made-up and powdered in what was apparently a laborious, but futile, attempt to conceal the ravages of time.

The woman introduced herself as Madame Contessa Cherie, "star of the classic foreign art film, *Mon Veneris*, and others."

With a quick embrace she welcomed Farika and Mara Marhoe to her home. "I'm just so delighted to finally meet you both," she bubbled in a somewhat dramatic fashion, her head quivering. "I've heard so much about you from Forrest Lawn! She's a truly delightful young lady with admirable talent, as I'm sure you already know. I must say, she just simply raved about you! Raved on and on. Oh, this is such a pleasure, indeed. I normally don't welcome non-fellow thespians into my humble abode, let alone complete strangers. But any friend of Forrest Lawn's is a friend of mine! I've always said that, you know. I trust you both had an enjoyable journey."

"Well, actually..." Farika started to say, her face grimacing. .

"Glad to hear it," pronounced Madame Contessa Cherie, interrupting Farika in mid-sentence. "There's no better tonic for the soul than a bit of globetrotting. Oh my, where are my manners? Do sit down and join me, won't you? I was just viewing one of my old motion pictures, *The Heartless Harlot*. It's a cinematic classic in every sense of the word with reviewers praising my performance, calling it 'a tragedian masterpiece!' Oh, I've heard some people say that silent movies are passé – a thing of the past. But don't let those vulgarians fool you with such utter nonsense. That thinking is nothing but a load of ordure! Talkies are nothing more than a fad that will come and go, my dear. You mark my words! A renaissance of silent films is on the horizon as we speak." Clapping her hands together, she suddenly shouted, "Draco! Pink champagne and Beluga caviar for everyone, and then you may attend to dinner."

Mara Marhoe looked jubilant.

"You do like pink champagne and Beluga caviar, I hope?" inquired the aged actress. Without waiting for an answer, she tossed her head back and chortled, "Of course you do! Doesn't everybody?" She then took a long drag on her Tiparillo. "Well, now that all of our pleasantries have been exchanged, let us get right down to the heart of the matter, shall we?"

"The heart of the matter?" repeated Farika, sounding a trifle bit confused.

"Yes," replied Madame Contessa Cherie. "The little matter of my compensation for your food and lodging."

The smile suddenly departed Mara Marhoe's face.

The silent film star gently tossed her head back and began to laugh. "My darling dears, you didn't honestly expect that your tenancy here, along with the champagne and caviar, were all going to be gratuitous, did you? If you did, I'm afraid you were quite mistaken!"

"But," protested Mara Marhoe, her voice sounding strained by distress, "we spent the last dollar we had traveling here from New York and now we're flat-busted broke. We have no money to pay you with."

Madame Contessa Cherie smiled. "I am well aware of all that. I know more than you give me credit for," she asserted. "But you needn't worry; you'll both be gainfully employed by this coming weekend."

Farika and Mara Marhoe simultaneously displayed looks of puzzlement.

"You see, my pretty pets, I've arranged for the both of you to work at my prestigious downtown entertainment establishment, The Castle de Sade, in exchange for your room and board here. You will start on Friday night, and whatever you make in tips will be yours to keep and use for your personal expenses."

"That's wonderful and very kind of you," enthused Farika, gleefully.. "But what kind of work will we be doing there?"

Madame Contessa Cherie's eyes sparkled like the ostentatious cocktail rings that she wore on each of her fingers. "You, my precious kitten, will be my star go-go dancer in a gilded cage. All you need to do is wear something short to show off your gams, stand in one spot, and gyrate your hips as the band plays. Oh, the bodily movements that pass for dancing these days! They're not at all like the Black Bottom or the Lindy Hop. Ahh, now that's when dancing really was dancing!"

"What about me?" Mara Marhoe inquired curiously, the distress in her voice gone. "Am I going to work as a go-go dancer at the club also? I'm a fantastic dancer, if I must say so myself. You should see me do the Funky Chicken!"

"Oh, my goodness, no," replied Madame Contessa Cherie, as a look of alarm swept across her face. "I don't have a cage large enough to fit you. Therefore, I've arranged for you to be a cigarette girl. All you need to do is simply walk around the club all night carrying a tray full of cigarettes, cigars, and various flagellation devices."

At that moment, Draco entered the room wearing a supercilious look and wheeling a vintage rosewood tea trolley upon which sat a bottle of imported French champagne, three fluted crystal glasses with gold rims, a plate containing small bits of buttered toast, a bowl of *creme fraiche*, and a Sterling silver caviar server filled with crushed ice and a black lump of pickled sturgeon eggs. As he poured some of the pink champagne into the glasses, Madame Contessa Cherie gazed upon him dotingly.

"Dear Draco," she sighed adoringly. "I just don't know how I'd ever manage without him. I've come to rely on him for so many things! You see, he came into my employ eons ago after my handmaiden, Tallulah, perished in that oh-so-tragic accident. The poor dear, she choked on a grape downstairs in the wine cellar. Draco's been my right-hand man ever since. Oh, believe me when I tell you that a woman of my stature just couldn't ask for a more loyal manservant. He performs multiple duties around the mansion: chauffeur, butler, chef, even groundskeeper!"

"I couldn't help but notice how beautiful the grounds were when we arrived!" said Mara Marhoe with a mouth full of caviar.

"Yes. I must admit that they were absolutely stunning," Farika chimed in, trying her utmost to refrain from rolling her eyes. She grinned sweetly and hoped that her hostess didn't detect the sarcasm that enveloped her words.

Seemingly oblivious to any impertinence on the part of her guests, Madame Contessa Cherie raised her fluted glass in the air and proposed a toast, to which Farika and Mara Marhoe happily drank: "To the start of an exciting new chapter in your lives!" She took a sip and then added, "And just to show you how generous I can be, I'm going to advance each of you lovely young ladies one-hundred dollars first thing tomorrow morning so you can go downtown and purchase some fabulous new clothes and fashion accessories for yourselves. And while you're at it, you might stop at a beauty parlor and get them to do something with your hair. I expect all the girls who work for me to be champions of haute couture."

* *

After the pink champagne had been drunk and the hor d'oeuvres consumed, Farika and Mara Marhoe were shown to their sparsely furnished shared quarters on the second floor by Madame Contessa Cherie's manservant. They locked the door after he left and proceeded to freshen themselves up for dinner in the formal dining room.

While Mara Marhoe was disrobing in preparation for a much-needed hot shower in the pink and black tiled en-suite bathroom, Doctor I's locked book with the royal blue leatherette cover fell out of her pocket onto the parquet flooring with a thump, attracting Farika's attention.

"Oh my goodness!" Farika exclaimed as her eyes looked down and met with the gold embossed letters on the cover that spelled out: *The Joy of Insanity*. "I had forgotten all about Doctor I's journal."

"I didn't," Mara Marhoe replied.

"What are you planning to do with it?"

"Well, I've been giving the matter quite a bit of thought since we left New York and I've come up with an ingenious plan. You and I are going to take that book and cash in on it," Mara Marhoe said with resolve.

"What are you talking about?"

Mara Marhoe let out a chuckle. "I'll bet you that over-sexed headshrinker at the Midtown nut hospital really freaked out when he found out that we made off with his book. And I can just about guarantee you that he'll be prepared to pay us a hefty ransom in exchange for getting it back into his grimy little hands."

"What makes you so sure he would do that?" Farika asked, picking up the book and staring at it intently. "What on earth could possibly be inside it that would be so valuable to him?"

"I haven't read it yet, so I couldn't tell you," confessed Mara Marhoe as she pulled open the bright, paisley-covered vinyl curtain and climbed into the claw-foot bathtub. "That damned thing has an indestructible lock on it which I haven't been able to pry open. But I can guarantee you that whatever's written inside is pretty important to the quack. All sorts of juicy, top secret information, no doubt!"

Farika tossed the mysterious book onto a tufted French provincial chair in the corner of the bedroom. "There's something about that book that makes me nervous. I'm not sure what it is, but I really wish you'd burn it."

"Burn it? Are you out of your freakin' mind, Farika?" Mara Marhoe inquired, sounding almost outraged. She then turned on the shower and began to lather up her portliness with a bar of fragrant, perfumed soap. "Well, I guess that was a rather dumb question to ask as it's quite obvious that you are. Do you seriously think I want to be hoofing around in some cheesy dive bar pushing cigarettes and whips every night for the rest of my life? And do you really want to be shaking your T and A for a bunch of weirdos in a big bird cage like some sort of epileptic canary until you're as wrinkled up as that rancid old harpy downstairs? Get with it, love. If we play our cards just right, there'll be two one-way tickets to paradise waiting for us inside that little blue book!"

Chapter Thirteen

The Leopard's Lair

Gazing upon her reflection in the full-length, baroque-framed mirror at the How Bizarre Boutique on Van Ness Avenue, Farika felt like she was barely able to recognize herself in the new outfit, personally hand-picked for her by the store's mustachioed wardrobe expert known as Max the Fashion Guru. The familiar-looking young woman staring back at her from the silvered glass was wearing a pleated light-gray tweed miniskirt into which was tucked a brown, button-down lace blouse accentuated by a long necklace of gold-plated stars that were linked together with large white pearls. Her once-long raven hair had been cut into a trendy, shoulder-length, layered shag with bangs, and, in her brown suede platform shoes, she stood slightly taller than Max, who hovered at arm's length in his bell-bottomed mauve velour jumpsuit, the back of his left hand resting against his hip.

Max lifted up his lavender-tinted wire rimmed

glasses and caressed Farika with his dreamy blue eyes. "Oh babe, you look *très* exquisite!" he intoned in a slightly effeminate voice. "Just look at you. Oh! You're *ab*-solutely fabulous! Ravishing! Oozing sex appeal! I guarantee you'll knock them dead."

Unable to take her eyes off the sight of her new self in the mirror, Farika turned her head slightly and cautiously touched her new hairstyle. "Do you really think so?" she asked, sounding unconvinced.

"Have a little faith in Max, baby," the fashion guru purred. "I've been in women's fashions, literally, way before Twiggy was even a seedling. They don't call me a fashion guru for nothing. I know what's hip, sweetie-pie."

Farika smiled approvingly. "You know, the more I see myself in this outfit, the more I grow to like it. I'll take it, then."

"Smashing!" enthused Max. "You're a star, baby. Now, would you like me to wrap up your new threads to go, or is your plan to wear them home?"

"Oh, I think I'd like to wear them home, if that's okay," said Farika. "They make me feel kind of... with it!"

"Whatever your little heart desires," replied Max, adding up the total cost of Farika's purchase. "I'd wear them home, too, if I were you. To be honest with you, babe, I wouldn't be caught dead in that get-up you came in here with. Ugh! Not only was it so yesterday; it looked like something someone who escaped from a mental institution would wear."

Startling one of the store's browsing customers, Mara Marhoe suddenly burst forth from the dressing room, her large frame testing the limits of a furry yellow top and an orange suede skirt. Her pudgy feet were squeezed into a pair of cork wedges with tangerine-colored leather straps, while a black crocheted, flapper-

The Amnesia Girl!

style cloche hat with a rhinestone butterfly hugged her head. Wrapped around her neck was a flamboyant multi-colored feather boa.

"Oh!" Max gasped as he laid his eyes upon Mara Marhoe modeling her new outfit. "*Très chic! Très chic!* The butterfly of beauty has emerged from its cocoon! Behold a seventies superstar! A true glamour goddess of the times! And who said there was no hope for you?"

"You did," sneered Mara Marhoe.

After paying for their new clothes with the money advanced to them by their new employer, Farika and Mara Marhoe bid Max the Fashion Guru goodbye and left the boutique, donned in their new fineries. As they stepped out onto the sidewalk and felt the cool, misty morning air of San Francisco embrace their senses, their eyes beheld an unwelcome sight that instilled within their hearts a feeling of dread.

Valerian's van, which they had driven to the boutique in and parked along the curb out front, was helplessly sandwiched between two black-and-white patrol cars with their "cherry top" lights flashing a constant rotating beacon of bright red. A gruff-appearing police officer was meticulously examining the exterior of the van and jotting down notes on a pad, while two other officers were busy conducting a search of the vehicle's interior.

"Oh crap!" grumbled Mara Marhoe, stopping dead in her tracks. "This is just what we needed today!"

"What are we going to do now?" asked Farika, her voice tinged with panic.

"We need to keep our cool," replied Mara Marhoe, "and just start walking nonchalantly over to that hotel on the corner."

However, before Farika and Mara Marhoe were able to make a break for it, the stern-faced cop with the notepad spotted them and shouted in their direction,

"Hey! You two over there! Are either of you ladies the driver of this vehicle?"

Mara Marhoe replied that neither she nor her girlfriend were the driver, while Farika forced a smile and shook her head from side to side, trying desperately to remain calm, cool, and collected.

The look on the police officer's face seemed to indicate that some amount of suspicion was afoot, as he then pressed them further, inquiring if either of them knew or had seen the person who had been driving the van. Again, they provided him with negative responses and smiles, and then promptly proceeded towards the Extravaganza Hotel just as a tow truck arrived on the scene to haul the van away to an impound lot.

Once inside the relative safety of the palatial golden-pillared lobby of the hotel, both women stopped and breathed a sigh of relief.

"Whew!" breathed Mara Marhoe, pretending to wipe away imaginary perspiration from her forehead with the end of her feather boa. "That sure was a close one!"

"Too close for comfort if you ask me," Farika responded, her body shivering as if it had been exposed to the chill of winter. "What's going to happen now?"

"Don't you worry your pretty little head over it, sexy mama," reassured Mara Marhoe, running her fingers lovingly through Farika's shag. "Everything is going to be just fine. I won't let anything bad happen to my Farika. Now you just sit down on one of those comfy-looking red chairs over there and pull yourself together while I go find a phone to call Madame Contessa Cherie."

"What are you going to tell her?"

"I'll tell her that we had an automobile accident or that someone stole the van or something, and get her to dispatch that chauffeur of hers with the million dollar smile down here to pick us up. No doubt in a long black funeral hearse. I can't imagine that creepy cretin behind the wheel of anything else!"

Farika smiled at Mara Marhoe's remark and then proceeded to sit down in one of the red chairs, which she discovered was indeed quite comfortable, while her friend took off in search of a pay phone.

The calm of the hotel's luxurious lobby with its oversized, potted palms and colossal, French Empire chandeliers of cut glass and ormolu sharply contrasted the flurry of worry that caused Farika's insides to tremble. Every now and then, the ringing of a telephone or the ding of the call bell at the front desk would break the placid stillness that Farika came to find had a soothing effect upon her frazzled nerves.

Whilst waiting for Mara Marhoe to return, Farika observed a number of well-dressed couples and singles with expensive luggage periodically gliding in and out of the hotel. Across the lobby from her, an older gentleman sat with his legs crossed, reading a newspaper and smoking a Sherlock Holmes-style pipe. He looked up from his page of stock market reports briefly to give Farika a curious look, then his eyes returned to the sanctum of his newspaper.

Just as Farika felt she was on her way to regaining her composure, the disconcerting sight of two uniformed police officers strolling into the hotel's lobby made her heart skip a beat. Their eyes seemed drawn to her face as they walked past her on their way up to the front desk. Feigning disinterest, Farika fidgeted with her fingernail cuticles, but listened intently as the cops asked the desk clerk if anyone who owned a black, 1973 Ford van with license plate number WARP-1227 was registered as a guest. The desk clerk carefully checked the hotel's guest registry, then shook his head and said no. At that point, one of the officers handed him a business card and instructed the man to phone him at the station immediately if anyone using that license plate number should check into the hotel, adding that it belonged to a vehicle that had been reported stolen in Nebraska. Then the two officers made their way back across the lobby, their eyes once again drawn to Farika's face as they walked past her on their way out.

As the pair exited the hotel, the younger of the two said to the other one, "Hey, Lieutenant, did you hear the latest rumor going around the station that all our squad cars are gonna get repainted baby blue and white?"

The older cop shook his head and chuckled. "Nah, it'll never happen, Keller."

No sooner had the inquisitive officers strolled out of the hotel and Farika once again breathed a sigh of relief, a bevy of kinetic, wild-eyed teenage girls armed with Polaroid cameras and autograph books clamored in, filling the lobby with giggles and excited chatter. Their boisterousness triggered the man with the pipe to peer over his newspaper and fire off a look of exasperation. He rose from his red chair, crossed the lobby in a huff, then disappeared up the red-carpeted grand staircase.

The trio of tittering teens paused briefly to survey their surroundings and then instantaneously gravitated toward Farika, who tried to pretend that she didn't notice them. Her ploy, however, failed to keep them at bay, and, before she knew it, they were standing just inches from her. She looked up at them and politely asked if they were in need of some help.

Animatedly, the three girls began talking all at once. "We just received word that he's staying here! Have you seen him yet? Did he speak to you? What's he like in person? Tell us! Did you get his autograph? What room number is he in?" Their questions hurled Farika into a mind-swirling state of perplexity.

"I'm sorry," Farika replied, sounding a bit stunned by the sudden and confusing interrogation. "I'm afraid I really don't have the slightest idea who or what you girls are talking about."

"She's lying!" hissed one of the trio, a dark-haired girl in a floral-patterned velvet mini-dress, black tights and a burgundy wide-brim floppy hat. "She's one of those renegade groupies with an agenda. I know her type!"

The second girl, who was in flared patchwork jeans and a halter-top decorated with hundreds of gold sequins, asked with bloodlust in her voice, "Should we kill her?"

"Keep your cool for now, Miss Wren," replied the third girl, a granny-booted, frizzy blonde, garbed in a crocheted top over a midi-length purple gauze Indian skirt. "I'll deal with this situation. After all, I'm in charge of the organization." She then turned to Farika and introduced herself as Miss Vixen Velour and her two friends as Miss Wren Russo and Miss Ferrari Fontana. "We heard through the grapevine that Leopard Man and his all-girl band, the Heavenly Blue, are in San Francisco to play a concert at the Richard Nixon Memorial Auditorium, and, according to our very reliable informant, they're secretly booked in here at the Extravaganza. Are you a groupie?"

"A groupie?" asked Farika with a slight chuckle. "I hardly think so."

"There's nothing wrong with being a groupie!" hissed Miss Ferrari Fontana.

"I never said there was," said Farika, taken aback by the girl's burst of anger. "I wasn't trying to offend you."

"It was the way you said it," responded Miss Wren Russo, accusingly. "You made it sound like a dirty word."

"People are always putting us down because they think groupies are trashy girls," declared Miss Ferrari Fontana. "Just because we like to ball pop stars!"

"Pop stars like Leopard Man!" Miss Wren Russo chimed in, licking her lips and giggling.

"I'm the founder and president of his fan club," Miss Vixen Velour, sternly pointed out, "so I get to ball him first. It's only fair."

Miss Wren Russo quickly returned her tongue to her mouth and frowned grumpily.

"I don't mean to come off as nosy," began Farika, "but you've all got me curious about this groupie thing you're into. It's kind of fascinating. Have you slept with a lot of famous musicians?"

"Tons of them!" crowed Miss Vixen Velour. "Bowie, Jagger, Clapton, Page, Alice, Ringo, the Mothers, T. Rex. I've balled just about every guy who's had a record in the charts... every guy except for Leopard Man. But then, of course, he's not your average rock and roll lay. He's something special."

"What makes him so special?" asked Farika, intrigued.

"Well, rumor has it," confided Miss Ferrari Fontana, "that he's from another planet. According to an article in *Ultra-Groove Magazine*, Leopard Man is a Jovian from Jupiter! And last month's issue of *Musicmonger Magazine* published a tell-all story that said he's a half-human/half-animal hybrid with a tail and leopard spots all over his body!"

"I'm saving up all of my money to go to Sweden and get a trans-animal operation so I can feel spiritually close to my pop idol," gushed Miss Wren Russo, beaming with pride.

"I don't know of any groupies in California that have balled him," stated Miss Vixen Velour, "but I intend to be the first. In fact, you might say it's my mission!"

"Wow!" exclaimed Farika. "That's a pretty wild way to get your kicks!"

"We don't do it just to get our kicks," explained Miss

Vixen Velour. "Sleeping with pop stars can be a very educational and lucrative business. Take Miss Ferrari here, for example. She makes good bread selling her him-prints at rock festivals, the avant garde galleries down in the Haight, and even some of the gay coffeehouses over in the Castro."

"What exactly are him-prints?" inquired Farika, growing more curious by the moment.

Miss Wren Russo began to giggle as Miss Vixen Velour explained, "Him-prints are intimate works of art created by dipping a pop star's genitalia into water-based paint and then firmly impressing it upon a canvas or a sheet of art paper. You frame it, and *voila*! You have a him-print!"

"Cha-ching!" voiced Miss Wren Russo, attempting to imitate the sound of a cash register.

"The ones autographed by the owners of the genitalia are worth a lot more," added Miss Ferrari Fontana. "And, naturally, the more famous the pop star and the larger the genitalia, the more money fans and collectors alike are willing to pay."

"Naturally," echoed Farika, nodding her head in agreement.

"Get the hell off these premises at once!" a male voice suddenly boomed out, as the hotel manager descended upon the gaggle of groupies, waving his plastic fly swatter in the air. A vein pulsated on his forehead and his eyes were like fiery balls of petulance. "I've told you goddamn groupies before, to stay away from this hotel! I won't have riff-raff like you disturbing our clientele and tarnishing the reputation of this fine establishment! Now hit the road before I ring for the vice squad and have you all carted off to jail!"

Within seconds, the three groupies made a mad dash for the exit and were gone. The cantankerous fly-swatter-wielding man returned to whatever compartment he had emerged from, and once again the golden-pillared lobby was swathed in soothing calm.

Farika began to grow restless and wondered what was taking Mara Marhoe so long to make a simple phone call, as it seemed she had been gone for quite some time. For several minutes she debated with herself whether she should remain seated in the red chair and continue to wait for her friend to return, or venture forth in search of her. Finally, giving in to her growing restlessness, she decided on the latter and rose to her platformed feet, only to be overcome once again by the peculiar sensation of her mind drifting away from her physical self. Her surroundings began to take on an unreal quality just as they had done back in the psychiatric hospital the very first time the nearly transparent outline of the crooning stranger with the golden glow appeared before her.

The moment seemed to be frozen in time and Farika waited to hear her name being softly sung as before. However, this time her ears were filled only with silence singing its wordless refrain. Even the sound of Farika's own heartbeat had vanished into the overpowering hush like a dream into the spun gold of dawn. Then the corner of her eye caught a movement and she turned her head to behold the hazy image of a man soundlessly descending the grand staircase. From his form emanated not only an aura of strange golden illumination, but an aura of mystery as well.

Farika shut her eyes tightly for a few moments in an attempt to regain reality. But when she opened her eyes she found that the hazy image had not dissipated as she had hoped. She wondered if she had, perhaps, fallen asleep in the red chair while waiting for Mara Marhoe, and had drifted into a dream, or could it be that she was experiencing another hallucination? Did the groupies somehow slip her some mind-altering psychedelic substance when she wasn't looking, or was she truly losing her mind? The latter possibility flooded her with anxiety.

Just then, time unfroze from its bizarre freeze-frame, the sounds of the environment resumed as normal, and Farika's anxiety fleeted away. The hazy image coming down the stairs came into crystal-sharp focus revealing a goateed man that Farika guessed to be in his early to mid-thirties. His legs were hugged by a pair of tight, black leather pants, and a shimmering, leopard-print shirt that was unbuttoned half the way down, and exposed a tantalizing thatch of chest hair that was as golden as the 14 karat gold chains that adorned his neck. His dark blond hair was long and flowing like the mane of a lion, and the contours of his face were handsomely chiseled; yet, at the same time, there was something almost feline about his looks and the way he moved.

The gaze of his piercing, hunter green eyes shifted to Farika, and her heart once again began to beat, albeit rather wildly. "Excuse me, Miss," he began, studying Farika's face curiously. "At the risk of this sounding like a cheesy pick-up line, don't I know you from somewhere? I feel like I've seen your face before, but I can't seem to place it."

Farika yearned to tell the handsome stranger that he looked familiar to her as well because somehow his doppelganger had been appearing to her as if some kind of premonition of this moment, and even serenading her. However, she feared he would think her insane if she did. Instead, she looked at him demurely and said, "You must be mistaken. I don't believe we've ever met before."

"My name is Leopard Man," he said, extending his right arm to offer a handshake. "I'm a singer with a musical group called The Heavenly Blue. We're on tour and in San Francisco to play at a rock concert."

"Leopard Man. That's a strange kind of name."

"I'm a strange kind of guy."

"My name is Farika. No last name. Just Farika."

"Farika. What a beautiful name. I've never known anyone named Farika before. Do you believe in déjà vu?" Leopard Man's words resounded with haunting familiarity and dispatched a wave of cold chills down Farika's spine.

"I think it's quite plausible," Farika replied. "This world is filled with a great number of mysterious happenings for which we have no explanations."

"I've always thought so myself," agreed Leopard Man, his hypnotic eyes transfixed on Farika's as though, at any moment, his gaze would pierce the very core of her soul. "I apologize if this sounds like I'm coming on too strong, but would it be at all possible for you to have dinner with me tonight and maybe we can explore some of these unsolved mysteries together? That is, of course, if you're not married or involved with anybody."

Farika felt her cheeks starting to blush. "I would be delighted to," she answered, trying hard to conceal her exhilaration behind a facade of coolness. "Thank you for the invitation. I'll be looking forward to our dinner date." She then gave Leopard Man the address in Pacific Heights where she was staying.

Leopard Man informed her he would pick her up at six-thirty and then, in true gentlemanly fashion, he took Farika's delicate hand and tenderly placed a single kiss upon the back of it. "Until tonight, sweet Farika," he said, still gazing into her eyes.

"What the hell is all this shit?" growled Mara Marhoe, breaking the magic spell. She stood behind Farika with her arms crossed. "And who the hell is this freak with the poof hair slobbering all over your hand?"

Doing her best to hide her embarrassment and ire at her girlfriend's rudeness, Farika forced a smile and ever so politely introduced Leopard Man to Mara Marhoe, who looked him up and down with disgust, and then flashed him a most evil glare.

"Let's go, Farika," Mara Marhoe said angrily, as her hand clamped onto Farika's arm and pulled her away from the startled singer. "We've got to get moving. Cherie's chauffeur is on his way over here to pick us up and take us back to the mansion." She turned her head and flashed Leopard Man one final look of disapproval as she and Farika headed towards the door leading out to the sidewalk.

Once outside the hotel, Mara Marhoe scolded Farika as they waited for their ride to arrive. "What the hell is wrong with you, girl? Did you forget that the pigs have a dragnet out for us? The last thing we need is for some mangy rock minstrel in search of a one-night stand to go poking around in our business, or in your panties! You can't trust him not to turn us in to the cops if he should suddenly remember where he's seen your face before!"

And, with that being said, Mara Marhoe retrieved a newspaper from her purse, opened it to the third page, and thrust it into Farika's face so she could see the headline in bold, black letters, which read:

STOLEN VAN LINKED TO ESCAPED MENTAL PATIENTS SPOTTED AT OAKLAND RACE RIOT

Below it was a black-and-white photo of a smiling Farika, alongside one of a frowning Mara Marhoe, followed by a story detailing their bold escape from the psychiatric facility in New York City, and the substantial number of cross-country crimes the pair had managed to amass in a short period of time, while on the run.

"You're a star, baby," said Mara Marhoe in her best

effeminate male voice, sarcastically echoing the words of Max the Fashion Guru.

* *

"Does my eyeliner look okay?" asked Farika, peering into the mirror on the bathroom medicine chest to do a final inspection of her eye makeup. "I hope I don't look like a raccoon."

"Why bother asking me?" snarled Mara Marhoe from the chair in the bedroom, where she sat with her face hidden in a book on abnormal psychology that she found in Madame Contessa Cherie's library. "My opinion obviously means nothing to you."

"Oh, stop being such a bitter pill," said Farika, nervously brushing her hair for the tenth time since getting dressed up for her evening out with Leopard Man. "It's just a dinner date. There's no harm in that."

"Well, I'm glad you can be so cavalier about this. I, on the other hand, can think of a whole slew of dangers and disasters that this thing could lead to. Listen to me. The best thing for you to do is to phone this Leopard Man guy and break the date. It's not too late to change your mind, Farika. It's a woman's prerogative."

"I can't," protested Farika. "He made reservations for us at the Swanky Chopstick and he's already on his way to pick me up. Besides, I don't want to break the date. I'm a big girl and I can go wherever I like, with whomever I like, whenever I like."

At that moment, the sound of eight-note Westminster chimes rang out from downstairs, followed shortly by Draco's voice calling up from the bottom of the stairs. "Miss Farika! You're, umm, gentleman caller is here."

"If you must insist on going through with this insanity," grumbled Mara Marhoe, "at least let me come along as your chaperone."

"My chaperone? Absolutely not!" cried Farika, incredulously. "Now, I told you before that I'll be careful and I won't let anything slip. So stop all your worrying over nothing. I've got to go; Leopard Man's waiting for me downstairs. Enjoy your abnormal psychology book."

"Up yours," groused Mara Marhoe, staring at the wall to avoid eye contact with Farika. "And up his too!"

Undaunted by any trepidation or Mara Marhoe's foul disposition, Farika took a deep breath to help calm the butterflies fluttering within her stomach before hurrying down the stairs and into the purple parlor, where Leopard Man awaited her with a single long-stem rose.

"I feel just like Cinderella on her way to the ball," Farika whispered dreamily into Leopard Man's ear as he escorted her to his gleaming, black Jaguar convertible with leopard-skin interior waiting at the curb. She climbed in, and, with a roar of the engine, they were off like a blazing rocket ship on a star-bound journey through the night.

Arriving at the Swanky Chopstick in the heart of San Francisco's Chinatown, Farika and her dinner date were greeted by a cordial doorman in a red and black uniform, who promptly opened the door to the restaurant for them while a valet parked the purring Jaguar. A middle-aged Oriental hostess in a long red silk dress with gold embroidery escorted them to a candle-lit table in a subdued corner, where a young, black-haired waitress dressed in similar traditional Chinese attire soon arrived to take their order.

After perusing the dragon-decorated menu for a minute, Farika and Leopard Man agreed upon the Chairman Mao platter for two, which consisted of Mao Goo Gai Pan with revolutionary rice, mystery egg rolls, and two bowls of won ton soup. Following the waitress' recommendation, Leopard Man also ordered for Farika and himself a round of Jade Tigers, which turned out to be a sweet blend of green crème de menthe, triple sec, lime juice, and powdered sugar. They arrived in white ceramic Buddha-shaped mugs, each with a straw protruding from the figure's bared pot belly.

"A toast," proposed Leopard Man, raising his booze-filled Buddha, "to mysteries... and bewitcheries." He took a sip of his green concoction and then placed the figural mug upon the table and gazed longingly into Farika's eyes, making her feel slightly self-conscious. "So, my beautiful, mystery woman," he said, "tell me all about Farika. What turns her on? What turns her off? What's her scene?"

"I wish I knew," replied Farika, glumly. "I'm still trying to figure that out myself."

"Aren't we all? By the way, I'm a Leo – a born romantic. What's your zodiac sign?"

"I'm not sure," Farika admitted, trying to come up with a quick explanation. "I've never really given much thought to astrology before. But I somehow have a feeling that whatever my sign is, it's very compatible with yours."

"You really are a woman of mystery," Leopard Man remarked, smiling and slowly stroking his goatee.

It was at that exact moment that a female restaurant patron, who happened to be passing by the table where Farika and her date were dining, paused to do a double take, and then, in response to her recognition of the golden-haired rock idol, screamed out his name in an ear-splitting decibel level. Without hesitation, she threw her body onto the tabletop, ripping open her blouse, spilling drinks, and overturning a bowl of won ton soup, which splashed all over Farika's new tweed skirt.

Fondling her bosoms through her eighteen-hour bra and working herself up into a frenzy, the crazed fan rolled around on the table and cried out, "Oh, sweet

Christ on the cross! It's Leopard Man! I love you! And I have all your records! Oh, I can't believe it's really you! I dream of performing sex acts with you every night! Oh, my God, take me right here and now! Manhandle me! I'm yours to be deflowered!"

Moments later, a muscular bouncer wearing a *lucha libre* wrestling mask rushed over, snatched the delirious woman from the surface of the table, and, while uttering something in Spanish, dragged her, screaming and kicking, out of the restaurant. Despite her vehement protests, he less-than-gracefully deposited her upon the sidewalk out front and motioned to her with his hand to vacate the premises.

The disruption left Farika visibly shaken, and having all eyes in the restaurant glued to her, as a myriad of voices whispered and giggled, rendered her embarrassed and self-conscious.

Leopard Man apologized profusely to her for the inexcusable behavior of his deranged devotee and lamented that he was no stranger to such incidents. "Fame," he stated, "is a double-edged sword. It's been both a blessing and a curse for me." He then suggested that they escape the gawking faces of The Swanky Chopstick for a more tranquil and less intrusive setting.

Farika was quite receptive to Leopard Man's suggestion and grabbed her purse. But as she rose from the table she suddenly became aware that her tweed skirt and the lower half of her blouse were drenched in a greenish combination of Jade Tiger cocktails and won ton soup. "Oh no!" she cried. My new clothes are ruined! And I need them for my new job on Friday night!"

In a comforting tone of voice, Leopard Man told her not to fret. "We can swing by the hotel where I'm staying," he volunteered. "The Extravaganza has a 24-hour laundry and dry cleaning service. They did a super job cleaning all of the Heavenly Blue's stage costumes. I guarantee they'll have your clothes looking as good as new. And it's a tax write-off for the record company, so it won't cost you a penny."

Farika said okay and was soon back in the front seat of Leopard Man's shiny black Jaguar and roaring down the neon-lit streets of the city, her ears pulsating with cosmic glitter music playing from the car's built-in, eight-track tape deck. She felt as though her body and mind were soaring at the speed of sound.

* *

Wrapped in a plush, white bath towel while waiting for her clothes to be dry-cleaned, Farika sat on the edge of the king-size bed in Leopard Man's hotel room on the thirteenth floor, gazing out the window and taking in the spectacular view of the lights of the city below. They extended as far as her eyes could see, spread out like an ocean of shining stars, some flickering and some glowing steadily, against the vast and still backdrop of night's ebony cloak.

Farika could not recall ever having seen such a magnificent sight before. She couldn't help but entertain the notion in the back of her mind that she might actually be dreaming all of this and could awaken at any moment to, sadly, find herself still in bed in Madame Contessa Cherie's hilltop mansion, or, worse yet, in her bed in the Midtown Psychiatric Hospital! However, such worrisome thoughts were quickly dispelled when Leopard Man walked into the room and handed her two small cards: one was a complimentary concert ticket for a front row seat and the other a backstage pass.

"I'd really like it... no, I'd really love it if you would come to my show at the Nixon on Saturday night so I could make love to you with my music," expressed

Leopard Man, hopefully. "Please say you'll come."

Farika was flooded with elation, but it rapidly evaporated as realization set in. "I would really love to," she replied sorrowfully, "but I'm afraid I have to dance at the Castle de Sade that night. I can't risk losing this new job and place to stay. I'm sorry, I can't go, but thank you just the same."

She handed the ticket and pass back to Leopard Man, but he gently closed her fingers around them while saying, "These are yours to keep, just in case, for whatever reason, you find yourself free this Saturday night."

He then kissed Farika on the cheek, sending an uncommon, but not unpleasant, wave of electricity racing through her body. It was a sensation she could not recall ever having felt before, but one that she unequivocally craved to experience again.

Before long, there came a knock at the door. It was one of the hotel's bellhops, and he presented Leopard Man with a light blue, cellophane garment bag containing Farika's freshly laundered and pressed clothes. Leopard Man rewarded him with a generous tip and shut the door.

"Here you go," smiled Leopard Man, as he handed the bag to Farika, who was still sitting on the bed. "That didn't take too long. Well, I suppose I'd better get Cinderella back to her wicked step-sister before the clock strikes twelve and the magic turns to dust and blows away."

"Who's afraid of a little dust?" asked Farika, smiling and sounding a bit vampish.

Responding to her cue, Leopard Man lit some scented pillar candles and a stick of wild cherry-scented incense, which filled the room with a sweet, smoky aroma. He then turned the lights down low and turned on a reel-to-reel tape player that sat upon a small round table in the corner, underneath a hanging swag light with a pleated, gold velvet shade. The song that began to play was a track from Leopard Man and the Heavenly Blue's latest album.

> *She is a gypsy, she is fire,*
> *She is a goddess of desire,*
> *On a gold throne she sat,*
> *Jade eyes like a cat,*
> *She hypnotized me with love.*

> *She is the night, she is the day,*
> *My love for her will never fade away,*
> *And when we make love,*
> *The heavens above*
> *Sing like a choir of cosmic fire.*

> *My lady, her love shines like the stars,*
> *Her soft voice like golden sitars*
> *Sings sweet, so sweet*
> *Like a love song in my heart.*

"I'm really glad you decided to stay," Leopard Man whispered into Farika's ear, "Are you ready to try on that glass slipper?" He wrapped his arms around Farika's slightly trembling body and held her close.

His manly aura and the touch of his warm fingertips on Farika's bare flesh kindled flames of passion deep within her, and soon the world beyond the fragrant, song-filled hotel room melted away into nothingness, and the sensation of Leopard Man's heart beating next to hers was the only thing that felt real to Farika. She could not imagine there being a more perfect moment in time and space, and found it impossible to convince herself that she and the man whose arms she was now in could have been anything other than lovers in another lifetime.

The Amnesia Girl!

But then, her mind, all at once, gave way to thoughts of an even more curious magnitude.

"Before we make love," said Farika, ambivalent with equal parts of embarrassment and curiosity, "There's something, uh, I need to ask you. This is going to sound, uh, really weird, but, umm, do you by any chance happen to have... a tail and leopard spots?"

Leopard Man smiled. "There's only one way for you to find out," he replied in a seductive voice as golden and velvet as the hanging swag light. With his spellbinding eyes gazing deeply into Farika's, he slowly began to unbutton his shirt.

Farika's bath towel fell to the floor as she surrendered to his animal magnetism. *If this is all just a dream, I don't ever want to wake up*, she thought.

Chapter Fourteen

Simply Smashing

Subsequent to a two-minute-long kiss, Farika bid Leopard Man goodnight and unlocked the front door of the mansion with the key Madame Contessa Cherie had given to her. Creeping as quietly as a cat in the shadows, she made her way across the unlit purple parlor and into the hall, taking great care not to bump into any furniture or to knock anything over and wake up the sleeping household. She silently ascended the stairs, and, upon reaching the entrance to her bedroom, slowly turned the crystal knob without making a sound and opened the door. As she began to tiptoe into the dark depths of the room, the light switched on, momentarily blinding her eyes with its assaulting brightness. She immediately squinted and instinctively held the back of her hand to her eyes to shield them from the glare.

"Did you sleep with him?" demanded Mara Marhoe. "Well, did you? Answer me!"

"Shhhh," whispered Farika. "Keep your voice down.

It's half past one and you'll wake everyone up."

"I know what bloody time it is!" Mara Marhoe yelled at the top of her lungs. "And I don't give a damn if I wake up the dead! Did you sleep with that... that mutated musician... that freak of nature? Oh God! I hope he didn't give you crabs!"

Farika was overcome by a tidal wave of indignation. "That's my business!" she snapped. "Now, it's late and I'm tired, so can we just drop this and go to bed? I'd really like to get some sleep. Okay?"

Outraged, Mara Marhoe began clawing at her own arms and face with her fingernails. "Ewww!" she cried nauseously. "Just the very thought of that man touching your body, it's so vomitory it makes my stomach curdle! It makes me want to go out and commit crimes!"

"Would you please compose yourself and keep your voice down? You're acting ridiculous. Do you want us to get kicked out of this house, and with no money and no car on top of that? Wouldn't that just be terrific?"

With tears streaming down her cheeks, which were now red from self-inflicted scratch marks, Mara Marhoe rushed to Farika and threw her arms around her. She hugged her tightly and said, "I love you Farika."

Farika's indignation quickly melted away. "I love you, too," she responded, as she bestowed upon Mara Marhoe a reciprocal embrace. "I consider you my best friend in the whole world. You're like the sister I never had. Or should I say, the sister I don't remember having. That is, if I even have a sister, which I may or may not have. Oh, I'm starting to sound certifiable. Well, you know what I'm trying to say."

"Yes, I do. But I don't think you know what I'm trying to say. I love you, Farika, but not like a friend or a sister. My feelings for you go much deeper than that. I love you with a mad passion I haven't felt for anyone since I fell for Paisley Pendleton. Do you now understand what I'm trying to tell you? I just don't love you, Farika. I'm *in love* with you!"

Stunned by Mara Marhoe's revelation, which left Farika at a loss for words, her eyes widened and her lower jaw dropped open. She took a deep breath and attempted to digest her friend's words. The thought that initially popped into her head was that the love-confession was nothing but a false statement to riddle Farika with guilt after enjoying a night out on the town with a famous rock star while Mara Marhoe was left to spend the evening alone with only a book for company. Another thought then occurred to her; perhaps the confession was simply said in jest, as an attempt to introduce a note of levity. However, when no grin or sound of laughter showed itself to be forthcoming from Mara Marhoe's lips, Farika soon realized that neither theory could be correct. Mara Marhoe was being altogether serious.

"Oh my goodness," declared Farika. "I never realized... I didn't know... I'm not quite sure what to say."

"Just say you'll be my loving lesbo forever," replied Mara Marhoe, smiling through her tears. "That's all you need to say. That's all I need to hear."

"I can't," admitted Farika. "Your friendship means the world to me and I owe you so much for all you've done for me. I mean, if it weren't for you, I'd still be in that psycho ward, and, who knows, maybe even dead by now. I do love you, Mara Marhoe. But it's not the kind of lesbo love that you're talking about. I could never love you or any other woman in that way."

"I wouldn't be so sure about that if I were you," argued Mara Marhoe. "Don't forget, love, you have amnesia and that means you could be anyone or anything, including a card-carrying, Joan Baez-approved, vagitarian. Have an open mind. I guarantee if you try it, you'll like it!"

"You make lesbianism sound like an Alka-Seltzer commercial," quipped Farika. "I was going to wait until tomorrow to tell you, but I guess I should tell you now before you say anything else. Something strange and wonderful happened today when Leopard Man and I first gazed into each other's eyes. I can't really explain it, but there was an instant mystical connection between us. And I knew at that very moment that he and I were soul-mates."

"That nomadic malefactor is not your soul-mate!" cried Mara Marhoe, picking up a French provincial chair. As she repeatedly dashed it against the bedroom wall, she screamed, "I am! I am!" She then snatched one of the down pillows from her bed and viciously ripped it apart. As the room filled with white duck feather fallout, she screamed out in a feigned, posh English accent a slightly skewed quote from *Romeo and Juliet*. "O serpent heart hiding behind Farika's flowering face, you are but a beautiful tyrant, an angelic fiend with hair like... feathers!"

"Calm down!" Farika ordered, affrighted by Mara Marhoe's sudden outburst. "You're acting unhinged!"

"Unhinged? I'll show you unhinged!" roared Mara Marhoe. And, with that being said, she made a beeline to the en-suite bathroom, grabbed hold of the pink enameled wood toilet seat, and, with a loud animalistic growl, ripped it from its hinges. "I won't take this sitting down!"

Farika gasped with horror and covered her mouth as if to prevent herself from screaming.

Mara Marhoe's facial muscles contorted themselves into a frightful portrait of raging madness. As if bellowing out a battle cry, she screamed yet another line from *Romeo and Juliet*, "Eyes look your last!" She then swung the toilet seat against the mirrored door of the medicine chest with all her might. With one blow, the glass shattered into dozens of pieces, some of which came crashing down into the sink below, while others landed on the floor around her feet. "Love is merely a madness!" she cried, looking over at Farika. "A violent delight always has a violent end!"

Farika frantically pleaded with Mara Marhoe to stop, but her begging fell on deaf ears. Instead, Mara Marhoe continued on her rampage, working herself up into such a frenzy that her eyes glazed over and from her mouth came foam like from a rabid beast. She swung at this and that, leaving a path of destruction in her wake while emitting an interesting array of grunts, howls, and random lines from various Shakespearean plays.

Terrified, Farika fled into the hallway and screamed repeatedly for help. She had never before seen Mara Marhoe react in such a violent manner and feared not only for her own well-being, but for Mara Marhoe's sanity as well.

Moments later, a half-awake Madame Contessa Cherie and her multi-purpose servant responded to Farika's cries and rushed up the stairs to find the guest bedroom in shambles with overturned furniture, broken lamps, crushed lampshades, and feathers strewn about the floor. From the bathroom, Mara Marhoe could be heard wailing out ominous words from *Macbeth*.

"This is absolutely appalling!" complained the now wide-awake lady of the manor, her golden bracelets jingling, as she waved her hands about in disgust. "This room has been transformed from a fashionable *chambre* into the unholy chambers of the demented!" She then stormed into the ravaged bathroom, her face livid with anger, only to have the toilet seat flung in her direction. Missing her head by mere inches, it landed on the floor with a thud. "Miss Marhoe! I must insist that you refrain from this imbecility at once!" she yelled. "I have quite an aversion to boorishness!"

"And why not death rather than living torment?" Mara Marhoe cried out, dramatically. "My life is nothing but a walking shadow! It signifies nothing!" She then began to climb out through the open bathroom window, stating her intention to jump to her death. However, her sizable frame proved to be far wider than the frame of the window and she was only able to squeeze her body halfway through the opening before becoming lodged and unable to advance in either direction. "Chaos has come again!" she yelled. "My stars shine darkly above my head. I crave that you leave me to bear my evils alone!"

"She's mad!" cried Madame Contessa Cherie. "She's gone stark raving mad!" She then clapped her hands to summon her manservant, who stood just outside of the doorway with his face void of expression. "Draco! Please remove this proletariat from the bathroom window and lock her in the closet while I decide which course of action to take."

"Yes, Madame," he replied, obediently. "At once."

Farika and Madame Contessa Cherie watched as Draco walked across the bathroom, grabbed hold of Mara Marhoe's kicking legs, and, with one powerful tug, yanked her out of the window frame. However, the force caused Mara Marhoe's body to launch into his, knocking him to the floor in a semi-dazed state. Seizing the opportunity, Mara Marhoe immediately wrapped her feather boa around Draco's neck and began strangling him with it while pummeling his ears with obscenities. He attempted to fight her off, but her weight kept him helplessly pinned to the floor. His face began to turn an alarming shade of purplish-red.

"Oh, my God!" shrieked Farika. "She's going to murder him with a fashion accessory!"

Madame Contessa Cherie took a quick look around

and spotted the hardcover guide to abnormal psychology on the floor. "What a godsend!" she exclaimed, crouching down to snatch it up. "This book will enable me to effectively treat her symptoms!" She then proceeded to clobber Mara Marhoe over the head with it, instantly knocking her out, cold.

Wasting no time, Madame Contessa Cherie rushed to the telephone and called the Presidio Psychiatric Hospital, who dispatched three, well-built orderlies clad in sterile white uniforms to collect Mara Marhoe. They arrived at the mansion just as she began to regain consciousness and resume her delirious recitation of Shakespeare.

"Thou are too wild, too rude, and too bold of voice," recited one of the orderlies, quoting *The Merchant of Venice* as he injected Mara Marhoe with a powerful sedative that took effect almost immediately. Switching to *Hamlet*, he then added, "Madness in great ones must not unwatched go!" With the assistance of the other two attendants, he then proceeded to strap her securely to a gurney and wheel her away.

"What's wrong with her?" asked Farika, her voice filled with great concern. "Is she going to be all right?"

"She appears to be suffering from a rare psychological condition known as schizoid-aggressive Shakespearean disorder, which is triggered by emotional stimuli," replied the orderly in charge. "But there's no need for you to worry. We'll have our expert dramaturges at the hospital evaluate her. They're well versed in Shakespeare, as well as in other classic works of literature, and specially trained to handle these sorts of cases. I'm sure with enough literary aversion therapy and psychotropic drugs, her mind can eventually be stabilized. Rest assured she'll be in good hands and will receive the best treatment available."

With tears welling up in her eyes, Farika waved

The Amnesia Girl!

goodbye to Mara Marhoe from the front door as the three psychiatric hospital employees whisked her into the back of a waiting ambulance and drove off into what was left of the night. "Parting is such sweet sorrow," she whispered to no one in particular, succumbing to a sinking feeling that she would never see Mara Marhoe again.

* *

A myriad of red and yellow tulips danced lazily in the gentle midday breeze as Farika and Leopard sat on the downy green grass of Golden Gate Park in the shade of an old Dutch windmill. A western tiger swallowtail butterfly meandered in the air and then landed on their picnic basket to savor a minute of relaxation before taking flight and disappearing among the fragrant flowerbeds of the Queen Wilhelmina Garden. Nearby, a shaggy teenage couple with a frisky, shaggy dog played a game of catch with a Frisbee while a young Asian woman in a floral sundress and yellow, rubber flip-flops sat on a bench synchronously eating a bag of shrimp-flavored chips and reading a Chinese newspaper.

"You've hardly touched your lunch," observed Leopard Man. "Is everything okay?"

"I just don't have much of an appetite today," replied Farika. "I guess I'm still pretty shaken up over what happened last night with Mara Marhoe. As mentally unbalanced as she was, she was still my best friend."

Leopard Man put his arm around Farika to console her. "I know it's tough," he empathized. "But, at least, she's finally getting the help she needs. Try to put what happened last night out of your mind. It was a bad scene, hun, but now it's all behind you."

"Everything in my life is so damn out of place, like a jigsaw puzzle with the pieces put together wrong," lamented Farika, as she stared at her uneaten piece of a baguette and fidgeted with it. "But, for some strange reason, whenever I'm with you, everything feels so right."

Leopard Man smiled. "Must be another one of those unexplained mysteries that boggle the mind."

"Must be."

"The funny thing is," mused Leopard Man, "I've been experiencing quite a few unexplained mysteries of my own ever since the moment I first saw you sitting in the lobby of the hotel." Reaching for his guitar, he continued, "I have a little surprise for you. Hopefully it'll help cheer you up."

As his fingertips caressed strings of steel, a mellow, yet haunting, arrangement of notes and chords thrummed from his musical instrument and resonated deep within Farika's body, mind, and spirit. He then gazed deeply into her eyes of green and triggered a wave of goose bumps that rolled across her flesh as these lyrics flowed dreamily from his lips:

> *Farika, child with an angel's face*
> *Farika, lost in time and in space*
> *Farika, sweet Farika*
> *Farika, soul of mystical flame*
> *Farika, omens whisper her name*
> *Farika, my Farika, sweet Farika*
> *Farika, child of silver moonbeams*
> *Farika, smile of stardust and dreams*
> *Farika, sweet Farika*
> *Farika, jade green cat-goddess eyes*
> *Farika, spellbound moon on the rise*
> *Farika, my Farika*
> *Farika, child of heavenly blue*
> *Farika, I will always love you*
> *Farika, my Farika, sweet Farika*

"That was the most beautiful thing I've ever heard," commented Farika, feeling flattered and wonderstruck all at the same time.

"It was written about you," responded Leopard Man, still gazing into Farika's eyes. "How could it be anything but beautiful?"

Farika could feel her cheeks blushing. "But those words... that melody... they sound so very familiar. It's as if I've heard them before, a long time ago... in a dream."

Leopard Man let out a slight chuckle as he laid his guitar on the ground next to him. "You couldn't have. I only wrote that song this morning after I woke up from dreaming about you. I haven't even played it for the band yet. I wanted you to be the first person to hear it. After all, sweet Farika, you were my muse." He then took her into his arms and gently guided her body down onto the soft blades of grass, where he pressed his lips against hers and took her breath away with an impassioned kiss.

Just then, something moved in Farika's peripheral vision. She turned her head slightly and her eyes focused on an old man in a yellow hooded rain slicker standing just a few feet away from her. She thought it odd that he should be dressed for inclement weather when the sky above was a cloudless canopy of sun-drenched turquoise-blue. But before she could utter a word, the stranger suddenly pulled his raincoat wide open, startling her with his scrawny nakedness and the sight of a tattooed elephant's face, strategically positioned from the bottom of his navel down to his clean-shaven pubic region to enable his flaccid uncircumcised member to serve as the elephant's trunk. With an impish grin, he pulled his raincoat closed and then dashed off through the tulips.

Farika immediately disengaged from Leopard Man's kiss and sprang up into a sitting position. "That dirty old man!" she exclaimed, pointing her finger at the fleeing pervert. "He just flashed me!"

Leopard Man also sat up and looked around.

The shaggy dog was jumping into the air to catch the flying Frisbee in its mouth and the Asian woman on the bench had set her newspaper down next to her to watch. The two shaggy teenagers were whistling and calling to the dog, and the tulips were still swaying ever so gracefully.

"What dirty old man?" Leopard Man inquired, turning his head from side to side with the side of his hand pressed against his forehead like a visor. "I don't see anyone, Farika. You must have imagined it. Are you having an acid flashback or something?"

"No! He really was there!" insisted Farika. "I didn't imagine him. I saw him as clearly as I can see you. But he's gone now."

"I think you're letting your friend's nervous breakdown get the best of you," pronounced Leopard Man, retrieving a bottle of Chianti from the picnic basket. He then proceeded to fill a plastic cup with the wine and handed it to Farika. "Things like that can really play tricks on your mind, you know? You should get into Zen. Meditation is where it's at."

Farika felt sure that the flasher she had witnessed was real, but the mystery of his sudden vanishing act began to gnaw at her thoughts. The tulip garden was quite a large area, but it offered no nearby spots in which a grown man could easily conceal himself – especially one wearing a bright yellow rain slicker! Plus, the other people in this section of the park were happily carrying on as if nothing odd had happened at all. Perhaps they did not see him, Farika said to herself in an attempt to find a rational explanation to keep at bay the creeping fear that it was madness for her not to think herself mad.

* *

Emerging from the back of the limousine driven by Madame Contessa Cherie's chauffeur, Farika found herself at the Castle de Sade, ready to start her first night on the job. From the outside, the place appeared to be a run-of-the-mill nightclub, with the exception of its somewhat tacky castle-like facade of phony gray stone. Above the main entrance, which was designed to look like a wooden drawbridge, the name of the club flashed continuously in bright red neon.

Upon entering a small vestibule, Farika was greeted by a cigarette vending machine and a pair of life-size suits of armor clutching pollaxes with blades that appeared to be stained with blood. Dismissing it as either a product of her runaway imagination or a trick of the dim lighting, Farika proceeded inside. She found the interior of the building had the look of a cavernous dungeon, with its faux stone walls displaying various devices of torture, along with hand and leg manacles, and tapestries depicting scenes of debauchery. Flickering wall-mounted torches of wrought iron cast eerie shadows all around as she walked across the cobblestone flooring, her footsteps echoing. The entire place seemed a setting more appropriate for a trial of the Spanish Inquisition than a 1970's discotheque, she thought as she took in the sights of her new place of employment.

On one side of the club was a bar, which was tended by a staff of drink-mixing dominatrices. And on the opposite side was a small stage that overlooked a dance floor surrounded by dark Spanish-style tables and chairs upholstered in black leather. To the left of the stage was a full-scale replica of a French Revolution guillotine where a mannequin made up to resemble Marie Antoinette was secured with stocks at the bottom of the heavy wooden frame, its plastic neck positioned directly below the angled blade in wait of its "execution." To the right of the stage and mounted on a small cylindrical platform encircled by a row of simulated human skulls with flashing red light bulbs in their eye sockets was Farika's go-go cage. Standing nine feet tall and four feet in diameter, its gold-colored metal bars resembled a giant birdcage with a domed top.

While waiting patiently inside her cage for the music of the club's mystery band to set her body into motion so she could begin earning her living, Farika couldn't help but feel rather self-conscious in the studded, black leather bikini with lace-up detail and red and black vinyl, thigh-high platform boots issued to her by the nightclub's surly manager – a beefy biker-type with a gear chain for a necklace and heavily tattooed arms protruding out of a black leather vest. *But a job is a job and money is money*, Farika told herself as she watched the nightclub slowly fill up with a boisterous Friday night crowd. Dancing in a cage scantily dressed in the tanned hide of dead livestock was a far better alternative than being homeless and hungry. And, even more so, it was preferable to being back in New York City under the thumbs of Doctor I and his sinister sidekick, Nurse Mars.

The conglomeration of idle chatter, occasional outbursts of laughter, and the clinking of glasses filled with alcoholic beverages were suddenly interrupted by the amplified voice of the club's master of ceremonies. "And now, for that magic moment you've all been waiting for!" the voice boomed enthusiastically. "Ladies and gentlemen of the Castle de Sade, it gives me great pleasure to introduce to you our special mystery band, all the way from Canoga Park: the psycho-delic, the psycho-tronic, the psycho-licious... Little Sadie & The Sadistics!"

A bright spotlight lit up the stage and the club's patrons clapped, whistled, and cheered with delight, for standing front and center stage with her band assembled behind her was Little Sadie – an attractive, leather-clad, black woman sporting a massive silver-colored afro wig sparkling with sprayed-on glitter. Her eyelids were painted with glittering silver eye shadow and her lips radiated from a coating of metallic, glow-in-the-dark silver lipstick. With a bullwhip in her right hand, she walked up to the microphone in her deadly stiletto-heeled shoes, and, with a scowl, glared at the applauding crowd for several moments before grabbing the mic from its stand and crying out, "Let there be music! Let there be pain!"

With a single crack of Little Sadie's bullwhip as a cue, The Sadistics proceeded to crank out a frenetic rock and roll tune. Multi-colored strobe lights started flashing and, from within the confines of her giant birdcage, Farika began performing the go-go dance routine that Madame Contessa Cherie had taught her.

The dance floor quickly filled with gyrating people garbed in the latest styles of bondage and fetish wear. Men in leather chaps and studded chest harnesses danced with women dressed up in leather mini-skirts, skin-tight latex rubber catsuits, and corsets of leather and lace. Some of the dancers also wore bizarre fashion accessories such as ball gags in their mouths, dog collars around their necks, gas masks, executioner hoods, and even chainmail coifs. It was a strange sight for Farika to behold, but she took it all in stride and even tried to imitate some of their unusual dance steps, which incorporated threatening hand gestures and bodily movements that mimicked various acts of physical violence.

From a pair of towering speakers mounted at each side of the stage, Little Sadie's soulful voice burst forth like an out-of-control locomotive. It vibrated throughout every inch of the discotheque, rattling the glasses at the bar and propelling the dancers into what could only be described as a mass mania of malevolent motions. She sang:

> *Everybody's dancing to a brand new beat now*
> *Come on baby, do the Sado-Motion*
> *So put on your black leather*
> *And your spiked high heels now*
> *Come on baby, do the Sado-Motion*
> *All the sado-masochists can do it with ease*
> *There's nothing more exciting than a dungeon of sleaze*
> *So come on, come on, do the Sado-Motion with me*

As the wild-eyed singer belted out her hit song, *The Sado-Motion*, the increasingly aggressive people on the dance floor rhythmically responded by slapping, punching, and kicking their partners in time to the music. Other dance moves they employed included hair-pulling, nipple-pinching, eye-gouging, throat-choking, gonad-squeezing, and the dripping of hot melted candle wax onto exposed flesh.

> *You've got to swing your fist now*
> *Come on baby, jump up, jump fast*
> *Before my whip cracks across your ass, whoa, whoa*
> *Now that you can do it, let's get a chain now*
> *Come on baby, do the Sado-Motion*
> *Burn me with your cigarette and go insane now*
> *Come on baby, do the Sado-Motion*
> *Subdue until you're queasy and go out of control*

The Amnesia Girl!

> *With masochistic rhythm and sadistic soul*
> *Come on, come on, do the Sado-Motion with me*

As the music continued to rage on, a large medieval-style torture wheel attached to four long chains began to lower from the ceiling above the center of the dance floor and stopped just above the heads of the Sado dancers. Farika could see that around its rim were dozens of metal hooks from which hung a wide assortment of wooden paddles, switches, leather straps, riding crops, and whips of various types and sizes. It was like a smorgasbord of corporal punishment.

Each person on the dance floor eagerly selected his or her favorite implement of torture from the wooden wheel, which was then slowly hoisted back up. The couples then commenced flogging and paddling each other as they danced to Little Sadie's song, while those without partners self-flagellated to the beat of the music until their bodies and faces were covered by welts and bruises.

> *Kick me to the floor with a Sado-Motion*
> *Come on baby, do the Sado-Motion*
> *Choke me with your hands if you get the notion*
> *Come on baby, do the Sado-Motion*
> *There's never been a dance that's so painful to do*
> *It really turns me on to beat you black and blue*
> *So come on, come on, do the Sado-Motion with me*

By this time, the Castle de Sade's crowd had been whipped into a ferocious frenzy, both figuratively and literally speaking, and droplets of spilled blood dotted the floor. As several fallen men and women were being mercilessly kicked and stomped on by hordes of feet in stiletto heels, platform shoes, and jackboots, they smiled and moaned with masochistic pleasure.

A group of dancers had Sado-Motioned their way over to Farika's golden go-go cage and were trying to whip and cane her through the vertical gaps between the metal bars. Terrified, she let out a loud scream, which only served to attract more of the demented dancers to descend upon her cage, striking her with their riding crops and trying to grab her by the hair. Several of them began to rock the cage violently from side to side as if to topple it from its platform.

Kicking at her attackers with her platform heels and clawing at their arms with her fingernails in a desperate effort to fend them off, Farika frantically screamed, "Help! Somebody help me, please!" The troubling thought then struck her that her kicking and clawing would more than likely be interpreted as dance moves by any of the club's patrons sitting at the bar or at one of the tables. It was also highly improbable, she told herself, that her screams and cries for help could be heard by anyone over the blaring music. Therefore, it seemed her only option was to open the door at the back of the cage, while the structure was still standing, and make a run for safety.

However, much to Farika's horror, she soon discovered that she was unable to get the door to open. She tried again and again, but no matter how forcefully she pushed against it, shook it, or kicked at it, the barred door refused to yield. It was as though someone had locked it from the outside. Farika's heart pounded wildly with fear and, feeling quite helpless, all she could do was continue screaming for help at the top of her lungs and hope that Little Sadie's deafening, violence-inciting musical number would quickly conclude and put an end to the madness and mayhem that had unfolded on the dance floor.

Farika suddenly heard a familiar-sounding voice call out her name. She turned and, to her surprise and relief, she saw Leopard Man pushing and shoving his way through the voluminous rabble of pirouetting inflictors of music-driven punishment. Upon reaching the cage that imprisoned his lover against her will, Leopard Man found it necessary to employ brute force in order to dissuade the assaultive sadists who were deriving twisted pleasures from the pain and torment of their trapped victim.

"The door is jammed!" shouted Farika. "I can't get it to budge!"

"That's because it's locked!" Leopard Man shouted back, examining the handle of the door at the back of the go-go cage. "Somebody put a padlock on it!"

"A padlock?" Farika sounded startled. "Who would want to lock me in this cage? And for what reason?"

Scanning the nightclub to find something with which to pry open the lock, Leopard Man spied a nearby mace hanging upon the wall alongside a framed portrait of the Marquis de Sade. Wasting no time, he retrieved it and proceeded to swing it against the padlock. The lock refused to budge, so he tried again, this time more forcefully, but found that he still couldn't get it to open. But, with the third mighty blow from the mace, the lock finally broke apart and the door swung open, liberating Farika from her confinement. She emerged and, with elation and gratitude, threw her arms around her savior.

"My knight in shining armor!" she swooned.

"My kitten in a leather bikini," Leopard Man purred, passionately. "The desk clerk at the Extravaganza told me that this place has a reputation for being a bit wild, so I thought I'd better swing by just to check on you. Plus, I couldn't pass up the opportunity to watch you perform that saucy dance number of yours."

"I'll never be able to thank you enough for saving me," gushed Farika. "I don't know what would have happened if you hadn't shown up when you did. These people here are absolutely psychotic!"

"I'll drive you home if you're ready to blow this scene. My Jag's parked out front."

Farika accepted Leopard Man's offer without any hesitation, and, after a quick stop in the dressing room to trade in her leather bikini and vinyl boots for her regular street clothes, she happily bid farewell to the Castle de Sade. As Leopard Man escorted her outside, the cool night air felt refreshing as it kissed her face and gently caressed her hair. But it couldn't prevent Farika from wondering, and worrying, what fate would have in store for her after the termination of her short-lived employment.

Through the phantom-like mist that shrouded the Pacific Heights District, the city lights to the east glowed like thousands of tiny luminous fragments of an exploded star. Gazing out at them from the car window, Farika imagined that each one was the burning ember of someone's broken dream, and that somewhere out there was at least one shining for hers.

She once again thanked Leopard Man for rescuing her, remunerated him with a tenderhearted, goodnight kiss, and then departed his car and made her way across the uninspiring front yard to the front door of the even more uninspiring mansion, which seemed to Farika to look as bleak and tired on the outside as she felt on the inside. After unlocking the door, she waved goodbye to Leopard Man and then proceeded inside, her nerves still rattled from her traumatic experience at the rampageous discotheque.

As she began to climb the stairs on her way to her sleeping quarters, she couldn't help but overhear the voice of Madame Contessa Cherie emanating from behind a closed pair of ornately carved pocket doors near the bottom of the staircase.

"I have some *mar*-velous news for you, Forrest

The Amnesia Girl!

Lawn!" Madame Contessa Cherie was saying, mirthfully and with her usual over-dramatization of speech. "Pop the cork on that bottle of bubbly and get ready to make merry! What I mean, darling, is that I've taken care of those two dregs of society for you like you asked. Yes, that's what I said. Oh, these long distance connections are just dreadful. Yes, I'll speak up. Can you hear me now? Good."

Farika paused on the second step and listened with growing interest.

"You'll be pleased to learn that Mara Marhoe is in a padded room at the local lunatic asylum where she belongs," Madame Contessa Cherie cheerfully continued. "And the best part of all is that Draco and I didn't even have to implement Operation Gaslight to do it! That crazy cow flipped out all on her own! Isn't that just divine? Oh, and as for that other spiteful little viper, I've arranged to sell her to a white slave trader from China. Couldn't you just simply die?" Madame Contessa let out a laugh. "At this very moment she's securely locked inside a giant birdcage at my prestigious nightclub downtown and probably quite black and blue I would imagine. Rest assured that before the rising of the sun, that little irritant will be sedated, crated, and on a freighter bound for Shanghai."

Farika let out a gasp of shock as the revelation of Madame Contessa Cherie's evil intentions spilled into her ears and flooded her mind. She quickly covered her mouth with her hand, hoping she hadn't been heard. She then tiptoed down to the bottom of the stairs and placed her ear against one of the doors and continued listening to the disquieting telephone conversation, her initial shock transforming into a mixed bag of churning emotions, with feelings of anger and betrayal vying for predominance.

"Oh yes, she fetched quite a handsome price, just as

I knew she would from the first moment I laid my eyes on her," boasted Madame Contessa Cherie. "Darling, I'm well aware that Jeffrey Piggist was your highest paying customer. Yes, I also know that the actions of those two mental deficients that attacked him for no good reason have made it difficult for you to now maintain that glorious lifestyle to which you grew accustomed. No, I don't blame you one bit for being angry and wanting sweet revenge. You're entitled to it, darling! Yes, yes. Of course I'll share half of the money with you, Forrest Lawn. Haven't I always provided you with a generous finder's fee? I will wire it to you in the morning, darling. Give my love to Topaz. Kiss, kiss! Ciao."

The sound of Madame Contessa Cherie's telephone receiver returning to its cradle triggered Farika's fight-or-flight response and, with her heart pounding from a rush of adrenaline, she turned to flee. However, to her shock and ultimate horror, she discovered Draco was standing directly behind her. Before she had a chance to react, the sinister servant seized her, restraining her with a chokehold. With a gloved hand, he slapped a chloroform-soaked rag over her mouth and nose, and held it firmly in place, forcing Farika to breathe in the sweet-smelling chemical. She struggled for a bit, but was unable to free herself from his overpowering grip. Her mind grew cloudy, then she felt limpness taking hold of her body as everything faded into numbing blackness.

Chapter Fifteen

Bringing Down the House

Farika awoke in semi-darkness and on a cold, cobblestone floor in a strange room. She was racked by nausea and a dull pain pounded persistently inside her cloudy head. As her eyes adjusted to the duskiness, Farika could make out that she was in what appeared to be an old, underground wine cellar. It was a long and narrow chamber, somewhat dungeon-like in its appearance, with dank walls of reddish-brown brick and dimly lit by the flickering flames of two candles in a rusty sconce at the far end. A row of cobweb-enshrouded wooden wine barrels lined one side of the cellar, directly across from a long and rickety rack of dust-covered corked bottles that extended along the opposite wall.

A sudden clanging captured Farika's attention and she instantly turned her head in the direction of the sound and beheld the sight of Madame Contessa Cherie's scar-faced manservant barring the entrance of the wine cellar with a pair of heavy, arched gates of intricate iron scrollwork, which he promptly locked with an old skeleton key. Farika quietly watched as he disappeared into the shadows, and she waited until his echoing footsteps could be heard no more before stumbling to her feet and staggering over to the gated threshold. After trying, unsuccessfully, to free herself from the locked wine cellar, she resigned herself to her fate and sat atop one of the wooden wine barrels with her back against the wall and cried herself to sleep.

In a curious dream, Farika observed her body floating weightlessly in a dazzling beam of multi-colored light. Higher and higher she rose until she found herself aboard a rotating, saucer-shaped spacecraft, where she was greeted by two female beings who looked exactly like her, but were dressed in matching two-tone uniforms made of a shimmering white and gold metallic material. Each of them wore a dark gray, thick-chained necklace that hung down to their midsections and from which was suspended a bizarre pendant-like object that resembled a large glass eyeball with a red, radiating iris and a spinning hexagonal pupil of black.

Farika's doubles communicated with her telepathically. "Welcome back to the starship," they said in unison. "Do not be afraid. You are one of us – a traveler of time and intergalactic space. We have been monitoring and analyzing the information collected and transmitted to the ship's built-in computer system by your dream-machine implant."

They went on to explain that during her mission to explore the Earth and to study its inhabitants at close range, her brain waves became altered and her memory temporarily erased by the high level of nitrogen within the planet's troposphere. They also informed her that her mission had been completed and that the time had at last arrived for her to return with them to their home planet.

"It's only fair if you examine and probe my anatomy, then I get to examine and probe yours as well, all in the name of scientific research, of course," blurted out a familiar male voice from within the spacecraft.

Farika suddenly became aware of a silvery, floating object behind her telepathic doubles. She focused her eyes upon it and saw that it was a metallic slab, and strapped to it, underneath a bright spotlight, was Scott Javelin. He was on his back in a spread-eagle position and quite naked; his wrists and ankles secured by restraints composed of laser beams.

"I need to know where you're taking me and how long you ladies plan on keeping me," he demanded. "I have an A.S.T.R.A.L. meeting this Tuesday."

"Our destination is the sixth closest moon to the planet that you Earth-dwellers call Jupiter," simultaneously retorted the two uniformed Farikas, this time speaking verbally. "Our lunar time dimension is neither linear or cyclical and does not correspond to your time perception. It is something completely beyond the realm of your human comprehension, Earth specimen."

For a brief moment Farika thought she heard Leopard Man's voice singing, ever so faintly, *"Farika, I will always love you."* She turned to the two other Farikas and said, "I do not wish to return home with you. I wish to remain on Earth. A change has come over me and I've fallen madly in love with a golden-haired human who calls himself Leopard Man."

"Leopard Man, the pop star?" asked Scott Javelin from his floating slab, snickering. "What are you? Some teeny-bopper?"

Once again communicating via a transfer of thoughts, Farika's doubles replied in unison, "This 'love' that you feel for this alien life form is nothing more than a primitive irrational emotion produced by a confluence of chemicals released by the neurons in the basolateral amygdala. Your brain cells have been infected by an overexposure to human electromagnetic fields and you will require an immediate and thorough electrostatic mind purge to cleanse the pathogens from your system and detoxify your cerebral hemispheres."

"I don't want a mind purge," said Farika. "My desire is to remain on planet Earth and to be with Leopard Man for the rest of my life."

"If you remain on Earth, your past will be permanently forgotten, as will the telepathic abilities that are your planetary birthright. They will be lost to you forever, and you will never again be able to return to your true home beyond the stars. Our mission on this planet is complete and we will not be returning any exploratory crafts to this sector of the galaxy again."

"If that is to be my fate, then so be it!" said Farika.

In the blink of an eye, Farika's body was once again floating in the beam of multicolored light emanating from the hull of the rotating spacecraft. She then felt herself descending at such a terrifying speed that she feared a crash landing was surely imminent. She shut her eyes tightly and braced herself for the impending impact.

At that moment, Farika awoke in a cold sweat and slowly raised her eyelids to find that she was still sitting on the wooden wine barrel with her back against the wall in Madame Contessa Cherie's tenebrous wine cellar with no foreseeable means of escaping. She had no idea what time it was or for how long she had been dreaming. She noticed that the candles in the sconce had burned more than half the way down, so she figured she must have been sleeping for quite a while. However, she felt anything but well rested. And then something moving in the corner of her left eye caught her attention and she quickly turned her head to see who or what it was.

The Amnesia Girl!

At the entrance of the wine cellar, just outside of the locked gates, stood a silhouetted figure wearing what appeared to be a long, hooded cape of grayish-white. Not a word did it utter as it watched Farika through the iron scrollwork that held her captive.

"Madame Contessa Cherie? Is that you?" asked Farika, straining her eyes in the dim candlelight to make out the figure's identity. "Please let me out of here."

The figure remained cloaked in silence.

Tears welled up in Farika's eyes and she began to sob, fearing she would never again see freedom or her beloved Leopard Man. As the wet droplets of sorrow cascaded down her cheeks, a sinking feeling of despair started to seep into Farika's every nook and cranny. She thought back to her recent dream, which was still vivid in her mind, and wished that she and Leopard Man were together on a spaceship and traveling far away from San Francisco at the speed of light.

Suddenly, and much to Farika's amazement, the hooded figure walked through the iron gates as if they weren't there and slowly advanced toward her without speaking a single word. As it drew closer, Farika could see that is was a woman with an ashen face that featured colorless lips and dark sunken eyes.

Farika let out a gasp. "This can't be real," she conjectured, disbelieving her own eyes. "I'm either still asleep and dreaming all of this or I've gone completely insane like Mara Marhoe!"

The hooded figure turned her head slowly from side to side as if to disagree.

"Are you an earthbound spirit, forced to walk the Earth for all eternity?" Farika inquired.

The hooded figure nodded her head.

Farika suddenly remembered Madame Contessa Cherie's story about the housekeeper who tragically met her end by choking on a grape. "Are you Tallulah, the maid?" she asked.

The spirit still did not speak, but once again nodded.

"Is this the place where you choked on the grape?"

Tallulah's spirit gave a negative response by turning her head from side to side. She then raised her hands and clasped them around her own throat and a look of terror swept across her face.

"Are you trying to tell me that you were strangled to death?" asked Farika. "Who was it that murdered you? Was it Draco?"

The spirit removed her hands from her throat and nodded her head.

"Oh, my God!" exclaimed Farika, feeling overwhelmed by a renewed sense of dread. "I've got to get out of this wine cellar and away from this horrible house before it's too late! But I'm locked in here without a key. Please, Miss Tallulah, I'm begging you. Help me to escape from here if you can! My life is in grave danger!"

Tallulah's spirit glided to the opposite end of the wine cellar and pointed to the sconce upon the wall.

Farika was puzzled by the strange gesture and asked Tallulah what it meant. However, the untalkative specter did not give a reply. Instead, she continued to point to the sconce and then gradually dematerialized until her ghostly image was no longer visible.

With her heart now pounding with anticipation, Farika leapt from the wine barrel and dashed over to the sconce. She lifted each of the candles from their holders, hoping to find underneath one of them a key with which to unlock the iron gates that imprisoned her. But, to her disappointment, there was no key to be found. The thought then popped into her head that perhaps the ghost of the murdered maid had tried to inform her that the key to her freedom was located inside a hidden compartment either within the sconce or behind it inside the wall. Farika placed both of her hands upon the sconce and attempted to pull and wriggle it from the bricks to which it was mounted, but to no avail.

She then noticed a small, rust-encrusted rosette located at the center of the sconce and, gripping it between two fingertips, attempted to unscrew it in the hope that it would release the sconce from the wall. However, regardless of the amount of force Farika exerted to make the rose-shaped decoration turn, it simply refused to budge.

Desperate and raging with frustration, Farika picked up one of the dusty bottles from the nearby rack and swung it against the sconce as hard as she could. With a slight click, a small and inconspicuous black button popped out from the center of the rosette and Farika immediately pressed it with her fingertip, not sure what to expect. Once again the button made a clicking sound, activating a secret panel in the ceiling directly above to slide open and a rope ladder to drop down.

After plucking one of the candles from the sconce and quickly ascending the rungs of the ladder, Farika climbed through the opening in the ceiling and into a crawlspace, which was dark and cobwebbed, and roughly fifteen feet in length. At the end of the narrow passage was a small, metal grille, which Farika kicked out with her feet. She crawled through the opening and found herself outside in the mansion's overgrown backyard garden, where she was coldly greeted by the unremitting stare of a sullen-faced cherub sitting atop a three-tiered water fountain in which floated dead leaves from autumns past and green patches of moss.

Farika took a quick look around to ensure that the coast was clear, and then took off running as fast as her legs could carry her, looking over her shoulder every so often to make sure that Draco wasn't in pursuit.

* *

Golden rays of dawn were beginning to break through the gray mist left over from the night, bringing a new day to San Francisco, when Farika arrived at the Presidio Psychiatric Hospital. Her footsteps echoed as she walked across the terra cotta-tiled floor of the lobby to the information desk, where sat a chunky receptionist with over-permed hair, inserting chocolate-covered maraschino cherries into her mouth. The woman peered at Farika through her Coke-bottle-glasses, which caused her squirrel-brown eyes to appear frighteningly colossal, and, with her mouth still savoring the remnants of her previous cherry, she asked, "May I help you with something?"

Farika replied that she had come to visit Mara Marhoe and then waited as the receptionist proceeded to extract a large black book from one of the drawers of her desk and look up her friend's name.

"I'm sorry," said the receptionist, her breath smelling sweet with chocolate and cherries. "That patient is no longer with us."

"No longer with you?" asked Farika, confused. "I'm afraid I don't understand what you mean. If she isn't here, then where is she?"

"According to the record book, Miss Marhoe was discharged from this facility into the custody of a Doctor Iotaplutoniumenzymaticastrophe."

Farika gasped with shock and the color drained from her cheeks.

At that moment, there came a loud, blood-curdling scream from a long corridor on the other side of a pair of bolted steel doors with wired, glass windows. It was followed by another scream and then a fit of maniacal laughter, which sent a cold chill down Farika's spine.

"Are you Farika?" asked the receptionist, as she

returned the black book to its drawer.

Farika nodded her head.

"I have something here for you." She pulled open a large drawer at the bottom of the desk and then handed Farika the fringed purse of Valerian Kiwanis. It contained Doctor I's locked book, *The Joy of Insanity*, a pack of cigarettes, a lighter, and a single Screaming Yellow Zonker. "Before she left, your friend instructed me to give this to you if you showed up. She said it was extremely important that you have it. 'A matter of life and death' I believe were her exact words."

Farika draped the leather strap of the purse over her left shoulder, thanked the receptionist for her help, and then exited the hospital stunned by the unexpected news of Mara Marhoe's discharge. The morning sun assaulted her eyes as she made her way down the cement steps, causing her to squint and wish for a pair of sunglasses. As she stepped onto the sidewalk, she suddenly felt a man's hand grab her by the arm. And then she heard Draco's roughshod voice whispering ominously into her ear.

"Keep your mouth shut, Farika, and get into the limousine," he said, "or else I'll have to use the chloroform again. Madame is quite displeased with you for leaving like that without saying goodbye."

Digging her fingernails into the back of Draco's hand, deep enough to draw blood, Farika began to struggle desperately to free her arm from his powerful grip. She saw him reaching into the pocket of his uniform with his other hand but, before he was able to extract his trusty chloroform-soaked rag with which to render her unconscious, she delivered a swift and painful kick to his shin with the heavy, square heel of her platform shoe. With a loud cry of "ouch!" he lost his grip on her arm and she took off running down the sidewalk, faster than the wind that was blowing across the bay. Draco immediately gave chase.

Across the street, a man with a ladies' stocking over his head and a gun in his hand had just dismounted from a "flamboyant red" Sting-Ray bicycle with high-rise handlebars and a banana seat, and leaned it against a lamp post before heading into a twenty-four-hour liquor mart. Viewing the unattended bike as the only means of escaping her rapidly gaining assailant, Farika turned and darted between two parked cars as she ran across the street, heading in the direction of the Sting-Ray. She was more than half the way across the thoroughfare, with Draco in hot pursuit, when, suddenly, she heard a loud screeching sound.

As if from out of nowhere, a red Super Stock Dodge cut the corner at a high rate of speed and came barreling down the boulevard towards Farika. The driver, a gray-haired elderly woman in a pillbox hat, accentuated by artificial white gardenias, swerved sharply to avoid hitting her and ran over Draco, instead. With her Firestone black-wall tires squealing, she sped off like a red streak and, within seconds, was gone from sight.

Farika paused on the curb to catch her breath.

With a black tire mark running down the length of his crushed body, Draco lay spread-eagled in the center of the westbound lane like road kill. A trickle of red flowed from the corner of his mouth and, soon, flies began to buzz about. A large puddle of blood, as shiny and red as the speeding Dodge, formed around his lifeless carcass and quickly spread across the asphalt. A loyal servant right up to the very end, his black chauffeur's cap was still affixed to his head.

The horrendous sight filled Farika with a sense of relief, as well as an inclination to vomit. She turned her face away and then ambled down the street to the bus stop, as police and ambulance sirens wailed, and a crowd of morbid sightseers gathered around the aftermath of the hit-and-run accident to gawk, jabber, and snap pictures.

* *

Sitting in her front row seat at the Richard Nixon Memorial Auditorium, Farika waited with baited breath for Leopard Man and the Heavenly Blue to grace the stage with their celestial presence and kick off the long-anticipated Rock Apocalypse Concert. But she was not only looking forward to watching and hearing the band perform live; she was anxious to discover what the mysterious announcement was that Leopard Man told her last night he was going to make during the show. He had aroused her curiosity, among other things, but, despite all of her playful bribery and pleading to know more, the only thing Leopard Man would reveal to her was that the message was guaranteed to be 'mind-blowing.'

At ground level, the auditorium was packed to the hilt with concertgoers of all ages, and vibrant with overlapping chattering voices, adolescent giggling, and widespread anticipation. The air above was hazy with the wafting smoke of cigarettes, incense, and fragrant euphoria-producing flowers and leaves. From the other side of the gold-colored, grand drapes that hung downstage, just behind the proscenium arch, came the sounds of last minute sound checks as the sound engineer worked to make minor modifications to the sound system settings and levels.

A smile appeared on Farika's face as her mind drifted back to the previous night spent in Leopard Man's luxurious lair. Snuggled next to his warm body and wrapped securely in his arms made Farika feel loved and safe, and light years away from the fear unleashed upon her by Draco and Madame Contessa Cherie, the alarming discharge of Mara Marhoe from the psychiatric hospital, and the persistent amnesia that continued to plague her own mind. The intoxicating memory made Farika's nether regions begin to tingle.

"Hey!" blurted out a familiar voice from behind Farika's head. "Aren't you that chick from the Extravaganza?"

Farika turned to look over her left shoulder, and there, sitting directly behind her in the second row, were the three teenage groupies she had encountered in the lobby of Leopard Man's hotel.

"Man, how did you manage to score a front row seat?" asked Miss Wren Russo incredulously. "My girlfriends and I tried getting one, but they were all sold out!"

"You might say I was just in the right place, at the right time," replied Farika with a hint of a smile.

"If I remember correctly," fumed Miss Vixen Velour, "you told us at the hotel that you didn't know who Leopard Man and the Heavenly Blue were. And now we find you here in this auditorium where they're playing. And sitting in a front row seat, no less!" She stared at Farika suspiciously. "If you ask me, I find that rather curious."

"Well," smiled Farika, "let's just say that I've developed an appreciation for their music since then."

"Their music rocks!" squealed Miss Wren Russo. "I get so hot every time Werewolf Wayne plays one of their songs on his syndicated radio show. In fact, I'm getting hot right now just thinking about it! Ooh, I hope we score some back stage action after the concert tonight!"

"Me too!" chimed in Miss Ferrari Fontana. "I brought my water-based paints along, just in case!"

"Go take a cold shower, you harlots," commanded Miss Vixen Velour. "If anybody scores with Leopard

Man tonight, it's going to be me! You got that? I didn't put on these crotchless leopard-skin panties from Frederick's of Hollywood tonight for nothing, you know."

"Yeah, well I get to do his him-print before you ball him," Miss Ferrari Fontana declared. "A worn-out dick just won't do the trick! My art print buyers always select erect."

As the salacious trio of groupies continued to verbalize their lewd intentions regarding the man with whom Farika was in love and believed to be her soul mate, her disdain for them began to surge, and soon feelings of anger and disgust were burning deep within her like bubbling magma straining to erupt. She found herself filled with a strange desire to pounce upon the girls, brutalize them, and silence them. She had never before experienced such a violent urge and it began to unnerve her. She took in a deep breath in an attempt to contain her raging emotions and reminded herself that the three girls in the row behind her were nothing more than a wayward threesome of star-struck teenage delinquents. She told herself that those kinds of girls could never be anything more to Leopard Man than mere fans, and that they posed no threat to her or to the romantic, almost mystical, connection that existed between the golden-haired singer and herself.

"There's a song on their *Blue Album* called *Brain Plastic Control*," Miss Vixen Velour whispered into Farika's left ear. "If you play it backwards and listen really carefully, during the last six seconds of the guitar solo, just before the final verse and chorus, you'll hear a faint voice in a foreign accent revealing when the world is going to end."

A small gust of laughter exited Farika's smiling mouth. "And when is this apocalypse supposed to take place?" she asked, unable to keep herself from looking amused.

Miss Vixen Velour went deathly silent for a few moments before giving a reply. "Tonight," she said, gravely.

"Oh, that's nothing but a lot of nonsense," replied Farika, dismissively, while shaking her head in response to the absurdity of the words her ears were receiving.

"Oh, you think so?" challenged Miss Vixen Velour. "Well, I happen to know that it isn't. Flash Garish, the music reviewer with a harelip, said it was totally true, and he never, ever lies. Plus, I played the record backwards on my turntable and heard the voice with my very own ears. You know, for a rock and roll groupie, you really aren't all that bright."

"First of all," responded Farika with a tone of annoyance revealing itself in her voice. "I've told you before that I am not a rock and roll groupie. And secondly..."

"Don't put me on," interjected Miss Vixen Velour, interrupting Farika in mid-sentence. "If you're not a groupie, then what the hell are you doing sitting in the front row of the Rock Apocalypse concert wearing those odd things that nobody else wears?"

"And just what do you mean by that?" demanded Farika, nettled by the teenager's insolence. "There's nothing 'odd' about what I have on. It's very stylish, and I'll have you know that this outfit was hand-picked for me by Max, the world-renowned fashion guru." Farika wrinkled up her nose and stuck out her tongue. "And if you really must know," she continued as Miss Vixen Velour sneered and then rolled her eyes, "Leopard Man, himself, invited me to watch him perform tonight at this concert. He even gave me a free backstage pass along with the front row seat ticket."

Miss Vixen Velour's eyes stopped rolling and the childish sneer quickly departed her face. Her mouth dropped open and her cheeks turned a whiter shade of pale. Speechlessly, she turned and looked at the other two girls in her small entourage of groupies. Their mouths, too, hung wide open and speechless; their faces, which wore expressions of shock, had also gone pallid.

At that moment, someone in the crowd began to chant:

Leopard Man, Leopard Man
Leopard Man and the Heavenly Blue!

Other people in the crowd immediately joined in and soon there were hundreds of voices chanting Leopard Man's name in unison like a sacred mantra:

Leopard Man, Leopard Man
Leopard Man and the Heavenly Blue!
Leopard Man, Leopard Man
Leopard Man and the Heavenly Blue!

Miss Vixen Velour rose from her seat and began shaking out a rhythm on a leopard-skin tambourine. Miss Ferrari Fontana and Miss Wren Russo also stood up, and then the three Leopard Man-enamored groupies began to sing loudly, over the chanting:

Leopard Man, I love you
I dig the way you move
You radiate on the stage
Kiss me and sign your name
Flash me a neon smile
Turn me on with your style
You get me high, it's no lie
Your love drives me wild

Yeah! Rock and roll me
Yeah! Rock and roll me
All night long

Farika listened as the three girls continued to perform their anthem. A number of others in the auditorium began to sing along with them, some clapping their hands and some stomping their feet to the fast and steady beat produced by the tambourine's silver jingles.

Leopard Man, I love you
Baby you know it's true
You're number one on the charts
And number one in our hearts
My love for you is strong
I faint when I hear your song
Your cosmic rock gets me hot
Rock me all night long
Yeah! Rock and roll me
Yeah! Rock and roll me
All night long

The house lights suddenly dimmed, the gold drapes lifted up, and, much to the delight of the audience, Leopard Man in his leopard-skin loincloth and necklace of faux leopard teeth appeared on the fog-covered stage, illuminated by ethereal blue beams shining down from multiple stage lights hanging high above on a batten. A few feet behind him, also bathed in blue spotlights, were the Heavenly Blue, shimmering in their futuristic costumes of blue lame.

Leopard Man grabbed the microphone from the stand in front of him and shouted out to the excited crowd. "Hello San Francisco! Blue is the color of your dreams tonight! Are you ready to rock the house down?"

The crowd gave an immediate response by screaming wildly, cheering, and producing ear-piercing whistles. They roared with such intensity that Farika feared her assaulted ears would go deaf at any moment from the noise. She turned her head and gazed out across what looked to be a sea of thousands of faces. Many of the fans were jumping up and down in a state of abandoned enthusiasm. Some of the girls in the audience could be seen sobbing hysterically, while others proudly demonstrated their undying loyalty to the band by tearing out strands of their own hair and fainting in their seats.

With a bright pyrotechnic flash, a thunderous blast of rock and roll music generated by the Heavenly Blue's instruments instantly permeated the auditorium. Amplified drums pounded out a fevered beat, accompanied by the electrifying wailing of a Gibson guitar, the thumping of a Rickenbacker bass, and the space-age sounds of a Moog modular synthesizer. The combined result of the raging instruments produced a tune of mind-expanding proportions, which, to Farika, was nothing short of ear candy dipped in magic.

Leopard Man's amplified voice sent a wave of chills through her body as he sang:

> *Everybody's grooving to the weirdest show in town*
> *Dancing feet are moving to a psychotropic sound*
> *Standing in the corner is a lonely little girl*
> *She lost her mind, she wants to find*
> *The key to her lost world*
> *Is sanity really dead? Or hiding inside her head?*

As Leopard Man belted out the lyrics to the song, a

number of fans got up and began to dance in the aisles, their heads bobbing and their bodies gyrating wildly to the beat of the drums. Throughout the concert hall, adrenaline was pumping, hearts were racing, and ears were ringing. A laser-light show sent multicolored laser beams zigzagging through the audience, creating a psychedelic effect.

Mesmerized, Farika found that she was unable to take her eyes off of Leopard Man as he sang and pranced about the stage in his patch of blue light, every so often making eye contact with her, winking his eye and flashing an impish smile. She felt, at that moment, that nothing in the world mattered except for the music, which encircled her from head to toe with a wall of sound, and seized her soul. As each note, each beat, and each word found its way into Farika's ears, she envisioned herself disappearing inch by inch into the music until she became one with it.

After the song was over, the crowd cheered and furiously slapped the palms of their hands together. The dazzling laser light show paused and a glistening Leopard Man gave thanks to his fans as a few female members of the audience tossed brassieres and panties, upon which were written their names and telephone numbers, onto the foggy stage.

"Before we kick out the jams with our next song," announced Leopard Man into the microphone. "I'd like to take a minute and introduce to you the talented, and very foxy, ladies of the Heavenly Blue. On lead guitar and backing vocals is Ann-dromeda. On the bass is Euphoria. On drums is Nebula. And last, but never least, is Galexia on synthesizer. Give it up for the rock-tastic Heavenly Blue!"

The crowd rose from their seats and presented the band members with a generous round of applause, and from those of the male gender with raging hormones emerged a chorus of wolf-whistles and crass catcalls. The Heavenly Blue smiled and graciously took a bow.

"Our next song is dedicated to a very special lady who's here tonight and sitting in the front row," Leopard Man stated. "But before we perform it for you, I have an important question that I need to ask her, right here, right now." He gazed into Farika's eyes from the edge of the stage. "Farika, sweet Farika, will you marry me?"

The three groupies sitting behind Farika gasped with horror and then an unnerving hush fell over the auditorium as Farika suddenly found herself in a blue spotlight with all eyes fixed upon her, anxiously awaiting her reply. A hot flash surged throughout her body and then she felt herself succumb to total numbness, except for the feeling of her heart pounding inside her chest. The environment melted into a scene as surreal as a dream and Farika was convinced, beyond the shadow of a doubt, that she would awaken at any moment to discover that none of this was real.

"What's your answer?" asked Leopard Man, his hypnotic, green eyes still transfixed on Farika's. "Will you be my leopardess of love for all eternity?"

The thousands of gawking eyes around Farika suddenly faded away into the shadows and her numbness gave way to overwhelming elation that exploded like Fourth of July fireworks deep within her. The thrill was so intense, she felt like she was about to burst into the sun. "Yes!" she cried out with great delight, as tears of joy began to well up in her eyes. "I'll marry you!"

Every person sitting in the audience, with the exception of Miss Vixen Velour, Miss Wren Russo and Miss Ferrari Fontana, instantly and simultaneously responded by cheering, clapping their hands and stomping their feet upon the floor. Leopard Man smiled and made a thumbs-up gesture, and then the Heavenly

Blue commenced to crank out the next song in their repertoire and the dizzying laser light show resumed.

"I knew it!" hissed Miss Vixen Velour, seething with jealousy and resentment. "I knew that lie-spewing little trollop was a star-baller! She didn't have me fooled for one minute!"

"She not only stole Leopard Man away from us," added Miss Ferrari Fontana, angrily and with tears streaming from her eyes, "she ripped off the entire groupie world!"

Miss Wren Russo reached down into her blouse and withdrew a switchblade knife from the center of her push-up bra. She pressed a button on the knife's iridescent mother- of-pearl handle and, with a click, its sharp blade popped out. "Should I cut her up?" she asked with an eager tone in her voice.

"Slice her and dice her!" shouted Miss Ferrari Fontana.

Miss Vixen Velour leaned forward and wrapped her arm firmly around Farika's throat, placing her in a rear naked chokehold that made breathing difficult. "When Miss Wren gets done with her special beauty regimen for your face, no pop star, including Leopard Man, will ever be able to look at you without expelling vomit!" She then turned to her switchblade-wielding friend and shouted out a command, which filled Farika with terror. "Carve up her face like a jack-o'-lantern!"

Farika struggled desperately, but was unable to break free from Miss Vixen Velour's forceful stranglehold. She knew that she had to act quickly, so she thrust her hand into the fringed purse that sat upon her lap and withdrew Mara Marhoe's cigarette lighter, which she promptly ignited and held up to her assailant's elbow. The very instant its flame touched the groupie's flesh, she let out a cry of pain and immediately withdrew her scorched limb from Farika's person.

The Amnesia Girl!

Farika sprung to her feet and took off running across the laser-flashing auditorium as fast as she could.

"After her!" yelled Miss Vixen Velour, her words bellowing out like a battle cry. The gang of groupies leapt from their seats and raced after Farika, hungering for her pain and thirsting for her blood. They pursued her up the aisle as she headed for a door with an exit sign mounted above it.

"Help me!" Farika cried, as the three, crazed teenagers started to catch up to her. However, her voice was no match for the thundering music of the Heavenly Blue, which pounded and rattled the auditorium and drowned out her cries for help.

From the amplifiers, Leopard Man's voice sang out:

Royal blue precision metal tubing rusts
The wires catch on fire in her engine of lust
Her brain plastic control is starting to explode
Love at fifty thousand volts can overload
Does your body move to rock and roll?
Can you operate your brain control?

Upon fleeing from the raucous auditorium, Farika found herself dashing through a twisting maze of long and empty corridors. She hadn't the slightest notion where they would lead her, but continued down the passageways, filled to the brim with fright and feeling as though she were trapped within a nightmare with no means of waking herself up. She could hear the echoing sound of running footsteps growing louder behind her and she feared that, at any given moment, the tempestuous trio would catch her and carry out their horrendous threat.

Rounding a corner, Farika came upon a red door that had the word, FIRE EXIT stenciled upon it in large white letters. She opened the door and found herself in yet another long hallway; however, unlike the others, this one turned into a dead end at which stood a grinning larger-than-life statue of Richard Milhaus Nixon displaying a two-fingered peace sign. Attached to the marble pedestal upon which the "Tricky Dick" replica stood was a large bronze plaque, which read: I AM NOT A CROOK.

Reaching the end of the line, Farika came to an abrupt stop and bent forward with the palms of her hands on her knees to catch her breath. She suddenly became aware that the sound of pursuing feet had ceased and all that could be heard now was her panting and her wildly beating heart. She slowly turned around, expecting to see the groupies and, in all probability, the fast-flying steel blade of Miss Wren Russo's switchblade knife. However, what her eyes beheld was far more terrifying to her than that. Shocked, she let out a loud gasp. She felt faint. Time seemed to stand still, but, at the same time, felt like it was rushing by like pages that fly off of calendars in old movies. Nothing made sense.

The unexpected sight of Doctor I and Nurse Mars standing in the corridor, no more than ten feet away from her, caused Farika's head to reel and her stomach to knot up. Unsure if the doctor and his nurse were really there or not, she squeezed her eyes shut for a moment, hoping that the hallucination, if that was what indeed it was, would vanish. However, upon reopening her eyes, Farika was filled with dread to find the pair still standing in front of her. She suddenly felt her mouth open up, and then, heard the spine-chilling sound of, "Doctor Iotaplutoniumenzymaticastrophe!" burst forth from her lips in her own voice, but as though someone else were speaking through her.

"Hello, Farika," said Doctor I. "We meet again."

"Keep away from me!" Farika cried. Her heart was

now thumping in her chest. "What are you doing here?"

"Don't you know, Farika?" asked Doctor I. "We're here to help you. You're a seriously ill young woman and pose a great danger of harming yourself as well as those around you. We can't very well leave you on your own to run amuck. No, we can't have that at all, now can we? You must understand, Farika, that it's imperative for you to return to the hospital at once with Nurse Mars and me and receive the proper treatment for your mind. You must trust that we only have your best interest at heart."

"But I'm *not* seriously ill *or* a danger to myself or others!" argued Farika, shaking her head. "I don't need to be committed to a mental hospital just because I have amnesia."

"Self-inflicted amnesia!" blurted out Nurse Mars, displaying a grin that was as malevolent as it was crooked.

"I'm afraid your mental afflictions run far deeper than a simple case of rare amnesic syndrome," said Doctor I, slowly taking a step towards Farika. "I've also diagnosed you as having what is known as a multiple personality disorder, and one of its many symptoms is dissociative memory loss, such as what you've been experiencing. Additionally, you've been exhibiting signs of anxiety and even persecutory delusions. It's like a trifecta of mental disorders with a bonus prize!" He continued to advance even closer.

Farika took several steps backwards, until her back was pressed against the base of the Richard Nixon statue. "Where's Mara Marhoe?" she asked, angrily; but her question went unanswered. "I don't know what you and Cunt-Zilla did with her, but you aren't going to get me, too!"

Nurse Mars now began to creep towards Farika, brandishing a horrendously long hypodermic syringe.

"Five milligrams of Haldol says we will," she said confidently. "We have our ways of dealing with non-compliant patients and absconders such as yourself."

Farika's mind suddenly reeled back to that hazy afternoon in New York, when she and Mara Marhoe made their daring escape from the Midtown Psychiatric Hospital, and she recollected her friend saying, as she snatched Doctor I's book from his desk, that she always liked to be insured. Something told Farika there was no time like the present to put that insurance to good use! She quickly opened her purse and extracted *The Joy of Insanity*, along with a disposable cigarette lighter, which she held just below the book, her thumb pressed against the spark wheel.

"Stay back! Both of you!" Farika shouted. "If you come any closer, I'll torch this precious book of yours! I swear it!"

Doctor I immediately took a step back, as a look of great concern swept across his face. However, Nurse Mars boldly took another step forward, and informed Farika, "We can either do this the easy way, or we can do this my way. The choice is up to you. But either way..."

At that moment, Farika ignited the lighter. The flame began to lick at Doctor I's book, scorching the royal blue cover.

The alarmed psychiatrist grabbed Nurse Mars by her arm and yanked her back towards him. "That will be enough, nurse," he said sternly, his eyes fixed nervously on the flickering flame of the lighter. "I will handle this situation from here on out."

A gentle smile suddenly appeared on the doctor's face. "It's all right now, Farika. No one will harm you. I promise," he tried to assure her. "If you extinguish that lighter for a moment, I will tell you what you wish to know about your friend, Mara Marhoe."

Farika released her thumb from the lighter and the flame went out.

"Thank you, my dear," responded Doctor I, looking much relieved. "Now, you'll need to get a grip on yourself, as this will, no doubt, come to you as somewhat a shock. But, the truth of the matter is, there is no Mara Marhoe. There never was."

Farika looked confused.

"You see," Doctor I continued, "that person doesn't exist... at least not outside of your own mind. Mara Marhoe is just one of the many distinct personalities that exist within the realm of your twisted brain. You could give Sybil a run for her money!"

"I don't believe you!" cried Farika. "Mara Marhoe is real and not some figment of my imagination!"

"But, I'm afraid it's quite true," said Doctor I, empathetically. "The Mara Marhoe personality emerged to help you cope with the traumatic event of waking up in an unfamiliar and frightening environment and not having any sense of your own identity. This facet of your own self represents your unresolved inner conflicts, as well as your latent lesbian tendencies. You really must come to terms with this, Farika, otherwise you will never be able to resolve your psychosis."

"I don't believe anything you've told me!" Farika stated vehemently. "Not a single word of it! They're all lies just to get me to go back to the hospital with you. Maybe Mara Marhoe was right. Maybe you and Nurse Mars really *are* working for the government, and my amnesia, and every strange thing that's happened to me since I woke up in your hospital, are all part of some bizarre, mind control experiment that the two of you are involved in."

"Just listen to yourself, Farika," empathized Doctor I. "You're filled with such deep denial and desperation, that you're even willing to give credence to the insane ramblings of a non-existent mental patient manufactured by your own mind. And one whom you, yourself, even said was the most neurotic person you knew."

A chill ran down Farika's spine like an icy finger. "How did you know I said those words to Mara Marhoe? What a minute... Valerian Kiwanis was there when I told her that. She must have called you to get even with us for taking her van at the bra-burning rally! Okay, this is all starting to make sense to me now. I know what you're trying to do. You're trying to confuse me and make me think I've gone mad. Is that part of the experiment?"

Doctor I shook his head, sadly. "There is no experiment, Farika. Stop deluding yourself."

"Then how did you know what I said to Mara Marhoe? Was Valerian's van bugged? Or did Mara Marhoe squeal to you? That's it, isn't it? Mara Marhoe works for you as some kind of spy! She reports back to you with everything I say and do, and that's why the hospital released her into your custody. I should have never trusted her, right from the start of this whole, crazy, whatever-it-is that's happening to me!"

"Farika, sweet Farika," intoned Doctor I. "You're upsetting yourself, needlessly. Haven't you had enough of all this folly? Return to New York with me, and, together, we will explore your repressed sexual desires."

"I won't go back to New York, ever!" shouted Farika. "There's not a thing you can say or do that will make me go with you. And if you try to force me, I'll scream for the police! I don't care if I end up behind bars. Jail would be preferable to being trapped in that snake pit of yours."

"Very well," uttered Doctor I. "If that's the way you feel about it, then I won't try to force you against your will." He then held out his hand. "Now, if you'd be gracious enough to return to me my royal blue treatise, *The Joy of Insanity*. It was very naughty of you to have stolen it."

"But I didn't steal your book!" said Farika. "Mara Marhoe was the one who took it. You must believe me!"

"There she goes again, demonstrating her inability to accept responsibility for her own actions," growled Nurse Mars, her thumb impatiently tapping against the plunger of her hypodermic syringe. "This is nothing but a waste of valuable time. I say we dispense with all of this ineffective babble and administer therapeutics to the patient!"

"Nurse Mars!" snapped Doctor I. "Would you kindly refrain from your haughtiness? Your attitude isn't helping the situation one bit. You'd do well to remember that I am the doctor here, and I shall decide when to administer therapeutics.

"Yes, doctor," Nurse Mars grumbled while giving Farika the evil eye. "Am I to assume, then, that your professional approach will be to reveal to your patient the truth concerning her past?"

"Nurse Mars!" Doctor I shouted angrily. "That will be quite enough!"

Nurse Mars smiled with malicious satisfaction.

"What about my past?" Farika asked. "What is it that you're both keeping from me? What do you know about my past? I demand that you tell me! I want to know! I have a right to know!"

"Haven't you yet figured it out, Farika?" asked Doctor I.

"Figured what out?" Farika was growing impatient. "For all I know, I might actually be a roller derby queen who got amnesia by being hit over the head with a folding chair during a match race... or possibly a secret agent whose recollection of the past was chemically deleted by nameless government scientists with disfigured faces. Or maybe, now that I think about it, a traveler of time and space whose memory was somehow eradicated when a distortion in the space-time continuum was encountered."

Doctor I applauded. "Those are all quite magnificent theories, Farika, which I have no doubt would make intriguing plot lines for paperback novels. However, none are very accurate. Perhaps I should have revealed this to you during our first session, but it was my intention to spare you from further emotional trauma until I felt you were more psychologically equipped to cope with the truth. You see, the real reason you can't remember your past is because you don't have one. It's really as simple as that. Up until the moment you awoke in the psychiatric hospital, you didn't exist."

Farika began to laugh, almost maniacally. "That's absurd! Do you actually expect me to believe that? Now who's the crazy one? You must think I'm awfully gullible. Just because I can't remember who I was or where I came from doesn't mean I was born yesterday."

"You may choose not to believe it," shrugged Doctor I. "That is certainly your prerogative. However, I can assure you that every bit of what I've just told you is the truth. And, in the interest of your own mental hygiene, you would do well to accept it."

Farika continued to laugh until tears streamed from her eyes. "If what you say is true, then prove it," she demanded. "Prove it to me right now!"

Doctor I stroked his beard for several moments as he contemplated. He then stopped and declared, "I must say, this is highly irregular. But, very well, if you insist." He reached into his jacket pocket and took out a small key, which he tossed in Farika's direction. It landed at her feet with a tiny ping. "That key," he explained, "unlocks *The Joy of Insanity*. Open it to page number 232 and read it for yourself."

Farika retrieved the key from the ground and promptly unlocked the book, keeping one suspicious eye

The Amnesia Girl!

on the doctor and his nurse, for she trusted neither. She opened the book to the requested page and her eyes met the words that had been written upon it. They read: *"If what you say is true, then prove it," she demanded. "Prove it to me right now!"*

Farika was overcome by a wave of terror. "No!" she screamed. "This can't be!"

Doctor I's head nodded slowly. "I'm afraid it is, my dear. You must accept it."

"I will *not* accept it!" Farika screamed, slamming the book shut. "I refuse to be merely a figment of some writer's demented imagination! I refuse to be a one-dimensional character in a work of fiction! I want to live and breathe as a real, flesh-and-blood person!"

"But, you do live and breathe," explained Doctor I, "within the pages of *The Joy of Insanity*."

"No!" screamed Farika. "I don't want to exist only on sheets of paper in words, sentences, and paragraphs. There's more to me than adjectives, interjections, and amusing alliterations! I'm not imaginary! I am real!"

"Calm down, Farika. You're getting your dangling participles all in a fluster," lectured the psychiatrist. "Of course you feel real. We all feel real. If we didn't, the world would simply melt into madness. There'd be no rhyme or reason to anything. Wake up to yourself, Farika. Reality is but an illusion."

"How do I know this book isn't some sort of trick?" insisted Farika. "I don't know what's true and what isn't anymore."

"You seek the truth," declared Doctor I, "but there is only one truth, and it is an unchangeable truth: You are but a character in a story. We are all just characters in a story... each and every one of us. Just as the author of this story is but a character in someone else's story, and so on, and so on."

Gripped by dread, Farika again opened the book and

flipped through its pages until she came upon a passage that mirrored Doctor I's words. It said: *We are all just characters in a story... each and every one of us. Just as the author of this story is but a character in someone else's story, and so on, and so on.*

Farika once again slammed the book shut and was left trembling. "I always felt there was something not right about this book," she mused, staring at the scorched cover. "I could never quite put my finger on it, but something about it felt unnatural, almost... evil. I even suggested that Mara Marhoe burn it, but she wouldn't hear of it. Perhaps if I burned it now, I'll awaken from this nightmare and regain my true identity and my past."

Doctor I suddenly looked panic-stricken. "Come to your senses, girl!" he shouted. "Can't you see you're allowing yourself to become deluded by the insecurity of your own un-reality? Accept your fictitiousness. You don't exist outside of that book which you now hold in your hand. Now, kindly hand it back to me before it's too late."

"No!" shrieked Farika with the utmost defiance. She then opened the book quite hurriedly and, to the horror of Doctor I and Nurse Mars, began ripping out the pages in a violent manner, all the while shouting, "I want to exist! I need to exist! I will exist!"

A loud, crackling sound filled the air and then what remained of *The Joy of Insanity* burst into a ball of flames. Farika let out a scream and immediately flung the burning book into the air. She watched as it landed on the floor just inches away from the feet of the psychiatrist, who desperately, but unsuccessfully, attempted to stamp out the flames. And then her ears detected a low and peculiar rumbling sound that seemed to rise up from out of the ground beneath her, growing louder and more ominous by the second.

The Amnesia Girl!

The floor began to vibrate and the hanging overhead light fixtures shimmied on their chains in a most dramatic fashion. With groans and creaks, the entire auditorium started to sway to and fro, doors swung open and shut by themselves, light bulbs flickered wildly, and chairs slid back and forth across the buffed floor.

The motion added a feeling of light-headedness to Farika's terror, and she heard the voice of some unseen person frantically cry out, "Earthquake!" A frightful roar then filled Farika's ears and the ground began to shake violently and the building rocked and rolled with such intensity, it was almost as if the earth had desired to tear it from its very foundation and thrash it into a heap of rubble. Farika fought to stay standing as the floor heaved underfoot, and she watched in horror as exit signs and light fixtures fell to the floor and smashed apart, followed by dusty showers of broken plaster, bricks, and mortar.

A gigantic fissure in the floor suddenly opened up with an explosive sound, belching forth dust and smoke. The force knocked Doctor I and Nurse Mars off their feet, and they plunged into the gaping rift, screaming for their lives. The fissure then closed shut and their screaming was no more.

Farika was holding on to the base of the Richard Nixon statue for dear life when she suddenly heard Leopard Man's voice calling out her name. She turned and spotted the rock star standing by the exit, struggling against the earthquake to remain in a standing position. He held out his hand to her.

"Take my hand!" Leopard Man shouted. Come away with me, Farika!" He continued to say something else, but his voice was drowned out by the sound of mass screaming and thundering eruptions as the auditorium started to break apart, piece by piece.

Farika watched his lips moving and thought they

were saying, "Farika, I will always love you."

She released her grip on the statue's base and attempted to flee to the exit where Leopard Man stood, beckoning to her. However, the force of the temblor threw her to the ground like a helpless rag doll. She instinctively covered her head with her hands in an effort to shield herself against the falling pieces of ceiling tiles, bits of shattered glass, and other debris that pelted her body without mercy.

The hall was now beginning to fill with swirling clouds of dust from disintegrating masonry and black, billowing smoke from a fire that was raging somewhere in the building. Farika's eyes and nostrils began to sting, and she coughed and gasped for air as her heart pounded with fear. She managed to get onto her knees, bracing herself with the palms of her hands pressed firmly against the lurching floor. She looked over towards the exit for Leopard Man but he was no longer there. Farika was alone, with only her terror to embrace her.

Amidst the clamor and apocalyptic sounds of destruction, a loud and rhythmic thumping noise caught Farika's attention and she turned her head to look. Through the hellish haze she could make out the image of the Richard Nixon memorial statue teetering precariously upon its marble base. Helplessly she watched as the support sprung multiple cracks until it crumbled away and the statue began plummeting to the ground in her direction. She scrambled to move out of its path, but not with adequate enough speed, and the peace sign-bearing fingers of the statue delivered a presidential blow to the back of her head, propelling her into an abyss of blackness.

* *

"Mara. What a beautiful name," whispered a voice

that was unknown, and yet, in a most peculiar way, not completely unfamiliar. "I've never known anyone named Mara before." The voice paused for a moment before continuing to speak in a hushed tone. "Do you believe in déjà vu?"

Mara Marhoe slowly opened her eyes.

"Insanity – a perfectly rational adjustment to an insane world."

R. D. Laing, Scottish psychiatrist, 1972

The Amnesia Girl!

About the Author

Born and raised in the Chicago area, Gerri R. Gray is a cemetery photographer and a lifelong aficionado of horror, dark humor, and high camp. She blames her twisted sense of humor on a wayward adolescence influenced by the likes of Monty Python, Charles Addams, Frank Zappa, and John Waters.

She began writing poetry, music, short stories and plays while a teenager in the 1970s. Her first notable publication occurred in October of 1976 and was an interview with Ides of March singer/songwriter, Jim Peterik (who went on to find even greater success with the rock group, Survivor.) Her poetry has appeared in a number of literary journals and anthologies, including *The Poet, Xenomorph, The Kindred Spirit*, and, most recently, *Beautiful Tragedies*.

In 1980 she founded a small publishing company called, Golden Isis Press, and did double duty as editor and publisher of *Golden Isis Magazine* until its discontinuation in the early 1990s.

Writing under a fictitious name inspired by an H.P. Lovecraft novel, she began a successful career as an occult author in the late 1980s and, over the course of two decades, had over two-dozen books on various New Age subjects published by Citadel Press, Penguin, New Page Books and Adams Media.

Her non-fiction article, "The House of Many Shadows," appeared in Lynda Lee Macken's book, *Ghost Hunting the Mohawk Valley* (Black Cat Press, 2012). It chronicled the paranormal activity and investigations which took place at the historic 19th century mansion in Upstate New York that she and her husband currently live in, and out of which they operated a bed and breakfast with a vampiric *Dark Shadows* theme.

    Gerri's love of writing and her warped imagination mated and spawned a bizarre love child, which turned out to be her first novel: *The Amnesia Girl*.

Other HellBound Books Titles Available at:
www.hellboundbookspublishing.com

The Cabin Sessions

A confronting, hard-hitting, dark psychological thriller told with acid wit. Themes of abuse are explored through minds distorted by fear and corrupted by hatred and delusion; this is a tale in which redemption is gained in unexpected ways.

It's Christmas Eve when hapless musician Adam Banks stands on the bridge over the river that cleaves the isolated village of Burton. A storm is rolling into the narrow mountain pass. He thinks of turning back. Instead, he resolves to fulfil his obligation to perform the guest spot at The Cabin Sessions. He should be looking forward to it, but fear stirs when he opens the door on the Cabin's incense-choked air

Philip Stone is already there, brooding. He observes with a ruthless eye the regulars, from sleazy barmaid Hannah Fisher, to old crone Cynthia Morgan. Meanwhile, Philip's sister, Eva, prepares to take a bath. It¿s a ritual - she's a breath holder. At twenty-eight, Eva has returned to Burton to finish the business of her past, as memories begin to surface concerning one fateful day by the river and the innocence of her beloved brother...

Psychological Breakdown
By
David Owain Hughes

Within this tome lies eighteen tales of mind-bending terror, as Hughes delves into the human psyche and dishes out stories of what becomes of the broken minded, spirited and downright irked.

Part these blood-drenched pages at your own peril, for you will find diseased minds geared towards revenge and bloody chaos, with a few twists, turns and surprises thrown in for good, fucked-up measures.

Keep the lights on!

Worship Me

Something is listening to the prayers of St. Paul's United Church, but it's not the god they asked for; it's something much, much older.

A quiet Sunday service turns into a living hell when this ancient entity descends upon the house of worship and claims the congregation for its own. The terrified churchgoers must now prove their loyalty to their new god by giving it one of their children or in two days time it will return and destroy them all.

As fear rips the congregation apart, it becomes clear that if they're to survive this untold horror, the faithful must become the faithless and enter into a battle against God itself. But as time runs out, they discover that true monsters come not from heaven or hell...

...they come from within.

No Rest For The Wicked

A modern day ghost story with its skeletons buried firmly in the past.

From beyond the grave, a murderous wife seeks to complete her revenge on those who betrayed her in life; a powerless domestic still fears for her immortal soul while trying to scare off anyone who comes too close; and the former plantation master - a sadistic doctor who puts more faith in the teachings of de Sade than the Bible

When Eric and Grace McLaughlin purchase Greenbrier Plantation, their dreams are just as big as those who have tried to tame the place before them. But, the doctor has learned a thing or two over his many years in the afterlife, is putting those new skills to the test, and will go to great lengths in order to gain the upper hand. While Grace digs into the death-filled history of her new home, Eric soon becomes a pawn of the doctor's unsavory desires and rapidly growing power, and is hell-bent on stopping her.

Blood and Kisses

The definitive short story collecting from James H Longmore - an eclectic mix of dark horror, bizarro and Twilight-Zone style tales of the downright disturbing.

Welcome to the long awaited collection from the writer of horror novels *'Pede* and *Tenebrion*; a forword by Richard Chizmar (co-author of *Gwendy's Button Box* and author of *A Long December*), 18 short stories, 5 flash fiction and even a poem - all skin-crawling, soul-shredding tales of terror, of the darkest things that skulk amongst the night's inky shadows, and of the everyday gone horribly awry.

Discover the alternative implication of technology becoming self-aware, enjoy the acquaintance of a charismatic new pastor who promises his flock a brand new place in which to worship his God, and spend a little time in the company of a nice young man who is inexorably caught up in his home town's terrible secret. Then there is Cupid's revelation that personally he has never experienced love, yet we discover that very emotion alive and not so well amongst the ruins of a post zombie apocalypse world, and we bear witness to a childhood innocence forever destroyed in a war-torn city. There is more, Dear Reader, much, much more; for within these pages we have devils, demons and ghosts, lycanthropes and demi-gods, all rubbing nefarious shoulders with vilest of Hell's offspring who have slithered from the netherworld to doff their caps and wish us all the sweetest of dreams…

Demons, Devils and Denizens of Hell Vol, 2

The second volume in HellBound Books' outstanding horror anthology fair teems with tales of Hades' finest citizens – both resident and vacationing in our earthly realm… -

Compiled by the inimitable P. Mattern and featuring: Savannah Morgan, Andrew MacKay, Jaap Boekestein, James H Longmore, Stephanie Kelley, Ryan Woods, James Nichols, P. Mattern, Marcus Mattern, Gerri R Gray, and legion more…

A HellBound Books LLC Publication

http://www.hellboundbookspublishing.com

Printed in the United States of America

www.ingramcontent.com/pod-product-compliance
Lightning Source LLC
Chambersburg PA
CBHW021121300426
44113CB00006B/239